Episcopal Church. African Methodist

Hymnal

adapted to the Doctrines and usages of the African Methodist Episcopal church.

Episcopal Church. African Methodist

Hymnal

adapted to the doctrines and usages of the African Methodist Episcopal church.

ISBN/EAN: 9783337100513

Printed in Europe, USA, Canada, Australia, Japan

Cover: Foto ©Lupo / pixelio.de

More available books at **www.hansebooks.com**

HYMNAL

ADAPTED TO THE

DOCTRINES AND USAGES

OF THE

AFRICAN METHODIST EPISCOPAL CHURCH.

Revised Edition.

PHILADELPHIA·
PUBLISHED BY THE A. M. E. BOOK CONCERN.
Rev. T. W. Henderson, D D, Business Manager.
No. 631 Pine Street.
1899.

PUBLISHER'S PREFACE.

THIS collection of hymns and sacred songs were gathered and arranged by REV. J. C. EMBRY, under the supervision of the REV. BISHOPS T. M. D. WARD, D. D., and B. T. TANNER, D. D., who were appointed by the Episcopal Counc l to execute the work, at their meeting held in Macon, Ga., January, 1892.

Concerning the work itself, we observe: 1. It is done in response to an almost universal demand. 2. This demand was for a cheaper book, and one of better arrangement than the old, in order that a music edition might be made. These requirements necessitated,—*a*) a smaller book to meet the demand for price; *b*) a grouping of the hymns metrically, so as to easily supply music for the same. 3. The collection is made chiefly from our own book and that of the M. E. Church. A few are from the Presbyterian, a few are from the Baptist Hymnal, and still a few others from miscellaneous sources. Finally, there are eighteen selections from the Psalmody of the U. P. Church, all of which have been reduced to popular meter.

The Wesleyan hymns prevail largely, and the whole collection will be found breathing a

PUBLISHER'S PREFACE.

pure orthodox and evangelical spirit. Original compositions by our own clergy are: BISHOPS PAYNE, TURNER and TANNER, and the REVS. H. T. JOHNSON, J. R. SCOTT and J. C. EMBRY. There are twelve Doxologies, the Liturgy of Baptism, the Lord's Supper and Reception of Members.

3. In the judgment of some, a collection of only 600 hymns may seem small for a large church. But to such we would say, Remember, first, that not more than two to three hundred compositions are ever used by any church in actual worship; the rest go for doctrine and sentiment; second, the multitude of song-book makers of the present day supply a large part of the songs and music used by all the churches. Hence a denominational hymnal stands for less to-day than formerly. But the church hymnal is the standard by which these others are gauged; it is the central core around which they are built up.

Everything will be found here that is needful for the service of praise in the house of God.

Now, therefore, to our venerable bishops, clergy and brethren the work is humbly committed for inspection and use, until it shall be finally passed upon by the General Conference itself.

PHILA., Oct. 3d, 1892.

NOTE OF APPROVAL

FROM THE BISHOPS

TO THE PASTORS AND MEMBERS OF THE A. M. E. CHURCH.

Dear Brethren :—We have examined the proofs of the revised and re-arranged Hymnal now ready for the press, as executed under our oversight by Dr. Embry. The sheets came to us as the work was in progress from week to week, and having inspected a copy, in proof, of the whole collection, we take pleasure in saying that we are highly gratified with the result of his rapid, but arduous labor. Most of these hymns are the same contained in our old book, in use the past seventeen years, and therefore not new or strange. The comparatively few collected from other sources are largely Wesleyan in authorship and spirit. The topical arrangement seems to be well chosen. and the hymns metrically grouped, so far as it was practicable, with a view to a music edition. At the suggestion of Bishop Ward, a few original pieces have been admitted or retained from the pens of our own authors. A small selection, also, has been made

NOTE OF APPROVAL.

from the Psalms, all of which teach sound doctrines and thus lend desirable aid to the devotional spirit. The chants of the former editions have been dropped, because impracticable for use, and the liturgy of Baptism and the Lord's Supper restored. The indexing has been executed with neatness and taste, and the whole work, typographically, is a gem. We pronounce it, therefore, highly creditable to the Church, and to those who have done the work. We commend the work to the whole Church until the General Conference of 1896 shall utter a final verdict. After all, the best test of any work, is the test of usefulness. May these hymns and sacred songs, issuing as a stream from the pure fountain of the Divine oracles, commend themselves in sweet satisfaction to the thousands of our Zion.

DANIEL A. PAYNE,
A. W. WAYMAN,
T. M. D. WARD,
H. M. TURNER,
W. J. GAINES,
B. W. ARNETT,
BENJ. T. TANNER,
A. GRANT,
B. F. LEE,
M. B. SALTER,
JAMES A. HANDY,
} Bishops of the A. M. E. Church.

TABLE OF SUBJECTS.

ORDER OF WORSHIP 1–8

SECTION.	HYMNS.

I. WORSHIP (Morning Service.) 1–42
Invocation and Praise.

II. THE HOLY SCRIPTURES 43–50
Their Excellence Exceeds the Glory of the Heavens, and Exhibits the Grace and Beauties of the Saviour.

III. BEING AND ATTRIBUTES OF GOD . . 51–78
Exhibit the Holy Trinity, and the Divine Majesty.

IV. OF CHRIST 79–125
The Advent, Atonement and the Resurrection.

V. THE HOLY SPIRIT 126–139
His Influences, Power and Offices Set Forth and Implored.

VI. GOSPEL INVITATIONS AND WARNING 140–181

VII. REPENTANCE AND CONVERSION . . 182–205

VIII. INTERNAL RELIGION 206–226
Justification and Adoption.

IX. CONSECRATION AND HOLINESS IMPLORED 227–243

X. CHRISTIAN PERFECTION 243–266
The Fullness of Love, and a Holy Heart.—(Chiefly Wesleyan.)

TABLE OF SUBJECTS.

SECTION.   HYMNS.

XI. THE CHURCH COMFORTED AND ENCOURAGED 267-287

XII. MINISTERIAL COMMISSION 288-300
    The Gospel for All Nations.

XIII. CHRISTIAN ORDINANCES 302-324
    Baptism —The Lord's Supper.

XIV. CHRISTIAN WARFARE AND FAITH UNDER TRIALS 325-371

XV. CHURCH ACTIVITIES 372-417
    Prayer.—Morning; Evening; The Seasons: New Year; Winter, etc.

XV. CHURCH ACTIVITIES, (Continued.) . . 418-431
    The Erection and Dedication of Churches.

XV. CHURCH ACTIVITIES, (Continued) . . 432-455
    Missions.—Dawn of the Millenium and Glory of the Latter Days.

XV. CHURCH ACTIVITIES, (Continued) . . 456-465
    Love Feasts and Social Worship.

XVI. FUNERALS, AND OTHER MEMORIAL OCCASIONS 466-513
    Death.—The Judgment.— Heaven.

XVII. DEVOTIONAL MISCELLANY 514-570
    Domestic and Social Worship.—Patriotic and National.— Prayer Meetings, etc., etc.

XVIII. THE SABBATH 571-581

XIX. SELECTIONS FROM THE PSALMS . . 583-600
    Doxologies —The Liturgy.- -Index.

ORDER OF CHURCH SERVICE.

The following order and arrangement of Divine Service will be observed by the Pastors of the A. M. E. Church whenever and wherever practicable. This is an abridgment of the old Wesley Prayer Book, which was adopted by the General Conference in May, 1880.

I.

Just before announcing the opening hymn, the Minister shall reverently rise and read one or more of the following sentences of Scripture:

I was glad when they said unto me, let us go into the house of the Lord, our feet shall stand within thy gates, O Jerusalem.

For a day in thy courts is better than a thousand. I had rather be a doorkeeper in the house of my God, than to dwell in the tents of wickedness

Because of the house of the Lord our God I will seek thy good.

Those that be planted in the house of the Lord, shall flourish in the courts of our God.

Blessed are they that dwell in thy house.

Lord, I have loved thy habitation, the place where thy honor dwelleth.

O, sing unto the Lord a new song, for he has done marvellous things —make a joyful noise unto the Lord, all the earth, and sing praises.

ORDER OF CHURCH SERVICE.

For the Lord is in his holy temple, let all the earth keep silence before him

Let the words of my mouth, and the meditation of my heart, be acceptable in thy sight O Lord. my strength and my redeemer.

1. Singing and prayer.
2. Immediately after prayer, organ play short prelude.

II.

1. Reading a chapter responsively, minister and people standing
2. Minister reading a chapter. or a part of a chapter, alone, people sitting.
3. Singing one stanza only, by choir and congregation.

Minister and people standing shall then say:

Minister. And God spake these words saying: I am the Lord thy God who brought thee out of the land of Egypt. out of the house of bondage; thou shalt have no other gods before me.

People. Lord have mercy upon us, and incline our hearts to keep this law.

M. Thou shalt not make to thyself any graven image. nor the likeness of anything that is in heaven above—or in the earth beneath, or in the water under the earth. Thou shalt not bow down to them, nor serve them; for I the Lord thy God am a jealous God, visiting the iniquity of the fathers upon the children, unto the third and fourth generation of them that hate me; and showing mercy unto thousands of them that love me and keep my commandments.

P. Lord have mercy upon us, and incline our hearts to keep this law.

M. Thou shalt not take the name of the Lord thy God in vain; for the Lord will not hold him guiltless, that taketh his name in vain.

P. Lord have mercy upon us and incline our hearts to keep this law.

M Remember the Sabbath day to keep it holy. Six days shalt thou labor, and do all thy work; but the seventh day is the Sabbath of the Lord thy God. In it thou shalt not do any work; thou, nor thy son, nor thy daughter, thy man-servant, nor thy maid-servant, nor thy cattle, nor the stranger that is within thy gates. For in six days the Lord made heaven and earth, the sea, and all that in them is and rested the seventh day: wherefore the Lord blessed the seventh day, and hallowed it.

P. Lord have mercy upon us, and incline our hearts to keep this law.

Sing:—

> Nearer my God, to Thee,
> Neare to Thee!
> E'en though it be a cross
> That raiseth me!
> Still all my song shall be—
> Nearer, my God, to Thee,
> Nearer to Thee!

Or this:—

> I need Thee every hour,
> Most gracious Lord;
> No tender voice, like thine
> Can peace afford.

ORDER OF CHURCH SERVICE.

I need Thee. O I need Thee;
Every hour I need Thee.
O bless me now my Saviour
I come to Thee.

M. Honor thy father and thy mother, that thy days may be long in the land which the Lord thy God giveth thee.

P. Lord have mercy upon us and incline our hearts to keep this law.

M. Thou shalt not kill.

P. Lord have mercy upon us, and incline our hearts to keep this law.

M. Thou shalt not commit adultery.

P. Lord have mercy upon us, and incline our hearts to keep this law.

M. Thou shalt not steal.

P. Lord have mercy upon us, and incline our hearts to keep this law.

M. Thou shalt not bear false witness against thy neighbor.

P. Lord have mercy upon us, and incline our hearts to keep this law.

M. Thou shalt not covet thy neighbor's house; thou shalt not covet thy neighbor's wife, nor his man-servant, nor his maid-servant, nor his ox, nor his ass, nor anything that is thy neighbor's.

P. Lord have mercy upon us, and write these laws upon our hearts.

ORDER OF CHURCH SERVICE.

> My soul, be on thy guard,
> Ten thousand foes arise;
> And hosts of sins are pressing hard,
> To draw Thee from the skies.

or this:—
> My God, my life, my love,
> To thee, to thee I call:
> I cannot live if thou remove,
> For thou art all in all.

M. Hear what Christ our Saviour saith. Thou shalt love the Lord thy God with all thy heart, and with all thy soul, and with all thy mind. This is the first and great commandment. And the second is like unto it: Thou shalt love thy neighbor as thyself. On these two commandments hang all the law and the prophets.

M. Glory be to the Father, and to the Son, and to the Holy Ghost.

P. As it was in the beginning, is now, and ever shall be, world without end. *Amen.*

1. *Choir chant or sing suitable hymn, people sitting.*
2. *Read and announce notices.*
3. *Preach the sermon or exhort as occasion may require.*

IV.

CLOSING SERVICES.

1. *The Lord's Prayer or an extempore prayer.*
2. *Lift the collection.*

Then shall be said the Apostles' Creed, the people standing.

I believe in God, the Father Almighty, Maker of heaven and earth; and in Jesus Christ, His only Son, our Lord, who was conceived by the Holy Ghost, born of the Virgin

ORDER OF CHURCH SERVICE.

Mary, suffered under Pontius Pilate, was crucified, dead and buried; he descended into the grave, the third day he arose from the dead; He ascended into heaven and sitteth on the right hand of God, the Father Almighty; from thence He shall come to judge the quick and the dead. I believe in the Holy Ghost, in the Holy Catholic Church,* the communion of saints, the forgiveness of sins, the resurrection of the body, and the life everlasting. *Amen.*

Doxology and benediction.

The following may be used at pleasure in lieu of the Decalogue, or even with it.

Where there are choirs the *Te Deum* should be chanted altogether, but if the people do not know how to chant it, let the minister and people use it alternately.

TE DEUM,

Minister. We praise Thee, O God, we acknowledge Thee to be the Lord.

People. All the earth doth worship Thee, the Father everlasting.

M. To Thee all angels cry aloud, the heavens and all the powers therein.

P. To Thee Cherubim and Seraphim continually do cry.

* By Holy Catholic Church is meant the Church of God in general.

ORDER OF CHURCH SERVICE.

M. Holy, holy, holy, Lord God of Sabaoth.

P. Heaven and earth are full of the majesty of Thy glory.

M. The glorious company of the apostles praise Thee.

P. The goodly fellowship of the prophets praise Thee.

M. The noble army of martyrs praise Thee.

P. The holy church, throughout all the world doth acknowledge Thee.

M. The Father of an infinite majesty.

P. Thine adorable, true and only Son.

M. Also, the Holy Ghost the Comforter.

P. Thou art the King of Glory, O Christ.

M. Thou art the everlasting Son of the Father.

P. When thou tookest upon Thee to deliver man, Thou didst humble Thyself to be born of a virgin.

M. When Thou hadst overcome the sharpness of death, Thou didst open the kingdom of heaven to all believers.

P. Thou sittest at the right hand of God, in the glory of the Father.

M. We believe that Thou shalt come to be our judge.

P. We therefore pray Thee, help Thy servants, whom Thou hast redeemed with Thy precious blood.

ORDER OF CHURCH SERVICE.

M. Make them to be numbered with Tl saints in glory everlasting.

P. O Lord, save Thy people and bless Thii heritage.

M. Govern and lift them up forever.

P. Day by day we magnify Thee.

M. And we worship Thy name ever, wor without end.

P Vouchsafe, O Lord, to keep us this d; without sin.

M. O Lord have mercy upon us, have mer(upon us.

P. O Lord, let Thy mercy be upon us as o' trust is in Thee.

M. O Lord, in Thee have I trusted; let n never be confounded.

M. Glory be to the Father, and to the So and to the Holy Ghost.

P. As it was in the beginning, is now, a ever shall be, world without end. *Amen.*

Gloria Patri.

Glory be to the Father, and | to ·· the | Son ¶ and | to ·· t
| Ho-ly | Ghost ;
As it was in the beginning, is now, and | ever | shall b(
world without end.—) A— | men.

Venite ad Meum.

1 Come unto me, all ye that labor and are | heav-y –lade
‖ and I · will | give ·· you | rest.
2 Take my yoke upon you and learn of me; for I s
meek and | lowly ·· in | heart, ‖ and ye shall find
rest— | unto ·· your | souls.
3 For my | yoke ·· is | easy ¶ and | my— | burden ·· is
light.

HYMNS.

SECTION I.

Worship.

Opening Worship.   C. M.

O FOR a thousand tongues to sing
   My great Redeemer's praise!
The glories of my God and King,
   The triumphs of his grace!

My gracious Master and my God,
   Assist me to proclaim,—
To spread through all the earth abroad
   The honors of thy Name.

Jesus! the Name that charms our fears,
   That bids our sorrows cease;
'Tis music in the sinner's ears,
   'Tis life, and health, and peace.

He breaks the power of cancelled sin,
   He sets the pris'ner free:
His blood can make the foulest clean;
   His blood availed for *me*.

He speaks—and, listening to his voice,
   New life the dead receive;
The mournful, broken hearts rejoice;
   The humble poor believe.

6 Hear him, ye deaf; his praise, ye dumb,
   Your loosened tongues employ;
 Ye blind, behold your Saviour come,
   And leap, ye lame, for joy.
                              C. Wesley

2 *Psalm lxiii. Opening morning service. C. M.*

EARLY, my God, without delay,
   I haste to seek thy face:
 My thirsty spirit faints away,
   Without thy cheering grace.

2 So pilgrims, on the scorching sand,
   Beneath a burning sky,
 Long for a cooling stream at hand;
   And they must drink or die.

3 I've seen thy glory and thy power
   Through all thy temple shine:
 My God, repeat that heavenly hour,
   That vision so divine.

4 Not all the blessings of a feast
   Can please my soul so well,
 As when thy richer grace I taste,
   And in thy presence dwell.

5 Not life itself, with all its joys,
   Can my best passions move,
 Or raise so high my cheerful voice,
   As thy forgiving love.

6 Thus, till my last expiring day,
   I'll bless my God and King!
 Thus will I lift my hands to pray,
   And tune my lips to sing.
                              Watts

INVOCATION AND PRAISE.

3 *Faithfulness of God.* C. M.

THE truth of God shall still endure,
And firm his promise stand;
Believing souls may rest secure
In his almighty hand.

2 Should earth and hell their forces join,
He would contemn their rage,
And render fruitless their design
Against his heritage.

3 The rainbow round about his throne
Proclaims his faithfulness;
He will his purposes perform,
His promises of grace.

4 The hills and mountains melt away,
But he is still the same:
Let saints to him their homage pay,
And magnify his name.
Beddome.

4 *Divine Guidance, and Rest.* C. M.

BEFORE thy mercy-seat, O Lord,
Behold, thy servants stand,
To ask the knowledge of thy word,
The guidance of thy hand.

2 Let thy eternal truths, we pray,
Dwell richly in each heart;
That from the safe and narrow way
We never may depart.

3 Lord, from thy word remove the seal,
Unfold its hidden store;
And, as we read, O may we feel
Its value more and more.

4 Help us to see the Saviour's love
Beaming from every page;

WORSHIP.

And let the thoughts of joys above
Our inmost souls engage.

5 Thus while thy word our footsteps guide
Shall we be truly blest;
And safe arrive where love provides
An everlasting rest.
William H. Bathurst.

5 *Joy of public worship.* L. M.

GREAT God, attend, while Zion sings
The joy that from thy presence springs;
To spend one day with thee on earth
Exceeds a thousand days of mirth.

2 Might I enjoy the meanest place
Within thy house, O God of grace,
Not tents of e se, nor thrones of power,
Should tempt my feet to leave thy door.

3 God is our sun, he makes our day;
God is our shield, he guards our way
From all assaults of hell and sin,
From foes without, and foes within.

4 All needful grace will God bestow,
And crown that grace with glory too;
He gives us all things, and withholds
No real good from upright souls.

5 O God, our King, whose sovereign sway
The glorious hosts of heaven obey,
And devils at thy presence flee;
Blest is the man that trusts in thee.
Isaac Watts.

6 *Praise for Loving-kindness.* L. M.

AWAKE, my soul, in joyful lays,
And sing thy great Redeemer's praise;
He justly claims a song from thee:
His loving-kindness, O! how free!

2 He saw me ruined in the fall,
   Yet loved me notwithstanding all;
   He saved me from my lost estate;
   His loving-kindness, O! how great!
3 Though numerous hosts of mighty foes,
   Though earth and hell my way oppose,
   He safely leads my soul along;
   His loving-kindness, O! how strong!
4 When trouble, like a gloomy cloud,
   Has gathered thick, and thundered loud,
   He near my soul has always stood;
   His loving-kindness, O! how good!
5 Soon shall I pass the gloomy vale,
   Soon all my mortal powers shall fail;
   Oh! may my last expiring breath
   His loving-kindness sing in death! *Medley.*

7   *God worthy of all Praise.*   L. M.

BE Thou exalted, O my God,
   Above the heavens, where angels dwell;
Thy power on earth be known abroad,
   And land to land thy wonders tell.
2 My heart is fixed; my song shall raise
   Immortal honors to his name;
   Awake, my tongue, to sound his praise,
   His wondrous goodness to proclaim.
3 High o'er the earth his mercy reigns,
   And reaches to the utmost sky;
   His truth to endless years remains,
   When lower worlds dissolve and die.
4 Be thou exalted, O my God,
   Above the heavens, where angels dwell;
   Thy power on earth be known abroad,
   And land to land thy wonders tell.
                                    Watts.

WORSHIP.

8 *The Sovereign Jehovah.* L. M.

BEFORE Jehovah's awful throne,
  Ye nations bow with sacred joy;
Know that the Lord is God alone;
  He can create, and he destroy.

2 His sovereign power, without our aid,
  Made us of clay, and formed us men;
And when, like wandering sheep, we strayed,
  He brought us to his fold again.

3 We are his people; we his care;
  Our souls, and all our mortal frame;
What lasting honors shall we r ar,
  Almighty Father, to thy name?

4 We'll crowd thy gates with thankful songs,
  High as the heaven our voices raise;
And earth, with her ten thousand tongues,
  Shall fill thy courts with sounding praise.

5 Wide as the world is Thy command,
  Vast as eternity thy love;
Firm as a rock thy truth shall stand,
  When rolling years shall cease to move.
               Watts.

9 *Majesty and Dominion of God.* L. M.

COME, O my soul, in sacred lays
  Attempt thy great Creator's praise:
But, O! what tongue can speak his fame,
What verse can reach the lofty theme?

2 Enthroned amid the radiant spheres,
  He glory like a garment wears;
To form a robe of light divine,
Ten thousand suns around him shine.

INVOCATION AND PRAISE.

3 In all our Maker's grand designs,
Almighty power, with wisdom, shines;
His works, through all this wondrous frame,
Declare the glory of his name.

4 Raised on devotion's lofty wing,
Do thou, my soul, his glories sing;
And let his praise employ thy tongue
Till listening worlds shall join the song.
Blacklock.

10 *Praise offered to God.* Psalm cxvii. L.M.

FROM all that dwell below the skies,
Let the Creator's praise arise;
Let the Redeemer's name be sung,
Through ev'ry land, by ev'ry tongue.
Eternal are thy mercies, Lord,
Eternal truth attends thy word;
Thy praise shall sound from shore to shore,
Till suns shall rise and set no more.

2 Your lofty themes, ye mortals bring,
In songs of praise divinely sing;
The great salvation loud proclaim,
And shout for joy the Saviour's name!
In ev'ry land begin the song;
To ev'ry land the strains belong:
In cheerful sounds all voices raise
And fill the world with loudest praise.
Watts.

11 *Take up thy cross.* L. M.

"TAKE up thy cross," the Saviour said,
"If thou wouldst my disciple be;
Deny thyself, the world forsake,
And humbly follow after me."

2 Take up thy cross; let not its weight
Fill thy weak spirit with alarm;

His streng h shall bear thy spirit up,
And brace thy heart and nerve thine arm

3 Take up thy cross, nor heed the shame;
Nor let thy foolish pride rebel;
Thy Lord for thee the cross endured,
To save thy soul from death and hell.

4 Take up thy cross, then, in his strength,
And calmly every danger brave;
'Twill guide thee to a better home,
And lead to victory o'er the grave.

5 Take up thy cross, and follow Christ;
Nor think till death to lay it down;
For only he who bears the cross
May hope to wear the glorious crown.
Charles W. Everest.

12 *Keeping the charge of the Lord.* S. M.

A CHARGE to keep I have,
A God to glorify;
A never-dying soul to save,
And fit it for the sky;

2 To serve the present age,
My calling to fulfil:
O may it all my powers engage,
To do my Master's will!

3 Arm me with jealous care,
As in thy sight to live;
And O, thy servant, Lord, prepare,
A strict account to give!

4 Help me to watch and pray,
And on thyself rely,
Assur'd, if I my trust betray,
I shall for ever die.
C. Wesley.

INVOCATION AND PRAISE.

13 - - *"Sing praises to God."*   S. M.

AWAKE, and sing the song
   Of Moses and the Lamb;
Tune every heart and every tongue,
   To praise the Saviour's name.

2 Sing of his dying love;
   Sing of his rising power;
Sing how he intercedes above
   For those whose sins he bore.

3 Tell, in seraphic strains,
   What he has done for you;
How he has taken off your chains,
   And formed your hearts anew.

4 His faithfulness proclaim
   While life to you is given;
Join hands and hearts to praise his name,
   Till we all meet in heaven.
                           Hammond.

14   *Met in his name.*   S. M.

JESUS, we look to thee,
   Thy promised presence claim;
Thou in the midst of us shalt be,
   Assembled in thy name.

2 Thy name salvation is,
   Which here we come to prove;
Thy name is l.fe, and health, and peace,
   And everlasting love.

3 Not in the name of pride
   Or selfishness we meet;
From nature's paths we turn aside,
   And worldly thoughts forget.

4 We meet the grace to take,
   Which thou hast freely given;

WORSHIP.

We meet on earth for thy dear sake,
  That we may meet in heaven.

5 Present we know thou art,
  But O thyself reveal!
Now, Lord, l t every bounding heart
  The m ghty comfort feel.

6 O may thy quickening voice
  The death of sin remove;
And bid our inmost souls rejoice,
  In hope of perfect love.

Charles Wesley

15   *Praise to the Trinity.*   6s & 4s

COME, thou Almighty King,
  Help us thy name to sing,
    Help us to praise;
  Father all glorious,
  O'er all victorious,
  Come, and reign over us,
    Ancient of Days.

2 Jesus, our Lord, descend;
  From all our foes defend
    Nor let us fall;
  Let thine almighty aid
  Our su e defence be made,
  Our souls on thee be stayed;
    Lord, hear our call.

3 Come, thou incarnate Word,
  Gird on thy mighty sword;
    Our prayer attend;
  Come, and thy people bless;
  Come, give thy word success;
  Spirit of holiness,
    On us descend

INVOCATION AND PRAISE.

4 Come, holy Comforter,
　Thy sacred witness bear,
　　In this glad hour;
　Thou, who almighty art,
　Now rule in every heart,
　And ne'er from us depart,
　　Spirit of power.
　　　　　　　　　　　Dobell's Col.

16　　*God of our Salvation.*　　8s & 7s.

PRAISE to thee, thou great Creator;
　Praise be thine from every tongue;
Join, my soul, with every creature,
　Join the universal song.
2 Father, source of all compassion,
　Free, unbounded grace is thine:
Hail the God of our salvation;
　Praise him for his love divine.
3 For ten thousand blessings given,
　For the hope of future joy,
Sound his praise through earth and heaven,
　Sound Jehovah's praise on high.
4 Joyfully on earth adore him,
　Till in heaven our song we raise;
There, enraptured, fall before him,
　Lost in wonder, love, and praise.
　　　　　　　　　　　Fawcett.

17　　　　　　8s & 7s, peculiar.
Christ the Lamb enthroned and worshipped.

HARK! ten thousand harps and voices
　Sound the note of praise above;
Jesus reigns, and heaven rejoices;
　Jesus reigns, the God of love:
See, he sits on yonder throne;
Jesus rules the world alone.

WORSHIP.

2 Jesus, hail! whose glory brightens
   All above, and gives it worth;
Lord of life, thy smile enlightens,
   Cheers, and charms, thy saints on earth:
When we think of love like thine,
Lord, we own it love divine.

3 King of glory, reign forever,
   Thine an everlasting crown:
Nothing from thy love shall sever
   Those whom thou hast made thine own.
Happy objects of thy grace,
Destined to behold thy face.

4 Saviour, hasten thine appearing;
   Bring, O, bring the glorious day,
When, the awful summons hearing,
   Heaven and earth shall pass away:
Then, with golden harps, we'll sing,
"Glory, glory to our King."

Kelly

18   *An Act of Thanksgiving.*   C. M.
    Psalm lxxxix. 26–37.

WHEN all the mercies of my God,
   My rising soul surveys;
Why, my cold heart, art thou not lost
   In wonder, love, and praise?

2 When in the slipp'ry paths of youth,
   With heedless steps I ran,
Thine arm, unseen, convey'd me safe,
   And led me up to man.

3 Through hidden dangers, toils and death,
   It gently clear'd my way,
And through the pleasing snares of vice,
   More to be fear'd than they.

INVOCATION AND PRAISE.

4 Through every period of my life,
 Thy goodness I'll pursue;
And after death, in distant worlds,
 The pleasing theme renew.

5 Through all eternity to thee
 A grateful song I'll raise;
But O! eternity's too short
 To utter all thy praise. *Addison*

19 "*My meditation of him shall be sweet.*" C. M.
Psalm civ. 34.

WHILE thee I seek, protecting Power!
 Be my vain wishes still'd;
And may this consecrated hour
 With better hopes be filled.

2 Thy love the power of thought bestow'd,
 To thee my thoughts would soar;
Thy mercy o'er my life has flow'd,
 That mercy I adore.

3 In each event of life, how clear
 Thy ruling hand I see;
Each blessing to my soul most dear,
 Because conferr'd by thee.

4 In every joy that crowns my days,
 In every pain I bear,
My heart shall find delight in praise,
 Or seek relief in pray'r.

5 When gladness wings the favor'd hour,
 Thy love my thoughts shall fill:
Resign'd, when storms of sorrow lower,
 My soul shall meet thy will.

6 My lifted eye, without a tear,
 The gath'ring storm shall see;
My steadfast heart shall know no fear—
 That heart will rest on thee. *Williams*

WORSHIP.

20   *The Desire of all nations.*   C. M

COME, thou Desire of all thy saints,
  Our humble s rains attend,
While with our praises and complaints,
  Low at thy feet we bend.
2 How should our songs, like those above
    With warm devotion rise!
  How should our souls on wings of love,
    Mount upward to the skies!
3 Come, Lord, thy love alone can raise
    In us the heavenly flame;
  Then shall our lips resound thy praise,
    Our hea ts adore thy name.
4 Now, Saviour, let thy glory shine,
    And fill thy dwellings here,
  Till life, and love, and joy divine,
    A heaven on earth appear.
5 Then shall our hearts, enraptured, say,
    "Come, great Redeemer, come,
  And bring the bright, the glorious day,
    That calls thy children home."
              Anne Steele

21   *Psalm* cxlviii.   C. M

PRAISE ye the Lord, y' immortal choirs
  That fill the worlds above;
Praise him who formed you of his fires,
  And feeds you with his love.

2 Shine to his praise, ye crystal skies,
    The floor of his abode;
  Or veil in shades your thousand eyes.
    Before your brighter God.
3 Thou restless globe of golden light,
    Whose beams create our days,

INVOCATION AND PRAISE.

Join with the silver queen of night
To own your borrowed rays.

4 Let the shrill birds his honors raise,
And climb the morning sky:
While grov'ling beasts attempt his praise
In hoarser harmony.

5 Thus while the meaner creatures sing,
Ye mortals take the sound:
Echo the glories of your King
Through all the nations round. *Watts.*

22 *Watchfulness and Prayer.* C. M.

ALAS! what hourly dangers rise,
What snares beset my way;
To heav'n I fain would lift my eyes,
And hourly watch and pray.

2 How oft my mournful thoughts complain,
And melt in flowing tears!
Striving against my foes in vain,
I sink amid my fears.

3 O gracious God, in whom I live,
My feeble efforts aid:
Help me to watch, and pray, and strive,
Nor let me be dismay'd.

4 Do Thou increase my faith and hope,
When fears and foes prevail;
And bear my fainting spirit up,
Or soon my strength will fail.

5 O keep me in Thy heav'nly way,
And bid the tempter flee:
And never, never let me stray
From happiness and Thee. *Steele.*

WORSHIP.

23 *Intercession of Christ.* H. M.
Rom. viii. 15; Heb. vii. 25.

ARISE, my soul, arise,
  Shake off thy guilty fears,
The bleeding sacrifice
  In my behalf appears;
Before the throne my Surety stands,
My name is written on his hands.

2 He ever lives above,
  For me to intercede,
His all-redeeming love,
  His precious blood to plead:
His blood atoned for all our race,
And sprinkles now the throne of grace.

3 Five bleeding wounds he bears,
  Received on Calvary;
They pour effectual pray'rs,
  They strongly speak for me:
Forgive him, O forgive, they cry!
Nor let that ransom'd sinner die.

4 The Father hears him pray,
  His dear anointed One;
He cannot turn away
  The presence of his Son;
His Spirit answers to the blood,
And tells me I am born of God.

5 My God is reconciled;
  His pardoning voice I hear:
He owns me for his child;
  I can no longer fear:
With confidence I now draw nigh,
And, "Father, Abba, Father," cry

Charles Wesley

INVOCATION AND PRAISE.

24 *Exhortation to Praise.*   H. M.

YE tribes of Adam, join
  With heaven, and earth, and seas,
And offer notes divine
  To your Creator's praise.
    Ye holy throng
    Of angels bright,
    In worlds of light
    Begin the song.

2 The shining worlds above
  In glorious order stand,
Or in swift courses move,
  By his supreme command:
    He spake the word,
    And all their frame
    From nothing came
    To praise the Lord.

3 Let all the nations fear
  The God that rules above;
He brings his people near,
  And makes them taste his love:
    While earth and sky
    Attempt his praise,
    His saints shall raise
    His honors high.   *Watts.*

25 *Renewing of a Covenant.* Jer. i. 4. C. M.

COME, let us use the grace divine,
  And all, with one accord,
In a perpetual cov'nant join
  Ourselves to Christ the Lord:

2 Give up ourselves through Jesus' pow'r
  His name to glorify;
And promise in this sacred hour,
  For God to live and die.

WORSHIP.

3 The cov'nant we this moment make
  Be ever kept in mind:
We will no more our God forsake,
  Or cast his words behind.
4 We never will throw off his fear,
  Who hears our solemn vow;
And if thou art well pleas'd to hear,
  Come down and meet us now!
5 Thee, Father, Son and Holy Ghost,
  Let all our hearts receive;
Present with the celestial host,
  The peaceful answer give.
6 To each the cov'nant blood apply,
  Which takes our sins away;
And register our names on high,
  And keep us to that day.
                            C. Wesley.

26   *Opening Worship.*   C. M.
ONCE more we come before our God;
  Once more his blessings ask:
O may not duty seem a load,
  Nor worship prove a task!
2 Father, thy quick'ning Spirit send
  From heaven in Jesus' name,
To make our waiting minds attend,
  And put our souls in frame.
3 May we rec ive the word we hear,
  Each in an honest heart:
And keep the precious treasure there,
  And never with it part.
4 To seek thee all our hearts dispose,
  To each thy blessings suit,
And let the seed thy servant sows
  Produce abundant fruit.   *Hart.*

INVOCATION AND PRAISE.

27 *Love of Christ celebrated.* **C. M.**

TO our Redeemer's glorious name
  Awake the sacred song!
O, may his love—immortal flame—
  Tune every heart and tongue.

2 His love what mortal thought can reach!
  What mortal tongue display!
Imagination's utmost stretch
  In wonder dies away.

3 Dear Lord, while we, adoring, pay
  Our humble thanks to thee,
May every heart with rapture say,
  "The Saviour died for me."

4 O, may the sweet, the blissful theme
  Fill every heart and tongue,
Till strangers love thy charming name,
  And join the sacred song. *Annie Steele.*

28 *"Wonderful in Counsel."* **C. M**

GOD moves in a mysterious way
  His wonders to perform:
He plants his footsteps in the sea,
  And rides upon the storm.

2 Deep in unfathomable mines
  Of never-failing skill,
He treasures up his bright designs,
  And works his sovereign will.

3 Ye fearful saints, fresh courage take:
  The clouds ye so much dread
Are big with mercy, and shall break
  In blessings on your head.

4 Judge not the Lord by feeble sense,
  But trust him for his grace;
Behind a frowning providence
  He hides a smiling face.

5 His purposes will ripen fast,
   Unfolding every hour;
The bud may have a bitter taste,
   But sweet will be the flower.

6 Blind unbelief is sure to err,
   And scan his work in vain;
God is his own interpreter,
   And he will make it plain.
Cowper.

29   *Praise to the Son.*   C. M.

O FOR a thousand seraph tongues
   To bless th' incarnate Word!
O for a thousand thankful songs
   In honor of my Lord!

2 Come, tune afresh your golden lyres,
   Ye angels round the throne;
Ye saints, in all your sacred choirs,
   Adore th' eternal Son.
C. Wesley.

30   *Psalm ciii. 8–12.*   S. M.

MY soul, repeat His praise,
   Whose mercies are so great;
Whose anger is so slow to rise,
   So ready to abate.

2 God will not always chide;
   And when his strokes are felt,
His strokes are fewer than our crimes,
   And lighter than our guilt.

3 High as the heavens are raised
   Above the ground we tread,
So far the riches of his grace
   Our highest thoughts exceed.

INVOCATION AND PRAISE.

4 His power subdues our sins;
   And his forgiving love,
Far as the east is from the west,
   Doth all our guilt remove.

5 While all his wondrous works,
   Through his vast kingdom, show
Their Maker's glory, thou, my soul,
   Shalt sing his graces too.
                              Watts.

31   *Exhortation to Praise.*   S. M.

ARISE, and bless the Lord,
   Ye people of his choice;
Arise, and bless the Lord your God,
   With heart, and soul, and voice.

2 Though high above all praise,
   Above all blessing high,
Who would not fear his holy name,
   And laud and magnify?

3 O for the living flame
   From his own altar brought,
To touch our lips, our souls inspire,
   And wing to heaven our thought.

4 God is our strength and song,
   And his salvation ours;
Then be his love in Christ proclaimed
   With all our ransomed powers.

5 Arise and bless the Lord:
   The Lord your God adore;
Arise, and bless his glorious name,
   Henceforth, forevermore.
                           Montgomery.

32 *Happiness of Heaven.* Psalm xlvii. S. M.

COME, ye that love the Lord,
 And let your joys be known:
Join in a song with sweet accord,
 While ye surround his throne:
Let those refuse to sing
 Who never knew our God;
But servants of the heav'nly King
 May speak their joys abroad.

2 The God that rules on high,
 That all the earth surveys,
That rides upon the stormy sky,
 And calms the roaring seas:
This awful God is ours,
 Our Father and our love,
He will send down his heav'nly pow'rs
 To carry us above.

3 There we shall see his face,
 And never, never sin!
There from the river of his grace,
 Drink endless pleasures in:
Yea, and before we rise
 To that immortal state,
The thoughts of such amazing bliss
 Should constant joys create. *Watts.*

33 *The Song of Heaven.* L. M.

THE countless multitude on high,
 Who tune their songs to Jesus' name
All merit of their own deny,
 And Jesus' worth alone proclaim.

2 Firm, on the ground of sovereign grace
 They stand before Jehovah's throne;
The only song in that blest place
 Is, "Thou art worthy, thou alone."

INVOCATION AND PRAISE.

3 With spotless robes of purest white,
  And branches of triumphal palm,
  They shout, with transports of delight,
  The ceaseless, universal psalm,—

4 "Salvation's glory all be paid
  To him who sits upon the throne,
  And to the Lamb, whose blood was shed
  Thou, thou art worthy, thou alone."
  Percy Chapel Col.

34 *Song of Gratitude and Praise.* L. M.

GOD of my life, through all my days
  I'll tune the grateful notes of praise;
  The song shall wake with opening light,
  And warble to the silent night.

2 When anxious care would break my rest,
  And grief would tear my throbbing breast,
  The notes of praise ascending high,
  Shall check the murmur and the sigh.

3 When death o'er nature shall prevail,
  And all the powers of language fail,
  Joy through my swimming eyes shall break,
  And mean the thanks I cannot speak.

4 But, O, when that last conflict 's o'er,
  And I am chained to earth no more,
  With what glad accents shall I rise,
  To join the music of the skies!

5 Then shall I learn th' exalted strains
  That echo through the heavenly plains,
  And emulate with joy unknown,
  The glowing seraphs round thy throne.
  Doddridge.

WORSHIP.

35 *Praise and Holy Fear.* L. M.

COME, let our voices join to raise
 A sacred song of solemn praise:
God is a sovereign King: rehearse
His honor in exalted verse.

2 Come, let our souls address the Lord,
Who framed our natures by his word;
He is our Shepherd: we, the sheep
His mercy chose, his pastures keep.

3 Come, let us hear his voice to-day,
The counsels of his love obey;
Nor let our hardened hearts renew
The sins and plagues that Israel knew.

4 Come, let us turn with holy fear,
To him who now invites us near;
Accept the offered grace to-day,
Nor lose the blessing by delay.

5 Come, seize the promise while it waits,
And march to Zion's heavenly gates;
Believe, and take the promised rest;
Obey, and be forever blest. *Watts.*

36 *For Zion's Peace.* L. M.

O THOU, our Saviour, Brother, Friend,
 Behold a cloud of incense rise;
The prayers of saints to heaven ascend,
Grateful, accepted sacrifice.

2 Regard our prayers for Zion's peace;
Shed in our hearts thy love abroad;
Thy gifts abundantly increase;
Enlarge, and fill us all with God.

3 Before thy sheep, great Shepherd, go,
And guide into thy perfect will;
Cause us thy hallowed name to know
The work of faith in us fulfill.

INVOCATION AND PRAISE.

4 Help us to make our calling sure;
  O let us all be saints indeed,
And pure, as thou thyself art pure,
  Conformed in all things to our Head.
5 Take the dear purchase of thy blood:
  Thy blood shall wash us white as snow:
Present us sanctified to God,
  And perfected in love below.
                            Charles Wesley.

37   *Access to God by a Mediator.*   C. M

COME, let us lift our joyful eyes
  Up to the courts above,
And smile to see our Father there,
  Upon a throne of love.
2 Come, let us bow before his feet,
  And venture near the Lord;
No fiery cherub guards his seat,
  Nor double-flaming sword.
3 The peaceful gates of heavenly bliss
  Are opened by the Son;
High let us raise our notes of praise,
  And reach th' almighty throne.
4 To thee ten thousand thanks we bring,
  Great Advocate on high,
And glory to th' eternal King,
  Who lays his anger by.   *Watts.*

38   *The Hope of Heaven.* Col. iii. 1.   C. M.

HOW happy ev'ry child of grace,
  Who knows his sins forgiv'n!
This earth, he cries, is not my place,
  I seek my place in heav'n:
A country far from mortal sight,
  Yet, O! by faith I see

WORSHIP.

The land of rest, the saints' delight,
  The heav'n prepared for me.
2 O what a blessed hope is ours!
  While here on earth we stay,
We more than taste the heav'nly pow'rs,
  And antedate that day;
We feel the resurrection near,
  Our life in Christ conceal'd,
And with his glorious presence here
  Our earthen vessels fill'd.
3 O would he more of heav'n bestow!
  And when the vessels break,
Our ransom'd spirits then shall go,
  To grasp the God we seek:
In rapt'rous awe on him I'll gaze,
  Who bought the sight for me.
And shout and wonder at his grace
  Through all eternity.
C. Wesley.

39   C. M.
Walking in the ways of Christ. Deut. v. 30–33.

HAPPY the souls to Jesus join'd,
  And sav'd by grace alone:
Walking in all his ways, they find
  Their heaven on earth begun.
2 The church triumphant in thy love,
  Their mighty joys we know;
They sing the Lamb in hymns above,
  And we in hymns below.
3 Thee, in thy glorious realm, they praise
  And bow before thy throne!
We in the kingdom of thy grace,
  The kingdoms are but one.

INVOCATION AND PRAISE.

1 The holy to the holiest leads,
  From thence our spirits rise;
  And he that in thy statutes treads,
  Shall meet thee in the skies.
                              C. Wesley.

40   *Worship of God in His Temple.*   C. M.

PRAISE waits in Zion, Lord, for thee;
  There shall our vows be paid;
Thou hast an ear when sinners pray;
  All flesh shall seek thine aid.

2 O Lord, our guilt and fears prevail;
  But pardoning grace is thine,
And thou wilt grant us power and skill
  To conquer every sin.

3 Blest are the men whom thou wilt choose
  To bring them near thy face;
Give them a dwelling in thy house,
  To feast upon thy grace.

4 In answering what thy church requests,
  Thy truth and terror shine;
And works of dreadful righteousness
  Fulfil thy kind design.

5 Thus shall the wondering nations see
  The Lord is good and just;
And distant islands fly to thee,
  And make thy name their trust.
                              Watts.

41   *Blest Hour of Prayer.*   L. M.

BLEST hour, when mortal man retires
  To hold communion with his God·
To send to Heaven his warm desires,
  And listen to the sacred word.

WORSHIP.

2 Blest hour, when God himself draws nigh,
  Well pleased his people's voice to hear;
  To hush the penitential sigh,
  And wipe away the mourner's tear.

3 Blest hour, for, where the Lord resorts,
  Foretastes of future bliss are given;
  And mortals find his earthly courts
  The house of God, the gate of heaven.

4 Hail, peaceful hour! supremely blest
  Amid the hours of worldly care;
  The hour that yields the spirit rest,
  That sacred hour, the hour of prayer.

5 And when my hours of prayer are past,
  And this frail tenement decays,
  Then may I spend in heaven at last
  A never-ending hour of praise.
  Thomas Raffles

42   *Acts* i. 9.   L. M.

THE mighty Conqueror leaves the dead,—
  Jesus the Lord ascends on high,
  The powers of hell are captive led,
  Dragged to the portals of the sky.

2 There his triumphal chariot waits,
  And angels chant the solemn lay:
  "Lift up your heads, ye heavenly gates;
  Ye everlasting doors, give way.

3 Loose all your bars of massy light,
  And wide unfold the radiant scene;
  He claims these mansions as his right,
  Receive the King of Glory in."

4 "Who is the King of Glory, who?"
  "The Lord, that all our foes o'ercame;
  The world, sin, death, and hell o'erthrew,
  And Jesus is the conqueror's name."

THE HOLY SCRIPTURES.

5 Lo! his triumphal chariot waits,
    And angels chant the solemn lay:
  "Lift up your heads, ye heavenly gates;
    Ye everlasting doors, give way."

6 " Who is the King of Glory, who?"
  " The Lord, of boundless power possessed,
    The King of saints and angels too,
    God over all, forever blessed."   *C. Wesley*

SECTION II.

The Holy Scriptures.

ON READING THE HOLY SCRIPTURES.

43   *Psalm* xix.   L. M.

THE heavens declare thy glory, Lord,
    In every star thy wisdom shines;
But when our eyes behold thy word,
    We read thy name in fairer lines.

2 The rolling sun, the changing light,
    And night and day thy power confess;
But the blest volume thou hast writ,
    Reveals thy justice and thy grace.

3 Sun, moon, and stars, convey thy praise
    Round the whole earth, and never stand
So when thy truth began its race,
    It touch'd and glanc'd on every land.

4 Nor shall thy spreading gospel rest,
    Till through the earth thy truth has run,
Till Christ has all the nations bless'd,
    That see the light, or feel the sun.

THE HOLY SCRIPTURES.

5 Great Sun of righteousness, arise!
   Bless the dark world with heav'nly light:
The gospel makes the simple wise;
   Thy laws are pure, thy judgments right.

Watts.

44 *The Saviour seen in the Scriptures.* **L. M.**

NOW let my soul, eternal King,
   To thee its grateful tribute bring;
My knee with humble homage bow;
   My tongue perform its solemn vow.

2 All nature sings thy boundless love,
   In worlds below and worlds above;
But in thy blessed word I trace
   Diviner wonders of thy grace.

3 There, what delightful truths I read;
   There, I behold the Saviour bleed:
His name salutes my listening ear,
   Revives my heart and checks my fear.

4 There Jesus bids my sorrows cease,
   And gives my laboring conscience peace;
He lifts my grateful thoughts on high,
   And points to mansions in the sky.

5 For love like this, O let my song,
   Through endless years, thy praise prolong;
Let distant climes thy name adore,
   Till time and nature are no more.

Ottiwell Heginbotham.

45 *Light and Glory of the Sacred Page.* **C. M**

WHAT glory gilds the sacred page!
   Majestic, like the sun,
It gives a light to every age;
   It gives, but borrows none.

2 The power that gave it still supplies
   The gracious light and heat;
   Its truths upon the nations rise:
   They rise, but never set.
3 Lord! everlasting thanks be thine
   For such a bright display,
   As makes a world of darkness shine
   With beams of heavenly day
4 Our souls rejoicingly pursue
   The steps of him we love,
   Till glory break upon our view
   In brighter worlds above.   *Cowper.*

46   *Before Sermon.*   C. M.

FATHER of all, in whom alone
   We live, and move, and breathe,
One bright, celestial ray dart down,
   And cheer thy sons beneath.
2 While in thy word we search for thee,
   (We search with trembling awe!)
   Open our eyes and let us see
   The wonders of thy law.
3 Now let our darkness comprehend
   The light that shines so clear;
   Now the revealing Spirit send,
   And give us ears to hear.
4 Before us make thy goodness pass,
   Which here by faith we know;
   Let us in Jesus see thy face,
   And die to all below.   *C. Wesley.*

47 *"Search the Scriptures."* John v. 39. C. M.

THE counsels of redeeming grace
   The sacred leaves unfold;
And here the Saviour's lovely face
   Our raptur'd eyes behold.

THE HOLY SCRIPTURES.

2 Here light descending from above
   Directs our doubtful feet;
Here promises of heavenly love
   Our ardent wishes meet.

3 Our numerous griefs are here redress'd,
   And all our wants supplied;
Naught we can ask to make us bless'd
   Is in this book denied.

4 For these inestimable gains,
   That so enrich the mind,
O may we search with eager pains,
   Assured that we shall find!
                                  S. Stennett.

48   *Delighting in the Word.*   C. M.

FATHER of mercies in thy word,
   What endless glory shines!
Forever be thy name adored
   For these celestial lines.

2 Here may the wretched sons of want
   Exhaustless riches find,
Riches above what earth can grant,
   And lasting as the mind.

3 Here the fair tree of knowledge grows
   And yields a free repast,
Sublimer sweets than nature knows
   Invite the longing taste.

4 Here the Redeemer's welcome voice
   Spreads heavenly peace around;
And life, and everlasting joys,
   Attend the blissful sound.

5 O may these heavenly pages be
   My ever dear delight;
And still new beauties may I see,
   And still increasing light!

THE HOLY SCRIPTURES.

6 Divine Instructor, gracious Lord,
   Be thou for ever near;
  Teach me to love thy sacred word,
   And view my Saviour there.   *Steele.*

49   *The Excellence of the Scriptures.*   C. M.

LADEN with guilt, and full of fears,
   I fly to thee, my Lord;
And not a glimpse of hope appears,
   But in thy written word.

2 The volume of my Father's grace
   Does all my grief assuage:
  Here I behold my Saviour's face,
   Almost in every page.

3 This is the field where hidden lies
   The pearl of price unknown;
  That merchant is divinely wise
   Who makes the pearl his own.

4 Here consecrated water flows
   To quench my thirst of sin;
  Here the fair tree of knowledge grows,
   Nor danger dwells therein.

5 O may thy counsels, mighty God,
   My roving feet command:
  Nor I forsake the happy road
   That leads to thy right hand.   *Watts.*

50 "*My tongue shall speak of thy word.*" 8s, 7s.
   Psalm cxix. 172.

PRECIOUS volume! what thou doest,
   Other books attempt in vain.
Plainest, fullest, sweetest, truest,
   All our good from thee we gain!

2 How thy living words refresh us!
   Words of truth and grace they are—

Than the finest gold more precious,
Than the honey sweeter far.
3 What lay hid from ancient sages,
What they sought, but fail'd to find,
This, unfolded in thy pages,
Now appears to all mankind.
4 Far too high for man to reach it,
'Tis reveal'd from heav'n above;
God himself alone could teach it:
'Tis the mystery of love.
5 Precious volume! all revealing,
All that we have need to know:
Nothing from our view concealing,
That can profit here below.
6 Hope we have: this hope is cheering,
That the things we know not now,
In the day of his appearing,
Christ will to his people show.

Kelly's Hymns.

SECTION III.

Being and attributes of God.

51   *Divine Excellence.*   C. M

HAIL, Father, Son, and Holy Ghost,
One God in persons three:
Of thee we make our joyful boast,
Our songs we make of thee!
2 Thou neither canst be felt nor seen
Thou art a spirit pure:
Thou from eternity hast been,
And always shalt endure.

3 Present alike in every place,
   Thy Godhead we adore:
   Beyond the bounds of time and space
   Thou dwell'st for evermore.
4 In wisdom infinite thou art,
   Thine eye doth all things see;
   And every thought of every heart
   Is fully known to thee.
5 Whate'er thou wilt, in earth below
   Thou dost in heaven above;
   But chiefly we rejoice to know
   Th' almighty God of love.   *C. Wesley.*

52   *The Trinity.*   C. M.

HAIL, holy, holy, holy Lord!
   Whom one in three we know:
By all thy heavenly host adored,
   By all thy Church below.

2 One undivided Trinity
   With triumph we proclaim:
   Thy universe is full of thee,
   And speaks thy glorious name.
3 Thee, holy Father, we confess:
   Thee, holy Son, adore:
   Spirit of truth and holiness,
   We praise thee evermore.
4 The incommunicable right,
   Almighty God, receive!
   Which angel-choirs, and saints in **light,**
   And saints embodied give.
5 Three persons, equally Divine,
   We magnify and love;
   And both the choirs ere long shall **join**
   To sing thy praise above.

BEING AND ATTRIBUTES OF GOD.

6 Hail, holy, holy, holy Lord,
(Our heavenly song shall be,)
Supreme, essential One, adored
In coëternal Three! *C. Wesley.*

53 *Grateful Praise.* Lev. xix. 30. C. M.

FREQUENT the day of God returns
To shed its quickening beams;
And yet how slow devotion burns;
How languid are its flames!

2 Accept our faint attempts to love,
Our frailties, Lord, forgive;
We would be like thy saints above,
And praise thee while we live.

3 Increase, O Lord, our faith and hope,
And fit us to ascend
Where the assembly ne'er breaks up,
The Sabbath ne'er shall end;—

4 Where we shall breathe in heavenly air,
With heavenly lustre shine,
Before the throne of God appear,
And feast on love divine;—

5 Where we in high seraphic strains,
Shall all our powers employ;
Delighted range the ethereal plains,
And take our fill of joy.

6 To Father, Son and Holy Ghost,
One God whom we adore,
Be glory as it was, is now,
And shall be evermore. *Browne.*

54 1 *Chron.* xxix. 10-13. C. M.

BLESS'D be our everlasting Lord,
Our Father, God, and King!
Thy sovereign goodness we record,
Thy glorious power we sing.

2 Thy goodness and thy truth to me,
  To every soul abound
  A vast unfathomable sea
  Where all our thoughts are drowned.
3 Its streams the whole creation reach,
  So plenteous is the store,
  Enough for all, enough for each,
  Enough for evermore.
4 Faithful, O Lord, thy mercies are!
  A rock that cannot move:
  A thousand promises declare
  Thy constancy of love. *C. Wesley.*

55   *God seen in his works.*   C. M.

FATHER above the concave sky,
  Enthroned in light profound,
At thy command, the lightnings fly,
  And thunders roar around.
2 O who can see the beaming Sun,
  The smiling moon at night,
  The snowy clouds, the countless stars,
  Enrob'd with dazzling light;
3 And yet refuse to sing thy praise,
  In sweetest notes of love?
  Or echo to angelic lays,
  Which fill the worlds above?
4 Whene'er I tread the blooming plains
  And pluck the fragrant flower,
  The luscious fruits, the yellow grains,
  I see thy matchless power.
5 What moves on earth, or wings the air,
  Or swims the swelling sea,
  Is but a ray of life to point
  Immortal man to Thee.
                    Bishop Payne.

BEING AND ATTRIBUTES OF GOD.

56   *Psalm* cxxxix. 1-6.   **C. M.**

LORD, all I am is known to thee:
   In vain my soul would try
To shun thy presence, or to flee
   The notice of thine eye.

2 Thy all-surrounding sight surveys
   My rising and my rest,
My public walks, my private ways,
   The secrets of my breast.

3 My thoughts lie open to thee, Lord,
   Before they're formed within,
And ere my lips pronounce the word,
   Thou know'st the sense I mean.

4 O wondrous knowledge! deep and high:
   Where can a creature hide?
Within thy circling arms I lie,
   Beset on every side.

5 So let thy grace surround me still,
   And like a bulwark prove,
To guard my soul from every ill,
   Secured by sovereign love.
                             Watts.

57   *The God of all Grace.*   **L. M.**
     [From the German.]

ETERNAL depth of love divine,
   In Jesus, God with us, displayed,
How bright thy beaming glories shine!
How wide thy healing streams are spread!

2 With whom dost thou delight to dwell?
   Sinners, a vile and thankless race:
O God! what tongue aright can tell
How vast thy love, how great thy grace?

BEING AND ATTRIBUTES OF GOD.

3 The dictates of thy sovereign will
 With joy our grateful hearts receive:
 All thy delight in us fulfill:
 Lo! all we are to thee we give.

4 To thy sure love, thy tender care,
 Our flesh, soul, spirit, we resign:
 O fix thy sacred presence there,
 And seal th' abode forever thine!
            Trans. by J. Wesley.

58   *Psalm* xxxvi. 5-9.   L. M.

HIGH in the heavens, eternal God,
   Thy goodness in full glory shines:
 Thy truth shall break through every cloud
   That veils and darkens thy designs.

2 Forever firm thy justice stands,
   As mountains their foundations keep:
 Wise are the wonders of thy hands:
   Thy judgments are a mighty deep.

3 Thy providence is kind and large,
   Both man and beast thy bounty share:
 The whole creation is thy charge,
   But saints are thy peculiar care.

4 My God! how excellent thy grace!
   Whence all our hope and comfort springs:
 The sons of Adam in distress
   Fly to the shadow of thy wings.

5 Life, like a fountain, rich and free,
   Springs from the presence of the Lord;
 And in thy light our souls shall see
   The glories promised in thy word.
            Watts.

BEING AND ATTRIBUTES OF GOD.

59   *Psalm cxlvii. 1–11.*   L. M.

PRAISE ye the Lord! 'tis good to raise
  Your hearts and voices in his praise:
His nature and his works invite
To make this duty our delight.

2 He formed the stars, those heavenly flames;
He counts their numbers, calls their names:
His wisdom's vast, and knows no bound,
A deep where all our thoughts are drowned.

3 Sing to the Lord, exalt him high,
Who spreads his clouds along the sky;
There he prepares the fruitful rain,
Nor lets the drops descend in vain.

4 He makes the grass the hills adorn;
He clothes the smiling fields with corn:
The beasts with food his hands supply,
And the young ravens when they cry.

5 What is the creature's skill or force,
The sprightly man, or warlike horse,
The piercing wit, the active limb?
All are too mean delights for him.

6 But saints are lovely in his sight;
He views his children with delight:
He sees their hope, he knows their fear;
He looks, and loves his image there.
                                        Watts.

60   *Opening Worship.*   L. M.

O THOU, whom all thy saints adore,
  We now with all thy saints agree,
And bow our inmost souls before
  Thy glorious, awful majesty.

2 The King of nations we proclaim:
Who would not our great Sovereign fear?

BEING AND ATTRIBUTES OF GOD.

We long t' experience all thy name,
And now we come to meet thee here.
3 We come, great God, to seek thy face,
And for thy loving-kindness wait;
And O, how dreadful is this place!
'Tis God's own house, 'tis heaven's gate!
4 Tremble our hearts to find thee nigh,
To thee our trembling hearts aspire;
And, lo! we see descend from high
The pillar and the flame of fire.
5 Still let it on th' assembly stay,
And all the house with glory fill;
To Canaan's bounds point out the way,
And lead us to thy holy hill.
6 There let us all with Jesus stand,
And join the general Church above,
And take our seats at thy right hand,
And sing thine everlasting love.
C. Wesley

61   *The Glory of God.*   L. M.
[From the German of Dr. Breithaupt.]

O GOD, thou bottomless abyss!
Thee to perfection who can know?
O height immense! What words suffice
Thy countless attributes to show?
2 Unfathomable depths thou art!
O plunge me in thy mercy's sea!
Void of true wisdom is my heart:
With love embrace and cover me!
3 While thee, all infinite, I set,
By faith, before my ravished eye,
My weakness bends beneath the weight:
O'erpowered, I sink, I faint, I die.

4   49

BEING AND ATTRIBUTES OF GOD.

4 Eternity thy fountain was
   Which, like thee, no beginning knew:
   Thou wast ere time began his race,
   Ere glowed with stars th' ethereal blue.

5 Greatness unspeakable is thine—
   Greatness, whose undiminished ray,
   When short-lived worlds are lost, shall shine
   When earth and heaven are fled away.
            Translated by J. Wesley.

62   *Divine Majesty.*   L. M.

ETERNAL Power, whose high abode
   Becomes the grandeur of a God;
   Infinite lengths beyond the bounds
   Where stars revolve their little rounds.

2 Thee while the first archangel sings,
   He hides his face behind his wings;
   And ranks of shining thrones around
   Fall worshipping, and spread the ground.

3 Lord, what shall earth and ashes do?
   We would adore our Maker too!
   From sin and dust to thee we cry,
   The Great, the Holy and the High!

4 Earth from afar hath heard thy fame,
   And worms have learned to lisp thy name;
   But, O! the glories of thy mind
   Leave all our soaring thoughts behind!

5 God is in heaven, and men below:
   Be short our tunes; our words be few!
   A solemn rev'rence checks our songs,
   And praise sits silent on our tongues.
                        Watts.

BEING AND ATTRIBUTES OF GOD.

63   *All Things are of God.*   L. M. 6 L.

THOU art, O God, the life and light
  Of all this wondrous world we see;
Its glow by day, its smile by night,
  Are but reflections caught from thee;
Where'er we turn, thy glories shine,
And all things fair and bright are thine.

2 When day, with farewell beam, delays
  Among the opening clouds of even,
And we can almost think we gaze,
  Through opening vistas, into heaven,—
Those hues, that mark the sun's decline,
So soft, so radiant, Lord, are thine.

3 When night, with wings of starry gloom,
  O'ershadows all the earth and skies,
Like some dark, beauteous bird, whose plume
  Is sparkling with unnumbered eyes,—
That sacred gloom, those fires divine
So grand, so countless, Lord, are thine.

4 When youthful Spring around us breathes,
  Thy Spirit warms her fragrant sigh;
And every flower that Summer wreathes
  Is born beneath thy kindling eye:
Where'er we turn, thy glories shine,
And all things fair and bright are thine.
Moore.

64   *Psalm* xxiii.   L. M. 6 L.

THE Lord my pasture shall prepare,
  And feed me with a shepherd's care:
His presence shall my wants supply,
And guard me with a watchful eye:
My noonday walks he shall attend,
And all my midnight hours defend.

2 When in the sultry glebe I faint,
Or on the thirsty mountain pant,
To fertile vales and dewy meads
My weary wandering steps he leads;
Where peaceful rivers, soft and slow,
Amid the verdant landscape flow.

3 Though in the path of death I tread,
With gloomy horrors overspread,
My steadfast heart shall fear no ill,
For thou, O Lord, art with me still:
Thy friendly crook shall give me aid,
And guide me through the dreadful shade.

4 Though in a bare and rugged way,
Through devious, lonely wilds I stray,
Thy bounty shall my pains beguile,
The barren wilderness shall smile,
With sudden greens and herbage crowned,
And streams shall murmur all around.
Addison.

65   *Wondrous Condescension.*   H. M

THE Lord Jehovah reigns,
  His throne is built on high;
The garments he assumes
  Are light and majesty:
His glories shine with beams so bright
No mortal eye can bear the sight.

2 The thunders of his hand
  Keep the wide world in awe;
His wrath and justice stand
  To guard his holy law;
And where his love resolves to bless,
His truth confirms and seals the grace.

3 Through all his mighty works
  Amazing wisdom shines;

Confounds the powers of hell,
And all their dark designs;
Strong is his arm, and shall fulfill
His great decrees and sovereign will.

4 And will this sovereign King
   Of glory condescend,
And will he write his name,
   My Father and my Friend?
I love his name, I love his word;
Join all my powers to praise the Lord.
                       Isaac Watts.

    Psalm xlvii. 5–9.   H. M.

GOD is gone up on high
   With a triumphant noise;
The clarions of the sky
   Proclaim th' angelic joys!
Join all on earth, rejoice and sing;
Glory ascribe to glory's King.

2 God in the flesh below,
   For us he reigns above:
Let all the nations know
   Our Jesus' conqu'ring love!
Join all on earth, rejoice and sing;
Glory ascribe to glory's King.

3 All power to our great Lord
   Is by the Father given;
By angel-hosts adored,
   He reigns supreme in heaven:
Join all on earth rejoice and sing;
Glory ascribe to glory's King.

4 Till all the earth, renewed
   In righteousness divine,
With all the hosts of God
   In one great chorus join,

Join all on earth, rejoice and sing;
Glory ascribe to glory's King.
C. Wesley.

67 *All-sufficiency.* S. M.

MY God, my life, my love,
 To thee, to thee I call:
I cannot live if thou remove,
 For thou art all in all.

2 Thy shining grace can cheer
 This dungeon where I dwell:
'Tis paradise when thou art here—
 If thou depart, 'tis hell.

3 The smilings of thy face,
 How amiable they are!
'Tis heaven to rest in thine embrace,
 And nowhere else but there.

4 To thee, and thee alone,
 The angels owe their bliss:
They sit around thy gracious throne,
 And dwell where Jesus is.

5 Thou art the sea of love,
 Where all my pleasures roll!
The circle where my passions move
 And centre of my soul.

6 To thee my spirits fly,
 With infinite desire:
And yet how far from thee I lie
 O Jesus, raise me higher!   *Watts*

68 *Opening Worship.* Psalm xcv. S. M

COME, sound his praise abroad
 And hymns of glory sing:
Jehovah is the sovereign God,
 The universal King.

2 He formed the deeps unknown,
   He gave the seas their bound:
The wat'ry worlds are all his own,
   And all the solid ground.
3 Come, worship at his throne:
   Come, bow before the Lord:
We are his work, and not our own,
   He formed us by his word.
4 To-day attend his voice,
   Nor dare provoke his rod:
Come, like the people of his choice,
   And own your gracious God. *Watts.*

69   *Psalm* xxiii.   S. M.

THE Lord my Shepherd is,
   I shall be well supplied;
Since he is mine, and I am his,
   What can I want beside?
2 He leads me to the place
   Where heavenly pasture grows,
Where living waters gently pass,
   And full salvation flows.
3 If e'er I go astray,
   He doth my soul reclaim,
And guides me in his own right way,
   For his most holy name.
4 While he affords his aid,
   I cannot yield to fear:
Though I should walk through death's dark
     shade,
   My Shepherd's with me there.
5 In spite of all my foes,
   Thou dost my table spread.
My cup with blessings overflows,
   And joy exalts my head.

6 The bounties of thy love
  Shall crown my following days;
Nor from thy house will I remove,
  Nor cease to speak thy praise.   *Watts*

70   *Psalm* ciii. 1–7.   S. M.

O BLESS the Lord, my soul:
  Let all within me join,
And aid my tongue to bless his name,
  Whose favors are divine.

2 O bless the Lord, my soul;
  Nor let his mercies lie
Forgotten in unthankfulness,
  And without praises die.

3 'Tis he forgives thy sins;
  'Tis he relieves thy pain;
'Tis he who heals thy sicknesses,
  And makes thee young again.

4 He crowns thy life with love,
  When ransomed from the grave;
He, who redeemed my soul from hell
  Hath sovereign power to save.

5 He fills the poor with good:
  He gives the sufferers rest:
The Lord hath judgment for the proud,
  And justice for th' oppre t.   *Watts*

71   .   *Glory, Mercy, Grace.*   C. M.

FATHER, how wide thy glory shines,
  How high thy wonders rise!
Known through the earth by thousand signs,
  By thousands through the skies.

2 Those mighty orbs proclaim thy power;
  Their motions speak thy skill:

BEING AND ATTRIBUTES OF GOD.

And on the wings of every hour
We read thy patience still.

3 Part of thy name divinely stands
On all thy creatures writ;
They show the labor of thy hands,
Or impress of thy feet:

4 But when we view thy strange design
To save rebellious worms,
Where vengeance and compassion join
In their divinest forms;

5 Here the whole Deity is known,
Nor dares a creature guess
Which of the glories brighter shone,
The justice or the grace.

6 Now the full glories of the Lamb
Adorn the heavenly plains;
Bright seraphs learn Immanuel's name,
And try their choicest strains.

7 O may I bear some humble part
In that immortal song!
Wonder and joy shall tune my heart,
And love command my tongue.
Isaac Watts.

72 *Psalm cxlv.* C. M.

LET every tongue thy goodness speak,
Thou sovereign Lord of all;
Thy strength'ning hands uphold the weak
And raise the poor that fall.

2 When sorrows bow the spirit down,
When virtue lies distressed,
Beneath the proud oppressor's frown,
Thou giv'st the mourner rest.

3 Thou know'st the pains thy servants feel,
   Thou hear'st thy children's cry;
   And their best wishes to fulfill,
   Thy grace is ever nigh.
4 Thy mercy never shall remove
   From men of heart sincere:
   Thou sav'st the souls whose humble love
   Is joined with holy fear.
5 My lips shall dwell upon thy praise,
   And spread thy fame abroad;
   Let all the sons of Adam raise
   The honors of their God.   *Watts.*

73   *God's Condescension.*   C. M.

O THOU, to whom all creatures bow
   Within this earthly frame,
Through all the world, how great art thou!
   How glorious is thy name!
2 When heaven, thy glorious work on high,
   Employs my wondering sight —
The moon, that nightly rules the sky,
   With stars of feebler light, —
3 Lord, what is man, that thou shouldst choose
   To keep him in thy mind?
Or what his race, that thou shouldst prove
   To them so wondrous kind?
4 O Thou, to whom all creatures bow
   Within this earthly frame,
Through all the world, how great art thou!
   How glorious is thy name!
                         Tate & Brady.

74   *Omnipresence of God.*   L. M.

FATHER of spirits, nature's God,
   Our inmost thoughts are known to thee:

BEING AND ATTRIBUTES OF GOD.

Thou, Lord, canst hear each idle word,
And every private action see.
2 Could we, on morning's swiftest wings,
Pursue our flight through trackless air
Or dive beneath deep ocean's springs,
Thy presence still would meet us there.
3 In vain may guilt attempt to fly,
Concealed beneath the pall of night;
One glance from thy all-piercing eye
Can kindle darkness into light.
4 Search thou our hearts, and there destroy
Each evil thought, each secret sin,
And fit us for those realms of joy,
Where nought impure shall enter in.
Spirit of the Psalms.

75 *Wisdom and Knowledge of God.* L. M.

AWAKE my tongue; thy tribute bring
To Him who gave thee power to sing;
Praise Him who has all praise above,
The source of wisdom and of love.
2 How vast his knowledge! how profound!
A depth where all our thoughts are drowned;
The stars he numbers, and their names
He gives to all those heavenly flames.
3 Through each bright world above, behold
Ten thousand thousand charms unfold;
Earth, air and mighty seas combine
To speak his wisdom all divine.
4 But in redemption, O, what grace!
Its wonders, O, what thought can trace!
Here wisdom shines forever bright;
Praise him, my soul, with sweet delight!
Needham.

BEING AND ATTRIBUTES OF GOD.

76   *The Lord's Prayer.*   L. M.

FATHER of all, whose powerful voice
  Called forth this universal frame!
Whose mercies over all rejoice,
  Through endless ages still the same:

2 Thou by thy word upholdest all;
  Thy bounteous love to all is showed:
Thou hear'st thy every creature's call;
  And fillest every mouth with good.

3 In heaven thou reign'st enthroned in light,
  Nature's expanse before thee spread:
Earth, air and sea before thy sight,
  And hell's deep gloom, are open laid:

4 Wisdom, and might, and love, are thine:
  Prostrate before thy face we fall,
Confess thine attributes divine,
  And hail thee sovereign Lord of all.

5 Thee, sovereign Lord, let all confess.
  That move in earth, or air, or sky;
Revere thy power, thy goodness bless,
  Tremble before thy piercing eye.

6 All ye who owe to him your birth,
  In praise your every hour employ:
Jehovah reigns: be glad, O earth,
  And shout, ye morning stars, for joy!
                              J. Wesley.

77   *God is Love.*   8s & 7s.

GOD is love: his mercy brightens
  All the path in which we rove;
Bliss he wakes, and woe he lightens;
  God is wisdom, God is love.

2 Chance and change are busy ever;
  Man decays, and ages move;

But his mercy waneth never;
   God is wisdom, God is love.

3 E'en the hour that darkest seemeth
   Will his changeless goodness prove;
   From the gloom his brightness streameth,
   God is wisdom, God is love.

4 He with earthly cares entwineth
   Hope and comfort from above:
   Everywhere his glory shineth;
   God is wisdom, God is love.   *Bowring.*

78   *Psalm cxlviii.*   8, 8, 6

BEGIN, my soul, th' exalted lay,
   Let each enraptured thought obey,
     And praise th' Almighty's name:
Lo! heaven and earth, and seas and skies,
In one melodious concert rise,
     To swell th' inspiring theme.

2 Ye fields of light, celestial plains,
   Where gay, transporting beauty reigns,
     Ye scenes divinely fair:
Your Maker's wondrous power proclaim,
Tell how he formed your shining frame,
     And breathed the fluid air.

3 Ye angels, catch the thrilling sound;
   While all the adoring thrones around
     His boundless mercy sing:
Let every list'ning saint above
Wake all the tuneful soul of love,
     And touch the sweetest string.

4 Let saints, redeemed from death and hell,
   In louder, loftier numbers, tell
     The wonders of his grace:

OF CHRIST.

Beyond creation's utmost bounds,
Above her noblest, sweetest sounds,
Declare Jehovah's praise. *Ogilvie.*

SECTION IV.
Of Christ.

79 *The Prince of Peace.* **C. M.**

TO us a child of hope is born,
  To us a Son is given:
Him shall the tribes of earth obey,
  Him, all the hosts of heaven.

2 His name shall be the Prince of peace,
  For evermore adored,—
The Wonderful the Counsellor,
  The great and mighty Lord.

3 His power. increasing, still shall spread:
  His reign no end shall know;
Justice shall guard his throne above,
  And peace abound below.

4 To us a child of hope is born;
  To us a Son is given;—
The Wonderful, the Counsellor,
  The mighty Lord of heaven.
J. Morrison.

80 *Psalm* xcviii. **C. M.**

JOY to the world—the Lord is come!
  Let earth receive her King:
Let every heart prepare him room,
  And heaven and nature sing.

62

2 Joy to the earth—the Saviour reigns!
   Let men their songs employ;
   While fields and floods, rocks, hills and plains,
   Repeat the sounding joy.

3 No more let sins and sorrows grow,
   Nor thorns infest the ground:
   He comes to make his blessings flow,
   Far as the curse is found.

4 He rules the world with truth and grace;
   And makes the nations prove
   The glories of his righteousness,
   And wonders of his love.   *Watts.*

81   *The Inauguration.*   C. M.

SEE, from on high, a light divine
   On Jesus' head descend;
   And hear the sacred voice from heaven,
   That bids us all attend: -

2 "This is my well-beloved Son,"
   Proclaimed the voice Divine:
   "Hear him," his Heavenly Father said,
   "For all his words are mine."

3 His mission thus confirmed from heaven,
   The great Messiah came,
   And heavenly wisdom taught to man,
   In God, the Father's name.

4 The path of heavenly peace he showed,
   That leads to bliss on high,
   Where all his faithful foll'wers here
   Shall live, no more to die.

5 O may we then, who own him Lord,
   And his loved name profess,
   By all our words and actions prove
   That we his mind possess.   *Unknown.*

OF CHRIST.

82 *The Incarnation.* C. M.

MORTALS, awake, with angels join,
  And chant the solemn lay:
Joy, love, and gratitude, combine
  To hail th' auspicious day.

2 In heaven the rapt'rous song began,
    And sweet seraphic fire
  Through all the shining legions ran,
    And strung and tuned the lyre.

3 Swift through the vast expanse it flew,
    And loud the echo rolled:
  The theme, the song, the joy was new,
    'Twas more than heaven could hold.

4 Down through the portals of the sky
    Th' impetuous torrent ran;
  And angels flew with eager joy
    To bear the news to man.

5 With joy the chorus we'll repeat,
    Glory to God on high!
  Good-will and peace are now complete:
    Jesus was born to die."

6 Hail Prince of Life, forever hail!
    Redeemer, brother, friend!
  Though earth, and time, and life, shall fail
    Thy praise shall never end. *Medley.*

83 *The Guiding Star.* C. M.

BRIGHT was the guiding star, that led,
  With mild, benignant ray,
The Gentiles to the lowly bed
  Where our Redeemer lay.

2 But, lo! a brighter, clearer light
    Now points to his abode;

OF CHRIST.

It shines through sin and sorrow's night,
To guide us to our Lord.

3 O, haste, to follow where it leads;
The gracious call obey,
Be rugged wilds, or flow'ry meads,
The Christian's destined way.

4 O, gladly tread the narrow path,
While light and grace are giv'n:
Who meekly follow Christ on earth,
Shall reign with him in heav'n.
Spir. of the Ps.

84 *Jude 24, 25.* S. M.

TO God, the only wise,
Our Saviour and our King,
Let all the saints below the skies
Their humble praises bring.

2 'Tis his almighty love,
His counsel and his care,
Preserves us safe from sin and death,
And every hurtful snare.

3 He will present our souls,
Unblemished and complete,
Before the glory of his face,
With joys divinely great.

4 Then all the chosen seed
Shall meet around the throne;
Shall bless the conduct of his grace,
And make his wonders known.

5 To our Redeemer, God,
Wisdom with power belongs,
Immortal crowns of majesty,
And everlasting songs.   *Watts.*

OF CHRIST.

85 *The Victory of the Cross.* S. M.

JESUS, the Conqueror, reigns,
  In glorious strength arrayed;
His kingdom over all maintains,
  And bids the earth be glad:

2 Ye sons of men, rejoice
  In Jesus' mighty love;
Lift up your heart, lift up your voice,
  To him who rules above.

3 Extol his kingly power;
  Kiss the exalted Son,
Who died, and lives to die no more,
  High on his Father's throne:

4 Our Advocate with God,
  He undertakes our cause,
And spreads through all the earth abroad
  The victory of his cross.
                        Charles Wesley.

86 *Atoning Sacrifice.* S. M.

NOT all the blood of beasts,
  On Jewish altars slain,
Could give the guilty conscience peace,
  Or wash away the stain.

2 But Christ, the heavenly Lamb,
  Takes all our sins away:
A sacrifice of nobler name,
  And richer blood than they.

3 My faith would lay her hand
  On that dear head of thine,—
While like a penitent I stand,
  And there confess my sin.
                        Watts.

OF CHRIST.

87   *" Unto us a Child is Born."*   S. M.

FATHER, our hearts we lift
　Up to thy gracious throne,
And thank thee for the precious gift
　Of thine incarnate Son!

2 The gift unspeakable
　We thankfully receive,
And to the world thy goodness tell,
　And to thy glory live.

3 Jesus, the holy child,
　Doth, by his birth, declare
That God and man are reconciled,
　And one in him we are.

4 A peace on earth he brings,
　Which never more shall end:
The Lord of hosts, the King of kings,
　Declares himself our friend.

5 His kingdom from above
　He doth to us impart,
And pure benevolence and love
　O'erflow the faithful heart.   *C. Wesley.*

88   *" Unto us a Son is given."*   L. M.

TO us a child of royal birth,
　Heir of the promises, is given!
Th' Invisible appears on earth,
　The Son of man, the God of heaven.

2 A Saviour born, in love supreme
　He comes, our fallen souls to raise:
He comes, his people to redeem,
　With all his plenitude of grace.

3 The Christ, by raptured seers foretold,
　Filled with th' eternal Spirit's power,

OF CHRIST.

Prophet, and Priest and King, behold,
And Lord of all the worlds adore.
4 The Lord of hosts, the God most high,
Who quits his throne on earth to live,
With joy we welcome from the sky,
With faith into our hearts receive.
C. Wesley

89　　　　*Gal. vi. 14.*　　　　L. M.

WHEN I survey the wondrous cross
On which the Prince of glory died,
My richest gain I count but loss,
And pour contempt on all my pride.
2 Forbid it, Lord, that I should boast,
Save in the death of Christ my God:
All the vain things that charm me most,
I sacrifice them to his blood.
3 See, from his head, his hands, his feet,
Sorrow and love flow mingled down!
Did e'er such love and sorrow meet?
Or thorns compose so rich a crown?
4 Were the whole realm of nature mine,
That were a present far too small;
Love so amazing, so Divine,
Demands my soul, my life, my all. *Watts*

90　　　　*His Exemplary Life.*　　　　L. M.

MY dear Redeemer, and my Lord,
I read my duty in thy word;
But in thy life the law appears,
Drawn out in living characters.
2 Such was thy truth, and such thy zeal,
Such def'rence to thy Father's will,
Such love, and meekness so divine,
I would transcribe, and make them mine.

OF CHRIST.

3 Cold mountains, and the midnight air,
Witness the fervor of thy prayer;
The desert thy temptations knew,
Thy conflict, and thy vict'ry too.

4 Be thou my pattern; make me bear
More of thy gracious image here:
Then God, the Judge, shall own my name
Among the foll'wers of the Lamb.   *Watts.*

91   *The Incarnation.*   7s.

HARK! the herald angels sing,
"Glory to the new-born King!
Peace on earth, and mercy mild;
God and sinners reconciled!"
Joyful all ye nations rise.
Join the triumphs of the skies;
With th' angelic hosts proclaim,
"Christ is born in Bethlehem!"

2 Christ, by highest heaven adored,
Christ, the everlasting Lord;
Late in time behold him come,
Offspring of a virgin's womb;
Veiled in flesh the Godhead see,
Hail th' incarnate Deity!
Pleased as man with men t' appear,
Jesus our Immanuel here.

3 Come, Desire of nations, come!
Fix in us thy humble home:
Rise, the woman's conqu'ring seed,
Bruise in us the serpent's head;
Adam's likeness now efface,
Stamp thine image in its place:
Second Adam from above,
Reinstate us in thy love.   *C. Wesley.*

OF CHRIST.

92   *Brazen Serpent.*   7s.

O THAT I could look to thee,
   Jesus, lifted up for me,
Me, a wounded Israelite,
Me, expiring in thy sight!
2 Guilt, the serpent's sting, I feel,
   Anguish inconceivable,
Bleeding, gasping on the ground,
Dying of the pois'nous wound.
3 But, with a believing eye,
   If I can my Lord espy,
Hanging on the sacred pole,
I, e'en I, shall be made whole.
4 Give me now to find thee near,
   Now as crucified appear:
Life is through thy wounds alone;
Mine to heal, display thy own.
                                   C. Wesley

93   *The Star of Bethlehem.*   L. M.

WHEN, marshall'd on the nightly plain,
   The gl'tt'ring hosts bestud the sky,
One star alone, of all the train,
Can fix the sinner's wandering eye.
2 Hark! hark! to God the chorus breaks,
   From every host, from every gem;
But one alone the Saviour speaks—
It is the Star of Bethlehem!
3 Once on the raging seas I rode;
   The storm was loud, the night was dark,
The ocean yawned, and rudely blow'd
The wind that tossed my foundering bark.
4 Deep horror then my vitals froze;
   Death-struck, I ceas'd the tide to stem;

OF CHRIST.

When suddenly a star arose—
It was the Star of Bethlehem!

5 It was my guide, my light, mine all;
It bade my dark forebodings cease;
And, through the storm and danger's thrall,
It led me to the port of peace.

6 Now, safely moor'd, my perils o'er,
I'll sing, first in night's diadem,
Forever, and for evermore—
The Star—the Star of Bethlehem!

H. K. White.

94 *Believe and be saved.* L. M.
John iii. 16, 17, 18.

NOT to condemn the sons of men,
Did Christ, the Son of God, appear:—
No weapons in his hands are seen,
No flaming sword, nor thunder there.

2 Such was the pity of our God,—
He lov'd the race of man so well,—
He sent his Son, to bear our load
Of sins, and save our souls from hell.

3 Sinners, believe the Saviour's word;
Trust in his mighty name, and live:
A thousand joys his lips afford;
His hands a thousand blessings give.

4 But vengeance and damnation lies
On rebels who refuse his grace;
Who God's eternal Son despise,
The hottest hell shall be their place.

Watts.

OF CHRIST.

95 *The Suffering and Crucifixion of Christ.* L. M.
Matt. xxvii. 26–53.

YE that pass by, behold the Man!
   The man of griefs condemned for you,
The Lamb of God, for sinners slain,
   Weeping to Calvary pursue!

2 See! how his back the scourges tear,
   While to the bloody pillar bound!
The ploughers made long furrows there,
   Till all his body is one wound.

3 Nor can he thus their hate assuage;
   His innocence to death pursued,
Must fully glut their utmost rage;
   Hark! how they clamor for his blood!

4 His sacred limbs they stretch, they tear,
   With nails they fasten to the wood!
His sacred limbs, exposed and bare,
   Or only cover'd with his blood!

5 See, there! his temples crown'd with thorns
   His bleeding hands extended wide!
His streaming feet transfixt and torn!
   The fountain gushing from his side!

6 Where is the King of Glory now?
   The everlasting Son of God!
The Immortal hangs his languid brow:
   The Almighty faints beneath his load!
                  C. Wesley.

96   *Dying, Rising, Reigning.*   L. M.

HE dies! the Friend of sinners dies!
   Lo! Salem's daughters weep around;
A solemn darkness veils the skies;
   A sudden trembling shakes the ground:

Come, saints, and drop a tear or two
  For him who groaned beneath your load:
He shed a thousand drops for you,
  A thousand drops of richer blood.

2 Here's love and grief beyond degree:
  The Lord of glory dies for man!
But lo! what sudden joys we see!
  Jesus, the dead, revives again!
The rising God forsakes the tomb;
  Up to his Father's courts he flies;
Cherubic legions guard him home,
  And shout him welcome to the skies!

3 Break off your tears, ye saints, and tell
  How high your great Deliv'rer reigns:
Sing how he spoiled the hosts of hell,
  And led the monster death in chains!
Say, "Live for ever, wondrous King!
  Born to redeem, and strong to save!"
Then ask the monster, "Where's thy sting?"
  And, "Where's thy vict'ry, boasting grave?"
                                Watts.

97   *"It is finished."*   L. M.

'TIS finished! The Messiah dies,
  Cut off for sins, but not his own!
Accomplished is the sacrifice,
  The great redeeming work is done.

2 'Tis finished! All the debt is paid:
  Justice Divine is satisfied:
The grand and full atonement made:
  God for a guilty world hath died.

3 The veil is rent in Christ alone:
  The living way to heaven is seen:
The middle wall is broken down,
  And all mankind may enter in.

OF CHRIST.

4 The types and figures are fulfilled:
  Exacted is the legal pain:
The precious promises are sealed:
  The spotless Lamb of God is slain.

5 Saved from the legal curse I am;
  My Saviour hangs on yonder tree:
See there the meek expiring Lamb!
  'Tis finished! He expires for me.
                                    C. Wesley.

98   *Rejoice evermore.*   H. M.

REJOICE, the Lord is King!
  Your Lord and King adore;
Mortals, give thanks and sing,
  And triumph evermore;
Lift up your hearts, lift up your voice;
Rejoice, again I say, rejoice.

2 Jesus, the Saviour, reigns,
  The God of truth and love;
When he had purged our stains,
  He took his seat above;
Lift up your hearts, lift up your voice;
Rejoice, again I say, rejoice.

3 His kingdom cannot fail,
  He rules o'er earth and heaven;
The keys of death and hell
  Are to our Jesus given;
Lift up your hearts, lift up your voice;
Rejoice, again I say, rejoice.

4 He sits at God's right hand
  Till all his foes submit,
And bow to his command,
  And fall beneath his feet;
Lift up your hearts, lift up your voice;
Rejoice, again I say, rejoice.

5 He all his foes shall quell,
    And all our sins destroy ;
    Let every bosom swell
      With pure seraphic joy ;
Lift up your hearts, lift up your voice;
Rejoice, again I say, rejoice.

6. Rejoice in glorious hope ;
    Jesus the Judge shall come,
    And take his servants up
      To their eternal home ;
We soon shall hear the archangel's voice;
The trump of God shall sound,—Rejoice!
                    Charles Wesley.

99   *Various Offices of Christ.*   H. M.

JOIN all the glorious names
    Of wisdom, love, and power,
That ever mortals knew,
    That angels ever bore :
All are too mean to speak his worth,
Too mean to set my *Saviour* forth.

2 But O ! what gentle terms,
    What condescending ways,
Doth our *Redeemer* use
    To teach his heavenly grace !
Mine eyes with joy and wonder see
What forms of love he bears for me.

3 Arrayed in mortal flesh,
    The *Cov'nant-Angel* stands,
And holds the promises
    And pardons in his hands :
Commissioned from his Father's throne
To make his grace to mortals known.

4 Great *Prophet* of my God,
    My tongue would bless thy name:

OF CHRIST.

By thee the joyful news
  Of our salvation came,—
The joyful news of sins forgiven,
Of hell subdued, and peace with Heaven.

5 Be thou my *Counsellor*,
  My *Pattern* and my *Guide;*
And through this desert land
  Still keep me near thy side:
O let my feet ne'er run astray,
Nor rove, nor seek the crooked way. *Watts.*

100   *High Priest.*   H. M.

JESUS, my great *High Priest*,
  Offered his blood and died.
My guilty conscience seeks
  No sacrifice beside:
His powerful blood did once atone,
And now it pleads before the throne.

2 My *Advocate* appears
  For my defence on high:
The Father bows his ears,
  And lays his thunder by:
Not all that earth or hell can say
Shall turn his heart, his love away.

3 O thou almighty *Lord*,
  My *Conqu'ror* and my *King*,
Thy sceptre, and thy sword,
  Thy reigning grace I sing:
Thine is the power: behold I sit
In willing bonds beneath thy feet.

4 Now let my soul arise,
  And tread the tempter down;
My *Captain* leads me forth
  To conquest and a crown:

A feeble saint shall win the day,
Though death and hell obstruct the way.

5 Should all the hosts of death,
   And powers of hell unknown,
Put their most dreadful forms
   Of rage and mischief on,
I shall be safe, for *Christ* displays
Superior power, and guardian grace. *Watts.*

101   *It is finished.*   8, 7, 4.

HARK! the voice of love and mercy
   Sounds aloud from Calvary;
See! it rends the rocks asunder,
   Shakes the earth, and veils the sky;
     "It is finished:"
   Hear the dying Saviour cry.

2 "It is finished!" O what pleasure
   Do these precious words afford!
Heavenly blessings, without measure,
   Flow to us from Christ the Lord:
     "It is finished:"
   Saints, the dying words record.

3 Tune your harps anew, ye seraphs;
   Join to sing the pleasing theme;
All on earth, and all in heaven,
   Join to praise Immanuel's name;
     Hallelujah!
   Glory to the bleeding Lamb.
                   Jonathan Evans.

102   *The Star in the East.*   30th 11, 10, 11, 10.

BRIGHTEST and best of the sons of the
   morning,
Dawn on our darkness, and lend us thine aid:
Star of the East, the horizon adorning,
   Guide where the infant Redeemer is laid.

2 Cold, on his cradle, the dew-drops are shining,
  Low lies his bed with the beasts of the stall;
  Angels adore him, in slumber reclining,—
  Maker, and Monarch, and Saviour of all.
3 Say shall we yield him in costly devotion,
  Odors of Eden and off'rings divine?
  Gems of the mountain, and pearls of the ocean,
  Myrrh from the forest, and gold from the mine?
4 Vainly we offer each ample oblation;
  Vainly with gifts would his favor secure;
  Richer by far is the heart's adoration;
  Dearer to God are the pray'rs of the poor.
                                        Heber.

103   *The Birth of Christ.* Luke ii. 11-16.   11s.

HITHER, ye faithful, haste with songs of triumph,
  To Bethlehem go, the Lord of Life to meet;
  To you, this day, is born a Prince and Saviour,
  O, come, and let us worship at his feet.
2 O, Jesus! for such wondrous condescension,
  Our praise and reverence are an offering meet.
  Now is the Word made flesh, and dwells among us,
  O, come, and let us worship at his feet.
3 Shout his almighty name, ye choirs of angels,
  Let the celestial courts his praise repeat;
  Unto our God be glory in the highest;
  O, come, and let us worship at his feet.

104   *The Incarnation.*   8, 7, 8, 7.

HARK! what mean those holy voices
  Sweetly sounding through the skies?
  Lo! th' angelic host rejoices,
  Heavenly hallelujahs rise.

2 Listen to the wondrous story
   Which they chant in hymns of joy:
   Glory in the highest glory!
   Glory be to God most high!

3 Peace on earth, good-will from heaven,
   Reaching far as man is found:
   Souls redeem'd and sins forgiven,
   Loud our golden harps shall sound.

4 Christ is born, the great Anointed,
   Heaven and earth his praises sing:
   O! receive whom God appointed
   For your Prophet, Priest and King.

5 Hasten, mortals, to adore him,
   Learn his name and taste his joy:
   Till in heaven ye sing before him,
   Glory be to God most high!

6 Let us learn the wondrous story
   Of our great Redeemer's birth:
   Spread the brightness of his glory
   Till it cover all the earth. *Cawood.*

105   *Luke* ii. 8–14.   C. M.

WHILE shepherds watch'd their flocks by night,
   All seated on the ground,
   The angel of the Lord came down,
   And glory shone around.

2 "Fear not," said he, (for mighty dread
   Had seiz'd their troubled mind,)
   "Glad tidings of great joy I bring
   To you and all mankind.

3 "To you, in David's town, this day,
   Is born of David's line,
   The Saviour, who is Christ the Lord;
   And this shall be the sign:

4 "The heavenly babe you there shall find
  To human view display'd,
All meanly wrapp'd in swathing bands,
  And in a manger laid." *Patrick.*

106 *Design and object of his Advent.*   C. M.

HARK, the glad sound! the Saviour comes—
  The Saviour, promis'd long;
Let every heart prepare a throne,
  And every voice a song.

2 He comes, the pris'ner to release,
  In Satan's bondage held;
The gates of brass before him burst,
  The iron fetters yield.

3 He comes, from thickest films of vice,
  To clear the mental ray,
And on the eyes oppress'd with night
  To pour celestial day.

4 He comes, the broken heart to bind,
  The wounded soul to cure,
And, with the treasures of his grace,
  T' enrich the humble poor.

5 Our glad hosannas, Prince of peace,
  Thy welcome shall proclaim,
And heaven's eternal arches ring
  With thy beloved name.   *Doddridge.*

107   *Stupendous love.*   C. M.

PLUNGED in a gulf of dark despair,
  We wretched sinners lay,
Without one cheering beam of hope,
  Or spark of glimm'ring day.

2 With pitying eyes the Prince of grace
  Beheld our helpless grief;
He saw, and (O amazing love)!
  He ran to our relief.

OF CHRIST.

3 Down from the shining seats above
   With joyful haste he fled,
Entered the grave in mortal flesh,
   And dwelt among the dead.

4 O for this love let rocks and hills
   Their lasting silence break!
And all harmonious human tongues
   The Saviour's praises speak.

5 Angels, assist our mighty joys,
   Strike all your harps of gold;
But when you raise your highest notes,
   His love can ne'er be told!   *Watts.*

108   *The Fountain of Atonement.*   C. M.

THERE is a fountain filled with blood,
   Drawn from Immanuel's veins;
And sinners, plunged beneath that flood,
   Lose all their guilty stains.

2 The dying thief rejoiced to see
   That fountain in his day;
And there may I, though vile as he,
   Wash all my sins away.

3 Dear dying Lamb, thy precious blood
   Shall never lose its power,
Till all the ransomed Church of God
   Be saved to sin no more.

4 E'er since, by faith, I saw the stream
   Thy flowing wounds supply,
Redeeming love has been my theme,
   And shall be till I die.

5 Then, in a nobler, sweeter song,
   I'll sing thy power to save,
When this poor lisping, stamm'ring tongue
   Lies silent in the grave.   *Cowper.*

109 *The Crucifixion.* **C. M.**

BEHOLD the Saviour of mankind
    Nailed to the shameful tree!
How vast the love that him inclined
    To bleed and die for thee!

2 Hark, how he groans! while nature shakes,
    And earth's strong pillars bend!
The temple's veil in sunder breaks,
    The solid marbles rend.

3 'Tis done! the precious ransom's paid!
    "Receive my soul!" he cries:
See where he bows his sacred head!
    He bows his head, and dies!

4 But soon he'll break death's envious chain,
    And in full glory shine:
O Lamb of God, was ever pain,
    Was ever love, like thine?   *S. Wesley, Sr*

110   *Coronation of Christ.*   **C. M.**

ALL hail the power of Jesus' name!
    Let angels prostrate fall:
Bring forth the royal diadem,
    And crown him Lord of all!

2 Ye chosen seed of Israel's race,—
    A remnant weak and small,—
Hail him who saves you by his grace,
    And crown him Lord of all.

3 Ye Gentile sinners, ne'er forget
    The wormwood and the gall:
Go, spread your trophies at his feet,
    And crown him Lord of all.

4 Let every kindred, every tribe
    On this terrestrial ball,
To him all majesty ascribe,
    And crown him Lord of all.

OF CHRIST

5 O that, with yonder sacred throng,
   We at his feet may fall!
We'll join the everlasting song,
   And crown him Lord of all. *Perronet.*

111   "*I am the Way.*"   L. M.

JESUS, my all, to heaven is gone,
   He whom I fix my hopes upon;
His track I see, and I'll pursue
   The narrow way, till him I view.

2 The way the holy prophets went,
   The road that leads from banishment,
The King's highway of holiness,
   I'll go, for all his paths are peace.

3 This is the way I long have sought,
   And mourned because I found it not:
My grief a burden long has been,
   Because I was not saved from sin.

4 The more I strove against its power,
   I felt its weight and guilt the more;
Till late I heard my Saviour say,
   "Come hither, soul, I AM THE WAY."

5 Lo! glad I come, and thou, blest Lamb,
   Shalt take me to thee as I am;
Nothing but sin have I to give,
   Nothing but love shall I receive

6 Then will I tell to sinners round
   What a dear Saviour I have found;
I'll point to thy redeeming blood,
   And say, "Behold the way to God!" *Cennick.*

112   "*Over all, God blessed forever.*"   L. M.

THE day of Christ, the day of God,
   We humbly hope with joy to see,
Washed in the sanctifying blood
   Of an expiring Deity—

OF CHRIST.

2 Who did for us his life resign:
 There is no other God but one;
 For all the plenitude divine
 Resides in the eternal Son.

3 Spotless, sincere, without offense,
 O may we to his day remain!
 Who trust the blood of Christ to cleanse
 Our souls from every sinful stain.

4 Lord, we believe the promise sure!
 The purchased Comforter impart!
 Apply thy blood to make us pure—
 To keep us pure in life and heart!

5 Then let us see that day supreme,
 When none thy Godhead shall deny!
 Thy sovereign majesty blaspheme,
 Or count thee less than the Most High.
 C. Wesley

113   L. M.
Praise to God for his Perfections and Providence.

PRAISE ye the Lord: my heart shall join
 In work so pleasant, so divine:
My days of praise shall ne'er be past,
While life, and thought, and being, last.

2 Happy the man whose hopes rely
 On Israel's God: he made the sky,
And earth, and seas, with all their train;
And none shall find his promise vain.

3 His truth forever stands secure;
 He saves th' oppressed, he feeds the poor,
He helps the stranger in distress,
The widow and the fatherless.

4 He loves the saints; he knows them well,
 But turns the wicked down to hell:

OF CHRIST.

Thy God, O Zion, ever reigns;
Praise him in everlasting strains. *Watts.*

114 *The Grace of Christ.* L. M.

NOW to the Lord a noble song!
Awake, my soul; awake, my tongue:
Hosanna to th' Eternal Name,
And all his boundless love proclaim.

2 See, where it shines in Jesus' face,
The brightest image of his grace:
God, in the person of his Son,
Has all his mightiest works outdone.

3 The spacious earth and spreading flood
Proclaim the wise the powerful God;
And thy rich glories, from afar,
Sparkle in every rolling star:

4 But in his looks a glory stands,
The noblest labor of thy hands;
The pleasing lustre of his eyes
Outshines the wonders of the skies. *Watts.*

115 *Resurrection.* C. M.

THE Sun of Righteousness appears,
To set in blood no more:
Adore the Scatt'rer of your fears,
Your rising Sun adore.

2 The saints, when he resigned his breath,
Unclosed their sleeping eyes;
He breaks again the bands of death,
Again the dead arise.

3 Alone the dreadful race he ran,
Alone the wine-press trod:
He dies and suffers as a man;
He rises as a God.

4 In vain the stone, the watch, the seal,
  Forbid an early rise
To him who breaks the gates of hell,
  And opens paradise.   *S. Wesley, Jr.*

116   *Rejoicing in the Risen Christ.*   C. M.

AWAKE, glad soul! awake! awake!
    Thy Lord has risen long;
Go to his grave, and with thee take,
    Both tuneful heart and song.

2 Where life is waking all around,
    Where love's sweet voices sing,
The first bright blossom may be found
    Of an eternal spring.

3 The shade and gloom of life are fled
    This resurrection day;
Henceforth in Christ are no more dead,
    The grave hath no more prey.

4 In Christ we live, in Christ we sleep,
    In Christ we wake and rise,
And the sad tears death makes us weep,
    He wipes from all our eyes.

5 Then wake, glad heart! awake! awake!
    And seek thy risen Lord!
Joy in his resurrection take,
    And comfort in his word!   *S. B. Monsell.*

117   *Ascension Day.*   7s.

HAIL the day that sees him rise,
    Ravished from our wistful eyes!
Christ, awhile to mortals given,
Re-ascends his native heaven.

2 There the pompous triumph waits:
  Lift your heads, eternal gates!

OF CHRIST.

Wide unfold the radiant scene;
Take the King of glory in!

3 Circled round with angel powers,
Their triumphant Lord and ours,
Conqueror over death and sin,—
Take the King of glory in!

4 Him though highest heaven receives,
Still he loves the earth he leaves;
Though returning to his throne,
Still he calls mankind his own.

5 See, he lifts his hands above!
See, he shows the prints of love!
Hark, his gracious lips bestow
Blessings on his Church below!

6 Saviour, parted from our sight,
High above yon azure height,
Grant our hearts may thither rise,
Following thee beyond the skies.
Charles Wesley.

118 *The Lord is Risen.* 7s.

CHRIST, the Lord, is risen again,
Christ hath broken every chain;
Hark! angelic voices cry,
Singing evermore on high,
  Hallelujah! Praise the Lord!

2 He who gave for us his life,
Who for us endured the strife,
Is our Paschal Lamb to-day!
We, too, sing for joy, and say,
  Hallelujah! Praise the Lord!

3 He who bore all pain and loss,
Comfortless, upon the cross,

OF CHRIST.

Lives in glory now on high,
Pleads for us, and hears our cry:
Hallelujah! Praise the Lord!

4 Now he bids us tell abroad
How the lost may be restored,
How the penitent forgiven,
How we, too may enter heaven!
Hallelujah! Praise the Lord!
[*Michael Weisse. Tr. by Miss C. Winkworth.*]

119   *The Lord is Risen.*   7s.

CHRIST. the Lord, is risen to-day,
  Sons of men and angels say;
Raise your joys and triumphs high;
Sing, ye heavens, – and earth, reply.

2 Love's redeeming work is done;
Fought the fight. the battle won:
Lo! the sun's eclipse is o'er;
Lo! he sets in blood no more.

3 Vain the stone the watch, the seal,
Christ has burst the gates of hell:
Death in vain forbids his rise;
Christ hath opened paradise.

4 Lives again our glorious King:
Where O Death. is now thy sting?
Once he died our souls to save;
Where's thy victory. boasting Grave?

5 Soar we now where Christ has led,
Following our exalted Head:
Made like him, like him we rise;
Ours the cross, the grave, the skies.
                       Charles Wesley.

OF CHRIST.

120   *Love which passeth Knowledge.*   L. M.
[From the Latin of St. Bernard.]

OF Him who did salvation bring
I could forever think and sing:
Arise, ye needy, he'll relieve;
Arise, ye guilty, he'll forgive.

2 Ask but his grace, and lo, 'tis given!
Ask, and he turns your hell to heaven:
Though sin and sorrow wound my soul,
Jesus, thy balm will make it whole.

3 To shame our sins he blushed in blood,
He closed his eyes to show us God:
Let all the world fall down and know
That none but God such love can show.

4 'Tis thee I love, for thee alone
I shed my tears and make my moan!
Where'er I am, where'er I move,
I meet the object of my love.

5 Insatiate to this spring I fly:
I drink, and yet am ever dry:
Ah! who against thy charms is proof?
Ah! who that loves can love enough?

121   *Rev. v. 12-14.*   L. M.

WHAT equal honors shall we bring
To thee, O Lord our God, the Lamb,
When all the notes that angels sing
Are far inferior to thy name?

2 Worthy is he that once was slain,
The Prince of life, that groaned and died;
Worthy to rise, and live, and reign
At his almighty Father's side.

3 Power and dominion are his due
Who stood condemned at Pilate's bar:

OF CHRIST.

Wisdom belongs to Jesus too,
  Though he was charged with madness here.
4 All riches are his native right,
  Yet he sustained amazing loss:
  To him ascribe eternal might,
  Who left his weakness on the cross.

5 Honor immortal must be paid,
  Instead of scandal and of scorn;
  While glory shines around his head,
  And a bright crown without a thorn.

6 Blessings forever on the Lamb,
  Who bore our sin, and curse, and pain:
  Let angels sound his sacred name,
  And every creature say, Amen! *Watts.*

122   *Rev.* v. 11–13.   C. M.

COME, let us join our cheerful songs
  With angels round the throne:
  Ten thousand thousand are their tongues,
  But all their joys are one.

2 Worthy the Lamb that died, they cry,
  To be exalted thus:
  Worthy the Lamb, our hearts reply,
  For he was slain for us.

3 Jesus is worthy to receive
  Honor and power divine;
  And blessings, more than we can give,
  Be, Lord, forever thine.

4 The whole creation join in one
  To bless the sacred name
  Of him that sits upon the throne,
  And to adore the Lamb.
                                Watts.

OF CHRIST.

123 *The Name of Jesus.* C. M.

HOW sweet the name of Jesus sounds
  In a believer's ear!
It soothes his sorrows, heals his wounds,
  And drives away his fear.

2 It makes the wounded spirit whole,
  And calms the troubled breast;
'Tis manna to the hungry soul,
  And to the weary, rest.

3 Dear Name, the rock on which I build,
  My shield and hiding-place;
My never-failing treasury, filled
  With boundless stores of grace.

4 Jesus, my Shepherd, Brother, Friend,
  My Prophet, Priest, and King;
My Lord, my Life, my Way, my End,
  Accept the praise I bring.

5 Weak is the effort of my heart,
  And cold my warmest thought;
But when I see thee as thou art,
  I'll praise thee as I ought.
                              Newton.

124 *The True Light.* 7s, 6L

CHRIST, whose glory fills the skies,
  Christ, the true, the only Light,
Sun of righteousness, arise,
  Triumph o'er the shades of night;
Dayspring from on high, be near,
Day-star, in my heart appear.

2 Dark and cheerless is the morn,
  Unaccompanied by thee;

Joyless is the day's return,
 Till thy mercy's beams I see;
Till thou inward life impart,
Glad my eyes, and warm my heart.

3 Visit then this soul of mine;
 Pierce the gloom of sin and grief;
Fill me, Radiancy divine;
 Scatter all my unbelief:
More and more thyself display,
Shining to the perfect day.

Charles Wesley.

125   *Rock of Ages.*   7s 6 lines.

ROCK of ages, cleft for me,
 Let me hide myself in thee:
Let the water and the blood,
From thy wounded side which flowed,
Be of sin the double cure,
Save from wrath and make me pure.

2 Could my tears forever flow,
Could my zeal no languor know,
These for sin could not atone;
Thou must save, and thou alone:
In my hand no price I bring,
Simply to thy cross I cling.

3 While I draw this fleeting breath,
When my eyes shall close in death,
When I rise to worlds unknown,
And behold thee on thy throne,
Rock of ages, cleft for me,
Let me hide myself in thee.

Toplady.

THE HOLY SPIRIT.

SECTION V.
The Holy Spirit.

126 *Sanctifying Influence.* S. M.

COME, Holy Spirit, come,
  Let thy bright beams arise;
Dispel the sorrow from our minds,
  The darkness from our eyes.

2 Convince us all of sin;
  Then lead to Jesus' blood,
And to our wondering view reveal
  The mercies of our God.

3 Revive our drooping faith,
  Our doubts and fears remove,
And kindle in our breasts the flame
  Of never-dying love.

4 'Tis thine to cleanse the heart,
  To sanctify the soul,
To pour fresh life in every part,
  And new-create the whole.

5 Dwell, Spirit, in our hearts,
  Our minds from bondage free;
Then shall we know, and praise, and love,
  The Father, Son, and Thee.
                                Hart.

127 *His Influences Sought.* S. M.

COME, Holy Spirit, come,
  With energy Divine,
And on this poor, benighted soul,
  With beams of mercy shine.

THE HOLY SPIRIT.

2 O melt this frozen heart;
　This stubborn will subdue;
　Each evil passion overcome,
　And form me all anew!

3 The profit will be mine,
　But thine shall be the praise;
　And unto thee will I devote
　The remnant of my days.
　　　　　　　　　　Beadome.

128　　　*Spirit of Faith.*　　　S. M.

SPIRIT of faith come down,
　Reveal the things of God;
And make to us the Godhead known,
　And witness with the blood:
'Tis thine the blood t' apply,
　And give us eyes to see.
Who did for every sinner die,
　Hath surely died for me.

2 No man can truly say
　That Jesus is the Lord,
Unless thou take the veil away,
　And breathe the living word:
Then, only then, we feel
　Our int'rest in his blood;
And cry with joy unspeakable,
　"Thou art my Lord, my God!"

3 O that the world might know
　That all-atoning Lamb!
Spirit of faith, descend, and show
　The virtue of his name:
The grace which all may find,
　The saving power, impart;
And testify to all mankind,
　And speak in every heart.
　　　　　　　　　　C. Wesley

THE HOLY SPIRIT.

129 *Revelations of the Spirit.* C. M.

SPIRIT Divine attend our prayer,
    And make our hearts thy home;
Descend with all thy gracious power:
    Come, Holy Spirit, come!

2 Come as the light, to us reveal
    Our sinfulness and woe;
And lead us in those paths of life
    Where all the righteous go.

3 Come as the fire, and purge our hearts,
    Like sacrificial flame:
Let our whole soul an offering be
    To our Redeemer's name.

4 Come as the wind, with rushing sound,
    With pentecostal grace;
And make the great salvation known
    To all the human race.

5 Spirit Divine, attend our prayer,
    And make our hearts thy home;
Descend with all thy gracious power:
    Come, Holy Spirit, come!
            Andrew Reed.

130 *The Enlightening Spirit.* C. M.

COME, Holy Ghost, our hearts inspire;
    Let us thine influence prove;
Source of the old prophetic fire,
    Fountain of life and love.

2 Come, Holy Ghost, for moved by thee
    The prophets wrote and spoke,
Unlock the truth, thyself the key;
    Unseal the sacred book.

3 Expand thy wings, celestial Dove,
    Brood o'er our nature's night;

THE HOLY SPIRIT.

On our disordered spirits move,
And let there now be light.
4 God, through himself, we then shall know
If thou within us shine;
And sound, with all thy saints below,
The depths of love divine.
Charles Wesley.

131 *Regeneration by the Spirit.* C. M.

NOT all the outward forms on earth,
Nor rites that God has given,
Nor will of man, nor blood, nor birth,
Can raise a soul to heaven.

2 The sovereign will of God alone
Creates us heirs of grace,
Born in the image of his Son,
A new, peculiar race.

3 The Spirit, like some heavenly wind,
Breathes on the sons of flesh,
Creates anew the carnal mind,
And forms the man afresh.

4 Our quickened souls awake and rise
From their long sleep of death,
On heavenly things we fix our eyes,
And praise employs our breath. *Watts.*

132 *Reviving Spirit.* C. M.

ETERNAL Spirit, God of truth,
Our contrite hearts inspire;
Revive the flame of heavenly love,
And feed the pure desire.

2 'Tis thine to soothe the sorrowing mind,
With guilt and fear oppressed;
'Tis thine to bid the dying live
And give the weary rest.

THE HOLY SPIRIT.

3 Subdue the power of every sin,
  Whate'er that sin may be,
That we, with humble, holy heart,
  May worship only thee.

4 Then with our spirits witness bear
  That we are sons of God,
Redeemed from sin, from death and hell,
  Through Christ's atoning blood.

Pratt's Col.

133   *His Quickenings Implored.*   C. M.

COME, Holy Spirit, Heavenly Dove,
  With all thy quick'ning powers,
Kindle a flame of sacred love
  In these cold hearts of ours.

2 Look how we grovel here below,
    Fond of these earthly toys;
  Our souls, how heavily they go,
    To reach eternal joys!

3 In vain we tune our formal songs,
    In vain we strive to rise;
  Hosannas languish on our tongues,
    And our devotion dies.

4 And shall we then forever live
    At this poor dying rate?
  Our love so faint, so cold to thee,
    And thine to us so great?

5 Come, Holy Spirit, Heavenly Dove,
    With all thy quick'ning powers;
  Come, shed abroad a Saviour's love,
    And that shall kindle ours.   *Watts.*

134   *The Interpreter. After Sermon.*   C. M.

THE Spirit breathes upon the word,
  And brings the truth to sight:

THE HOLY SPIRIT.

Precepts and promises afford
A sanctifying light.
2 A glory gilds the sacred page,
Majestic like the sun;
It gives a light to every age,
It gives—but borrows none.
3 The Hand that gave it still supplies
The gracious light and heat;
His truths upon the nations rise,—
They rise, but never set.
4 Let everlasting thanks be thine
For such a bright display,
As makes a world of darkness shine
With beams of heavenly day.
Cowper.

135   *The Promised Comforter.*   L. M.

JESUS, we on the words depend,
   Spoken by thee while present here,
" The Father in my name shall send
The Holy Ghost, the Comforter."
2 That heavenly Teacher of mankind,
That Guide infallible, impart,
To bring thy sayings to our mind,
And write them on our faithful heart.
3 That peace of God, that peace of thine,
O might he now to us bring in,
And fill our souls with power divine,
And make an end of fear and sin!
4 The length and breadth of love reveal,
The height and depth of Deity;
And all the sons of glory seal,
And change and make us all like thee.
C. Wesley.

THE HOLY SPIRIT.

136 *Our Guide.* L. M.

COME, gracious Spirit, heavenly Dove,
With light and comfort from above;
Be thou our Guardian, thou our Guide;
O'er every thought and step preside.

2 To us the light of truth display,
And make us know and choose thy way;
Plant holy fear in every heart,
That we from God may ne'er depart.

3 Lead us to holiness—the road
Which we must take to dwell with God;
Lead us to Christ—the living way;
Nor let us from his pastures stray;—

4 Lead us to God,—our final rest—
To be with him forever blest;
Lead us to heaven, its bliss to share—
Fullness of joy forever there. *Browne.*

137 *The work of the Holy Spirit.* 7s.

HOLY GHOST, with light divine,
Shine upon this heart of mine;
Chase the shades of night away,
Turn my darkness into day.

2 Holy Ghost, with power divine,
Cleanse this guilty heart of mine;
Long hath sin, without control,
Held dominion o'er my soul.

3 Holy Ghost, with joy divine,
Cheer this saddened heart of mine;
Bid my many woes depart,
Heal my wounded bleeding heart.

4 Holy Spirit, all divine,
Dwell within this heart of mine;

THE HOLY SPIRIT.

Cast down every idol-throne,
Reign supreme—and reign alone.
Andrew Reed.

138 *Earnest of Endless Rest.* 7s.

GRACIOUS Spirit, Love divine,
  Let thy light within me shine!
All my guilty fears remove;
Fill me with thy heavenly love.

2 Speak thy pardoning grace to me;
Set the burdened sinner free;
Lead me to the Lamb of God;
Wash me in his precious blood.

3 Life and peace to me impart;
Seal salvation on my heart;
Breathe thyself into my breast,
Earnest of immortal rest.

4 Let me never from thee stray;
Keep me in the narrow way;
Fill my soul with joy divine;
Keep me, Lord, forever thine.
John Stocker.

139 *Receive ye the Holy Ghost.* L. M. 6 l.
John 20: 22.

COME, Holy Ghost, our souls inspire,
  And lighten with celestial fire;
Thou the anointing Spirit art,
Who dost thy sevenfold gifts impart:
Thy blessed unction from above
Is comfort, life, and fire of love.

2 Enable with perpetual light
The dullness of our blinded sight;
Anoint and cheer our soiled face
With the abundance of thy grace;

Keep far our foes, give peace at home;
Where thou art guide, no ill can come.

3 Teach us to know the Father, Son,
And thee, of both, to be but one;
That through the ages all along,
This may be our endless song:
Praise to thy eternal merit,
Father, Son, and Holy Spirit.
      Gregorian Chant—Tr. by J. Cosin.

SECTION VI.

Gospel Invitations and Warning.

140   *The hearty welcome.*   L. M.

COME, sinners, to the gospel feast;
    Let every soul be Jesus' guest;
Ye need not one be left behind,
For God hath bidden all mankind.

2 Sent by my Lord, on you I call;
The invitation is to all:
Come, all the world! come, sinner, thou;
All things in Christ are ready now.

3 Come, all ye souls by sin oppressed,
Ye restless wand'rers after rest,
Ye poor, and maimed, and halt, and blind,
In Christ a hearty welcome find.

4 My message as from God receive:
Ye all may come to Christ and live:
O let his love your hearts constrain,
Nor suffer him to die in vain.

5 See him set forth before your eyes,
That precious, bleeding sacrifice!
His offered benefits embrace,
And freely now be saved by grace! *C. Wesley.*

141   *The Gospel Supper.*   L. M.

SINNERS, obey the gospel word!
  Haste to the supper of my Lord!
Be wise to know your gracious day;
All things are ready; come away.

2 Ready the Father is to own,
And kiss his late-returning son:
Ready your loving Saviour stands,
And spreads for you his bleeding hands.

3 Ready the Spirit of his love
Just now your hardness to remove;
T' apply and witness with the blood,
And wash and seal the sons of God.

4 Ready for you the angels wait,
To triumph in your blest estate:
Tuning their harps, they long to praise
The wonders of redeeming grace.

5 The Father, Son, and Holy Ghost,
Are ready with their shining host:
All heaven is ready to resound,
"The dead's alive! the lost is found!"
                              C. Wesley.

142   *Invitation and Warning.*   S. M.

THE Lord declares his will,
  And keeps the world in awe;
Amidst the smoke on Sinai's hill
Breaks out his fiery law.

2 The Lord reveals his face,
And, smiling from above,

GOSPEL INVITATIONS AND WARNING.

 Sends down the gospel of his grace,
 Th' epistles of his love.
3 These sacred words impart
 Our Maker's just commands;
 The pity of his melting heart,
 And vengeance of his hands.
4 We read the heavenly word,
 We take the offered grace,
 Obey the statutes of the Lord,
 And trust his promises. *Watts.*

143   *The Spirit Inviting.*   S. M.

THE Spirit, in our hearts,
 Is whispering, "Sinner, come;"
The bride, the church of Christ, proclaims
 To all his children, "Come!"
2 Let him that heareth say
 To all about him, "Come;"
 Let him that thirsts for righteousness
 To Christ, the fountain, come.
3 Yes, whosoever will,
 O, let him freely come,
 And freely drink the stream of life;
 'Tis Jesus bids him come.
4 Lo! Jesus, who invites,
 Declares, "I quickly come:"
 Lord, even so; we wait thy hour;
 O blest Redeemer, come.
       Epis. Col.

144   *The Warning.*   S. M.

AND will the Judge descend?
 And must the dead arise?
And not a single soul escape
 His all-discerning eyes?—

GOSPEL INVITATIONS AND WARNING.

2 And from his righteous lips
  Shall this dread sentence sound,
And through the millions of the damned
  Spread black despair around?—
3 " Depart from me. accursed,
  To everlasting flame.
For rebel-angels first prepared,
  Where mercy never came."
4 How will my heart endure
  The terrors of that day.
When earth and heaven before his face,
  Astonished, shrink away?
5 But ere that trumpet shakes
  The mansions of the dead,
Hark, from the gospel's gentle voice
  What joyful tidings spread!
6 Ye sinners, seek his grace,
  Whose wrath ye cannot bear;
Fly to the shelter of his cross,
  And find salvation there. *Doddridge*

145 *Living temples.* S. M

AND will the mighty God,
  Whom heaven cannot contain,
Make me his temple and abode,
  And in me live and reign?
2 Come, Spirit of the Lord.
  Teacher and heavenly Guide!
Be it according to thy word,
  And in my heart reside.
3 O Holy, Holy Ghost!
  Pervade this soul of mine:
In me renew thy Pentecost,
  Reveal thy power divine!

4 Make it my highest bliss
   Thy blessed fruits to know;
Thy joy, and peace, and gentleness,
   Goodness and faith to show.

5 Be it my greatest fear
   Thy hol ness to grieve;
Walk in the Spirit even here,
   And in the Spirit live. *George Rawson.*

146   *Isaiah lv. 1–3.*   C. M.

LET every mortal ear attend,
   And every heart rejoice;
The trumpet of the gospel sounds
   With an inviting voice.

2 Ho! all ye hungry, starving souls,
   That feed upon the wind,
And vainly strive with earthly toys
   To fill an empty mind.

3 Eternal wisdom hath prepared
   A soul-reviving feast,
And bids your longing appetites
   The rich provision taste.

4 Ho! ye that pant for living streams,
   And pine away and die,
Here you may quench your raging thirst
   With springs that never dry.

5 Rivers of love and mercy here,
   In a rich ocean, join;
Salvation in abundance, flows
   Like floods of milk and wine.

6 The happy gates of gospel grace
   Stand open night and day:
Lord, we are come to seek supplies,
   And drive our wants away. *Watts.*

147   *Come to Jesus.*   C. M

COME, humble sinner, in whose breast
    A thousand thoughts revolve,
Come, with your guilt and fear oppressed,
    And make this last resolve:

2 I'll go to Jesus, though my sin
    Hath like a mountain rose;
I know his courts, I'll enter in,
    Whatever may oppose:

3 Prostrate I'll lie before his throne,
    And there my guilt confess;
I'll tell him I'm a wretch undone,
    Without his sovereign grace.

4 I'll to the gracious King approach,
    Whose sceptre pardon gives;
Perhaps he may command my touch,
    And then the suppliant lives.

5 Perhaps he may admit my plea,
    Perhaps he'll hear my prayer;
But if I perish, I will pray
    And perish only there.

6 I can but perish if I go,
    I am resolved to try;
For if I stay away, I know
    I must forever die.

7 But if I die with mercy sought,
    When I the King have tried,
This were to die delightful thought!)
    As sinner never died.   *E. Jones.*

148   *The Free Invitation.*   C. M.

THE Saviour calls,—let every ear
    Attend the heavenly sound;
Ye doubting souls, dismiss your fear,
    Hope smiles reviving round.

2 For every thirsty, longing heart,
  Here streams of bounty flow;
  And life, and health, and bliss, impart
  To banish mortal woe.

3 Here springs of sacred pleasure rise
  To ease your every pain;
  (Immortal fountain! full supplies!)
  Nor shall you thirst in vain.

4 Ye sinners come; ' is mercy's voice;
  The gracious call obey:
  Mercy invites to heavenly joys,—
  And can you yet delay?

5 Dear Saviour, draw reluctant hearts!
  To thee let sinners fly,
  And take the bliss thy love imparts;
  And drink, and never die. *Steele.*

149 *Revelation iii. 20.* C. M.

COME, let us who in Christ believe,
  Our common Saviour praise:
To him, with joyful voices give
  The glory of his grace.

2 He now stands knocking at the door
  Of every sinner's heart;
  The worst need keep him out no more,
  Or force him to depart.

3 Through grace we hearken to thy voice,
  Yield to be saved from sin;
  In sure and certain hope rejoice
  That thou wilt enter in.

4 Come quickly in, thou heavenly Guest,
  Nor ever hence remove;
  But sup with us, and let the feast
  Be everlasting love. *C. Wesley.*

150   *The Year of Jubilee.*   H. M.

BLOW ye the trumpet, blow,
   The gladly solemn sound!
Let all the nations know,
   To earth's remotest bound,
The year of jubilee is come!
Return, ye ransomed sinners, home.

2 Jesus, our great High Priest,
   Hath full atonement made:
Ye weary spirits, rest;
   Ye mournful souls, be glad:
The year of jubilee is come!
Return, ye ransomed sinners, home.

3 Extol the Lamb of God,
   The all-atoning Lamb;
Redemption in his blood
   Throughout the world proclaim:
The year of jubilee is come!
Return, ye ransomed sinners, home.

4 Ye slaves of sin and hell,
   Your liberty receive,
And safe in Jesus dwell,
   And blest in Jesus live:
The year of jubilee is come!
Return, ye ransomed sinners, home.

5 Ye who have sold for naught
   Your heritage above,
Shall have it back unbought,
   The gift of Jesus' love:
The year of jubilee is come!
Return, ye ransomed sinners, home.

6 The gospel trumpet hear,
   The news of heavenly grace·

And, saved from earth, appear
Before your Saviour's face:
The year of jubilee is come!
Return, ye ransomed sinners, home.
C. Wesley.

151 *Jesus, the all-atoning Lamb.* H. M.

LET earth and heaven agree,
   Angels and men be joined,
To celebrate with me
   The Saviour of mankind:
To adore the all-atoning Lamb,
And bless the sound of Jesus' name.

2 Jesus! transporting sound!
   The joy of earth and heaven;
No other help is found,
   No other name is given.
By which we can salvation have;
But Jesus came the world to save.

3 Jesus! harmonious name!
   It charms the hosts above;
They evermore proclaim
   And wonder at his love:
'Tis all their happiness to gaze,—
'Tis heaven to see our Jesus' face.

4 His name the sinner hears,
   And is from sin set free;
'Tis music in his ears;
   'Tis life and victory;
New songs do now his lips employ,
And dances his glad heart for joy.

5 O unexampled love!
   O all-redeeming grace!
How swiftly didst thou move
   To save a fallen race!

What shall I do to make it known,
What thou for all mankind hast done?
C. Wesley.

152 *Transcendent Grace.* S. M.

GRACE! 'tis a charming sound!
   Harmonious to my ear!
Heaven with the echo shall resound,
   And all the earth shall hear.

2 Grace first contrived the way
   To save rebellious man;
And all the steps *that* grace display
   Which drew the wondrous plan.

3 Grace taught my wand'ring feet
   To tread the heavenly road;
And new supplies each hour I meet
   While pressing on to God.

4 Grace all the work shall crown,
   Through everlasting days:
It lays in heaven the topmost stone,
   And well deserves the praise. *Doddridge.*

153 *Our debt paid upon the cross.* S. M.

WHAT majesty and grace
   Through all the gospel shine!
'Tis God that speaks, and we confess
   The doctrine most divine.

2 Down from his throne on high,
   The mighty Saviour comes;
Lays his bright robes of glory by,
   And feeble flesh assumes.

3 The debt that sinners owed,
   Upon the cross he pays;
Then through the clouds ascends to God,
   'Midst shouts of loftiest praise.

4 There our High Priest appears
 Before his Father's throne;
 Mingles his merits with our tears,
 And pours salvation down.

5 Great Sovereign, we adore
 Thy justice and thy grace,
 And on thy faithfulness and power
 Our firm dependence place.
                      Samuel Stennett.

154   *The gift unspeakable.*   L. M.

HAPPY the man who finds the grace,
 The blessing of God's chosen race,
The wisdom coming from above,
The faith that sweetly works by love.

2 Wisdom divine! who tells the price
 Of wisdom's costly merchandise?
 Wisdom to silver we prefer,
 And gold is dross compared to her.

3 Her hands are filled with length of days,
 True riches and immortal praise;
 Her ways are ways of pleasantness,
 And all her flowery paths are peace.

4 Happy the man who wisdom gains;
 Thrice happy who his guest retains:
 He owns, and shall forever own,
 Wisdom, and Christ, and heaven, are one.
                      Charles Wesley.

155   *The Divine Teacher.*   L. M.

HOW sweetly flowed the gospel's sound
 From lips of gentleness and grace
While listening thousands gathered round,
And joy and reverence fill'd the place.

GOSPEL INVITATIONS AND WARNING.

2 From heaven he came, of heaven he spoke,
　To heaven he led his followers' way:
Dark clouds of gloomy night he broke,
　Unveiling an immortal day.
3 "Come, wanderers, to my Father's home;
　Come, all ye weary ones, and rest."
Yes, sacred Teacher, we will come,
　Obey, and be forever blest.
4 Decay, then, tenements of dust!
　Pillars of earthly pride, decay!
A nobler mansion waits the just,
　And Jesus has prepared the way.
　　　　　　　　　Sir John Bowring.

156　*Before Preaching to the Young.*　C. M.

GRACE is a plant, where'er it grows,
　　Of pure and heavenly root;
But fairest in the youngest shows,
　　And yields the sweetest fruit.

2 Ye careless ones, O hear betimes
　　The voice of sovereign love!
Your youth is stained with many crimes,
　　But mercy reigns above.

3 True, you are young, but there's a stone
　　Within the youngest breast,
Or half the crimes which you have done
　　Would rob you of your rest.

4 For you the public prayer is made;
　　O join the public prayer!
For you the secret tear is shed;
　　O shed yourselves a tear!

5 We pray that you may early prove
　　The Spirit's power to teach:
You cannot be too young to love
　　That Jesus whom we preach.　　*Cowper.*

157   *Before an Inviting Sermon.*   C. M

JESUS, Redeemer of mankind,
  Display thy saving power;
Thy mercy let these outcasts find,
  And know their gracious hour.

2 Ah! give them, Lord, a longer space,
  Nor suddenly consume;
But let them take the proffered grace,
  And flee the wrath to come.

3 O wouldst thou cast a pitying look,
  On every stony heart,
Like that which faithless Peter's broke,
  All goodness as thou art.

4 Who thee beneath their feet have trod,
  And crucified afresh,
Touch with thine all-victorious blood,
  And turn the stone to flesh.

5 Open their eyes thy cross to see,
  Their ears to hear thy cries:
Sinner, thy Saviour weeps for thee,
  For thee he weeps and dies.   *C. Wesley.*

158   *Grieving for the transgressors.*   L. M.

ARISE, my tend'rest thoughts, arise;
  To torrents melt, my streaming eyes!
And thou, my heart, with anguish feel
Those evils which thou canst not heal.

2 See human nature sunk in shame:
See scandals poured on Jesus' name;
The Father wounded through the Son,
The world abused the soul undone.

3 See the short course of vain delight
Closing in everlasting night—

In flames, that no abatement know,
Though briny tears for ever flow.

4 My God, I feel the mournful scene;
My bowels yearn o'er dying men;
And fain my pity would reclaim,
And snatch the firebrands from the flame.

5 But feeble my compassion proves,
And can but weep where most it loves;
Thy own all-saving arm employ,
And turn these drops of grief to joy.
Doddridge.

159 *Before an inviting sermon.* L. M

SHEPHERD of souls, with pitying eye,
The thousands of our Israel see;
To thee, in their behalf, we cry:
Ourselves but newly found in thee.

2 See where o'er desert wastes they err,
And neither food nor feeder have;
Nor fold nor place of refuge near;
For no man cares their souls to save.

3 Thy people, Lord, are sold for naught;
Nor know they their Redeemer nigh:
They perish whom thyself hath bought;
Their souls for lack of knowledge die.

4 Why should the foe thy purchase seize?
Remember, Lord, thy dying groans:
The need of all thy suff'rings these:
O claim them for thy ransomed ones!
C. Wesley.

160 *All things are ready.* Matt. xxii. 4. S. M

"ALL things are ready," come.
  Come to the supper spread;

GOSPEL INVITATIONS AND WARNING.

Come, rich and poor, come, old and young,
  Come, and be richly fed.
2 "All things are ready," come,
  The invitation's given,
  Through Him who now in glory sits
  At God's right hand in heaven.

3 "All things are ready," come,
  The door is open wide;
  O feast upon the love of God,
  For Christ, his Son, hath died.

4 "All things are ready," come,
  To-morrow may not be;
  O sinner, come, the Saviour waits
  This hour to welcome thee. *Albert Midlane.*

161 *Seek him while he may be found.* S. M.

MY son, know thou the Lord,
  Thy father's God obey;
Seek his protecting care by night,
  His guardian hand by day.

2 Call, while he may be found:
  Seek him while he is near:
Serve him with all thy heart and mind,
  And worship him with fear.

3 If thou wilt seek his face,
  His ear will hear thy cry:
Then shalt thou find his mercy sure,
  His grace forever nigh.

4 But if thou leave thy God,
  Nor choose the path to heaven,
Then shalt thou perish in thy sins,
  And never be forgiven.
      Robert C. Brackenbury.

162 *Come, ye disconsolate.* 10, 11, 10, 11.

COME, ye disconsolate, where'er ye languish,
  Come, and at God's altar fervently kneel;
Here bring your wounded hearts, here tell your anguish;
  Earth has no sorrow that Heaven cannot heal.

2 Joy of the desolate, Light of the straying,
  Hope of the penitent, fadeless and pure,
Here speaks the Comforter, in God's name saying,
  Earth has no sorrow that Heaven cannot cure.

3 Go, ask the infidel what boon he brings us—
  What charm for aching hearts *he* can reveal,
Sweet as the heavenly promise hope sings us,
  Earth has no sorrow that God cannot heal.
  Moore.

163 *The Healing Fountain.* 8, 7, 7.

COME to Calvary's holy mountain,
  Sinners ruined by the fall;
Here a pure and healing fountain,
  Flows to you, to me, to all,
    In a full perpetual tide,
    Opened when our Saviour died.

2 Come, in sorrow and contrition,
  Wounded, impotent, and blind;
Here the guilty, free remission,
  Here the lost a refuge find.
    Health this fountain will restore;
    He that drinks need thirst no more.

3 Come, ye dying, live forever;
  'Tis a soul-reviving flood;

God is faithful; he will never
  Break his covenant sealed in blood;
Signed when our Redeemer died,
Sealed when he was glorified.
                    James Montgomery

164   *Hear, and Live.*   8, 7, 4.

SINNERS, will you scorn the message
  Sent in mercy from above?
Every sentence, O how tender!
  Every line is full of love:
    Listen to it;
  Every line is full of love.

2 Hear the heralds of the gospel
    News from Zion's King proclaim:
  "Pardon to each rebel sinner,
    Free forgiveness in his name:"
      How important!
    "Free forgiveness in his name."

3 Tempted souls they bring you succor;
    Fearful hearts, they quell your fears,
  And, with news of consolation,
    Chase away the falling tears:
      Tender heralds!
    Chase away the falling tears.

4 O ye angels, hovering round us,
    Waiting spirits, speed your way;
  Haste ye to the court of heaven,
    Tidings bear without delay,
      Rebel sinners
    Glad the message will obey.
                    Jonathan Allen.

GOSPEL INVITATIONS AND WARNING.

165   *The Desire of Nations.*   8, 7.

COME, thou long-expected Jesus,
  Born to set thy people free;
From our fears and sins release us,
  Let us find our rest in thee.

2 Israel's Strength and Consolation,
  Hope of all the earth thou art;
Dear Desire of every nation,
  Joy of every longing heart.

3 Born thy people to deliver,
  Born a child and yet a King,
Born to reign in us forever,
  Now thy gracious kingdom bring.

4 By thine own eternal Spirit,
  Rule in all our hearts alone;
By thine all-sufficient merit,
  Raise us to thy glorious throne.
                    Charles Wesley.

166   *Even Me.*   8, 7, 3.

LORD. I hear of showers of blessing
  Thou art scattering full and free;
Showers the thirsty land refreshing:
  Let some drops now fall on me,
    Even me.

2 Pass me not, O God, my Father,
  Sinful though my heart may be;
Thou might'st leave me, but the rather
  Let thy mercy light on me,
    Even me.

3 Pass me not, O gracious Saviour,
  Let me live and cling to thee;

GOSPEL INVITATIONS AND WARNING.

 I am longing for thy favor;
  Whilst thou'rt calling, O call me,
   Even me.
4 Pass me not, O mighty Spirit,
 Thou canst make the blind to see;
Witnesser of Jesus' merit,
 Speak the word of power to me,
  Even me.
5 Love of God, so pure and changeless,
 Blood of Christ, so rich so free,
Grace of God, so strong and boundless,
 Magnify them all in me,
  Even me. *Mrs. Elizabeth Codner.*

167 *The Issues of Life and Death.*   S. M.

O WHERE shall rest be found,
 Rest for the weary soul?
'Twere vain the ocean depths to sound,
 Or pierce to either pole:
  The world can never give
  The bliss for which we sigh.
'Tis not the whole of life to live,
 Nor all of death to die.

2 Beyond this vale of tears
 There is a life above;
Unmeasur'd by the flight of years;
 And all that life is love:
  There is a death whose pang
  Outlasts the fleeting breath;
O! what eternal horrors hang
 Around "the second death!"

3 Lord God of truth and grace,
 Teach us that death to shun,
Lest we be banish'd from thy face,
 And evermore undone.

GOSPEL INVITATIONS AND WARNING.

Here would we end our quest:
Alone are found in thee
The life of perfect love—the rest
Of immortality. *Montgomery.*

168   *Quench not the Spirit.*   L. M.
(1 Thess. v. 19.)

SAY, sinner, hath a voice within
  Oft whispered to thy secret soul,
Urged thee to leave the ways of sin,
And yield thy heart to God's control?

2 Sinner, it was a heavenly voice.
  It was the Spirit's gracious call;
It bade thee make the better choice,
  And haste to seek in Christ thine all.

3 Spurn not the call to life and light;
  Regard in time the warning kind:
That call thou may'st not always slight,
  And yet the gate of mercy find.

4 God's Spirit will not always strive
  With hardened, self-destroying man;
Ye, who persist his love to grieve,
  May never hear his voice again.

5 Sinner, perhaps this very day
  Thy last accepted time may be;
O shouldst thou grieve him now away,
  Then hope may never beam on thee.
   Mrs. Ann B. Hyde.

169   *Haste, Traveler, haste!*   L. M.

HASTE, traveler, haste! the night comes on,
  And many a shining hour is gone;
The storm is gathering in the west,
And thou art far from home and rest.

GOSPEL INVITATIONS AND WARNING.

2 O far from home thy footsteps stray;
Christ is the life, and Christ the Way,
And Christ the Light; thy setting sun
Sinks ere thy morning is begun.

3 The rising tempest sweeps the sky;
The rains descend, the winds are high:
The waters swell, and death and fear
Beset thy path, nor refuge near.

4 Then linger not in all the plain,
Flee for thy life, the mountain gain;
Look not behind. make no delay,
O speed thee, speed thee on thy way.
William B. Collyer.

170   *The Invitation.*   8, 7, 8, 7, 4, 7.

COME, ye sinners, poor and needy,
  Weak and wounded, sick and sore,
Jesus ready stands to save you,
  Full of pity, love and power:
   He is able,
  He is willing, doubt no more.

2 Now, ye needy, come and welcome,
  God's free bounty glorify;
True belief and true repentance,
  Every grace that brings you nigh,
   Without money,
  Come to Jesus Christ and buy.

3 Let not conscience make you linger;
  Nor of fitness fondly dream;
All the fitness he requireth
  Is to feel your need of him:
   This he gives you,
  'Tis the Spirit's glimm'ring beam.

4 Come, ye weary, heavy-laden,
  Bruised and mangled by the fall;

GOSPEL INVITATIONS AND WARNING.

If you tarry till you're better,
You will never come at all:
Not the righteous,
Sinners Jesus came to call.
5 Agonizing in the garden,
Lo! your Maker prostrate lies!
On the bloody tree behold him!
Hear him cry before he dies,
"It is finished!"
Sinners, will not this suffice? *Hart.*

171 *The Christian Pilgrim.* 7s.

PILGRIM burdened with thy sin,
Haste to Zion's gate to-day;
There, till mercy let thee in,
Knock and weep and watch and pray.
2 Knock—for mercy lends an ear,
Weep—she marks the sinner's sigh;
Watch—till heavenly light appear;
Pray—she hears the mourner's cry.
3 Mourning pilgrim! what for thee
In this world can now remain?
Seek that world from which shall flee,
Sorrow, shame, and tears, and pain.
4 Sorrow shall forever fly;
Shame shall never enter there;
Tears be wiped from every eye—
Pain in endless bliss expire. *Geo. Crabbe.*

172 8 lines 7's.
Exhorting to turn to God. Why will ye Die? O house of Israel! Ezek. xviii. 31.

SINNERS, turn, why will ye die?
God, your Maker, asks you why:
God, who did your being give,
Made you with himself to live:

He the fatal cause demands,
Asks the work of his own hands;
Why, ye thankless creatures, why,
Will ye cross his love and die?

2 Sinners, turn, why will ye die?
God, your Saviour, asks you why;
God, who did your souls retrieve,
Died himself, that you might live.
Will you let him die in vain?
Crucify your Lord again?
Why, ye ransom'd sinners, why,
Will ye slight his grace and die?

3 Sinners, turn, why will ye die?
God, the Spirit, asks you why;
He, who all your lives hath strove,
Woo'd you to embrace his love:
Will you not the grace receive?
Will you still refuse to live?
Why, ye long-sought sinners, why,
Will ye grieve your God, and die?
C. Wesley.

173   *The Works of Sin.*   7, 6 L.

HEARTS of stone, relent, relent!
Break, by Jesu's cross subdued;
See his body mangled, rent,
Covered with his flowing blood!
Sinful soul, what hast thou done?
Crucified the Eternal Son?

2 Yes, thy sins have done the deed,
Driven the nails that fixed him there,
Crowned with thorns his sacred head,
Pierced him with a soldier's spear,
Made his soul a sacrifice:
For a sinful world he dies.

3 Wilt thou let him die in vain?
 Still to death pursue our God?
 Open all his wounds again?
 Trample on his precious blood?
 No; with all my sins I'll part;
 Saviour, take my broken heart. *C. Wesley.*

174   *The Power of Truth.*   L. M.

THIS is the word of truth and love,
 Sent to the nations from above;
Jehovah here resolves to show
What his almighty grace can do.

2 This remedy did wisdom find,
 To heal diseases of the mind—
 This sovereign balm, whose virtues can
 Restore the ruined creature, man.

3 The gospel bids the dead revive;
 Sinners obey the voice, and live;
 Dry bones are raised and clothed afresh;
 And hearts of stone are turned to flesh.

4 May but this grace my soul renew,
 Let sinners gaze and hate me too;
 The word that saves me does engage
 A sure defence from all their rage. *Watts.*

175   *Gospel liberty proclaimed.*   L. M
     Isaiah lii. 1-15.

AWAKE, Jerusalem, awake!
 No longer in thy sins lie down;
The garment of salvation take,
 Thy beauty and thy strength put on.

2 Shake off the dust that blinds thy sight,
 And hides the promise from thine eyes;
 Arise, and struggle into light,
 Thy great Deliv'rer calls, arise!

3 Shake off the bands of sad despair,
   Sion, assert thy liberty;
  Look up, thy broken heart prepare,
   And God shall set the captive free.
4 Vessels of mercy, sons of grace,
   Be purged from every sinful stain;
  Be like your Lord, his word embrace,
   Nor bear his hallow'd name in vain.
5 The Lord shall in your front appear,
   And lead the pompous triumph on;
  His glory shall bring up the rear,
   And perfect what his grace begun.
                                  C. Wesley.

176   *Returning to Christ.*   C. M.

MY head is low, my heart is sad,
   My feet with travel torn,
  Yet, O my Saviour, thou art glad
   To see thy child return!
2 It was thy love that homeward led,
   Thy arm that upward stayed;
  It is thy hand which on my head
   Is now in mercy la'd.
3 O Saviour, in this broken heart
   Confirm the trembling will,
  Which longs to reach thee where thou art,
   Rest in thee and be still.
4 Within that bosom which hath shed
   Both tears and blood for me,
  O let me hide this aching head,
   Once pressed and blessed by thee.
                              John S. B. Monsell.

177   *"Prepare to meet thy God."*   8, 7, 8, 4, 7.

DAY of judgment, day of wonders!
   Hark! the trumpet's awful sound,

Louder than a thousand thunders,
Shakes the vast creation round!
How the summons
Will the sinner's heart confound!
2 See the Judge our nature wearing,
Clothed in majesty divine!
You who long for his appearing
Then shall say, "This God is mine."
Gracious Saviour,
Own me in that day for thine!
3 At his call the dead awaken,—
Rise to life from earth and sea;
All the powers of nature, shaken
By his looks, prepare to flee:
Careless sinner,
What will then become of thee. *Newton.*

178 Isaiah lv. 1-3. L. M
Come ye to the waters.

HO! every one that thirsts, draw nigh;
'Tis God invites the fallen race:
Mercy and free salvation buy:
Buy wine, and milk, and gospel grace.
2 Come to the living waters, come!
Sinners, obey your Maker's call;
Return, ye weary wanderers, home,
And find my grace is free for all.
3 See from the rock a fountain rise;
For you in healing streams it rolls;
Money ye need not bring, nor price,
Ye lab'ring, burdened, sin-sick souls.
4 Nothing ye in exchange shall give;
Leave all you have, and are, behind.
Frankly the gift of God receive,
Pardon and peace in Jesus find.

5 I bid you all my goodness prove;
  My promises for all are free:
  Come, taste the manna of my love,
  And let your souls delight in me.
6 Your willing ear and heart incline,
  My words believingly receive;
  Quickened your souls by faith divine,
  An everlasting life shall live.
                                        C. Wesley.

179   *Revelation* iii. 20.   L. M.

BEHOLD a Stranger at the door!
  He gently knocks, has knocked before;
Has waited long—is waiting still:
You treat no other friend so ill.

2 O lovely attitude! He stands
  With melting heart and bleeding hands:
  O matchless kindness! and he shows
  This matchless kindness to his foes!

3 But will he prove a Friend indeed?
  He will: the very Friend you need;
  The Friend of sinners—yes, 'tis he,
  With garments dyed on Calvary.

4 Rise, touched with gratitude Divine;
  Turn out his enemy and thine,
  That soul-destroying monster, sin,
  And let the heavenly Stranger in.

5 Admit him, ere his anger burn;
  His feet departed, ne'er return;
  Admit him, or the hour's at hand
  You'll at his door rejected stand.   *Gregg.*

180   *" Escape for thy life."*   7s.

HASTEN, sinner, to be wise:
  Stay not for the morrow's sun,

Wisdom, if thou still despise,
Harder is she to be won.

2 Hasten, mercy to implore:
Stay not for the morrow's sun;
Lest thy season should be o'er
Ere this evening's stage be run.

3 Hasten, sinner, to return;
Stay not for the morrow's sun;
Lest thy lamp should cease to burn
Ere salvation's work is done.

4 Hasten, sinner, to be blest:
Stay not for the morrow's sun:
Lest the curse should thee arrest
Ere the morrow is begun. *T. Scott.*

181 *Psalm* 1. 16, 17, 20, 21. 8, 7, 8, 7, 4, 7.

WHY, O sinner, me profaning,
Why, says God, my statutes name?
Why, my cov'nant grace disdaining,
Still my cov'nant grace proclaim?
Hating counsel;
All my laws exposed to shame.

2 Long in silence I have waited,
Long thy guilt in secret grown;
Till thy heart, with pride elated,
Thought my counsels like thy own:
I'll reprove thee,
Till thy crimes, to thee, are known.

3 Sinners, hear Jehovah speaking!
Ye who, thoughtless, God despise!
Hear, lest, in his wrath awaking,
Vengeance rend you as it flies;
None can save you,
If his arm to judgment rise. *Goode.*

REPENTANCE AND CONVERSION.

SECTION VII.
Repentance and Conversion.

182   *Hardness of heart lamented.*   L. M.

O FOR a glance of heavenly day,
    To take this stubborn heart away,
And thaw with beams of love Divine,
This heart, this frozen heart of mine!

2 The rocks can rend; the earth can quake;
The seas can roar; the mountains shake:
Of feeling, all things show some sign,
But this unfeeling heart of mine.

3 To hear the sorrows thou hast felt,
O Lord, an adamant would melt!
But I can read each moving line,
And nothing moves this heart of mine.

4 Thy judgments, too, unmoved I hear,
(Amazing thought!) which devils fear:
Goodness and wrath in vain combine
To stir this stupid heart of mine.

5 But something yet can do the deed;
And that blest something much I need.
Thy Spirit can from dross refine,
And melt and change this heart of mine.
                                   Hart.

183   *Psalm li. 13-19.*   L. M.
   A broken heart for sacrifice.

A BROKEN heart, my God, my King,
    To thee a sacrifice I bring:
The God of grace will ne'er despise
A broken heart for sacrifice.

REPENTANCE AND CONVERSION.

2 My soul lies humbled in the dust,
And owns thy dreadful sentence just:
Look down, O Lord, with pitying eye,
And save the soul condemned to die.

3 Then will I teach the world thy ways,
Sinners shall learn thy sovereign grace;
I'll lead them to my Saviour's blood,
And they shall praise a pard'ning God.

4 O may thy love inspire my tongue!
Salvation shall be all my song;
And all my powers shall join to bless
The Lord, my strength and righteousness.
Watts.

184 *Pity of the Lord.* Psalm li. 1–4. L. M.

SHOW pity, Lord, O Lord, forgive,
　Let a repenting rebel live;
Are not thy mercies large and free?
May not a sinner trust in thee?

2 My crimes are great, but don't surpass
The power and glory of thy grace:
Great God, thy nature hath no bound,
So let thy pard'ning love be found.

3 O wash my soul from every sin!
And make my guilty conscience clean!
Here on my heart the burden lies,
And past offences pain mine eyes.

4 My lips with shame my sins confess,
Against thy law, against thy grace;
Lord, should thy judgments grow severe,
I am condemned, but thou art clear.

5 Yet save a trembling sinner, Lord,
Whose hope, still hov'ring round thy word,
Would light on some sweet promise there,
Some sure support against despair. *Watts.*

REPENTANCE AND CONVERSION.

185   *Seeking perfect rest in Christ.*   L. M.

O THAT my load of sin were gone!
   O that I could at last submit
At Jesus' feet to lay it down!
   To lay my soul at Jesus' feet!

2 Rest for my soul I long to find:
   Saviour of all, if mine thou art,
Give me thy meek and lowly mind,
   And stamp thine image on my heart.

3 Break off the yoke of inbred sin,
   And fully set my spirit free;
I cannot rest till pure within,
   Till I am wholly lost in thee.

4 Fain would I learn of thee, my God,
   Thy light and easy burden prove,
The cross, all stained with hallowed blood,
   The labor of thy dying love.

5 I would, but thou must give the power;
   My heart from every sin release;
Bring near, bring near the joyful hour,
   And fill me with thy perfect peace.

6 Come, Lord, the drooping sinner cheer,
   Nor let thy chariot wheels delay:
Appear, in my poor heart appear!
   My God, my Saviour, come away!
                       C. Wesley.

186   *Struggling after Christ.*   S. M.

AH! whither should I go,
   Burdened, and sick, and faint!
To whom should I my troubles show,
   And pour out my complaint?
My Saviour bids me come;
   Ah! why do I delay?

He calls the weary sinner home,
And yet from him I stay!

2 What is it keeps me back,
From which I cannot part?
Which will not let the Saviour take
Possession of my heart!
Some cursed thing unknown
Must surely lurk within;
Some idol which I will not own,
Some secret bosom-sin.

3 I now believe in thee
Compassion reigns alone;
According to my faith, to me
O let it, Lord, be done!
In me is all the bar,
Which thou wouldst fain remove;
Remove it, and I shall declare
That God is only love. *C. Wesley.*

187 *Giving All for Christ.* S. M.

AND can I yet delay
My little all to give?
To tear my soul from earth away
For Jesus to receive?

2 Nay, but I yield, I yield!
I can hold out no more:
I sink, by dying love compelled,
And own thee, conqueror!

3 Though late, I all forsake;
My friends, my all resign:
Gracious Redeemer, take, O take,
And seal me ever thine!

4 Come, and possess me whole,
Nor hence again remove:

Settle and fix my wav'ring soul
With all thy weight of love.

5 My one desire be this,
Thy only love to know;
To seek and taste no other bliss,
No other good below. *C. Wesley.*

188 *Praying for Faith.* C. M.

FATHER, I stretch my hands to thee,
No other help I know;
If thou withdraw thyself from me,
Ah! whither shall I go?

2 What did thine only Son endure,
Before I drew my breath!
What pain, what labor, to secure
My soul from endless death!

3 O Jesus, could I this believe,
I now should feel thy power!
Now my poor soul thou wouldst retrieve,
Nor let me wait one hour.

4 Author of faith, to thee I lift
My weary, longing eyes:
O let me now receive that gift,
My soul without it dies!

5 Surely thou canst not let me die,
O speak, and I shall live;
And here I will unwearied lie,
Till thou thy Spirit give.

6 The worst of sinners would rejoice,
Could they but see thy face;
O let me hear thy quick'ning voice,
And taste thy pard'ning grace!
C. Wesley

REPENTANCE AND CONVERSION.

189   *Surrendering at the Cross.*   C. M.

ALAS! and did my Saviour bleed?
  And did my Sovereign die?
Would he devote that sacred head
  For such a worm as I?

2 Was it for crimes that I have done
  He groaned upon the tree?
Amazing pity! grace unknown!
  And love beyond degree!

3 Well might the sun in darkness hide,
  And shut his glories in,
When Christ, the mighty Maker, died
  For man, the creature's sin!

4 Thus might I hide my blushing face,
  While his dear cross appears;
Dissolve my heart in thankfulness,
  And melt mine eyes to tears.

5 But drops of grief can ne'er repay
  The debt of love I owe:
Here, Lord, I give myself away,
  'Tis all that I can do.   *Watts.*

190   *Seeking the Power.*   C. M.

STILL, for thy loving-kindness, Lord,
  I in thy temple wait:
I look to find thee in thy word,
  Or at thy table meet.

2 Here in thine own appointed ways,
  I wait to learn thy will;
Silent I stand before thy face,
  And hear thee say, "Be still!"

3 "Be still! and know that I am God!"
  'Tis all I live to know;

To feel the virtue of thy blood,
And spread its praise below!

4 I wait my vigor to renew,
Thine image to retrieve!
The veil of outward things pass through,
And gasp in thee to live.

5 I work; and own the labor vain,
And thus from works I cease:
I strive; and see my fruitless pain,
Till God create my peace.   *C. Wesley.*

191 C. M.
"*O that I knew where I might find him.*" Job xxiii.
Sins and sorrows laid before God.

O THAT I knew the secret place
Where I might find my God!
I'd spread my wants before his face,
And pour my woes abroad.

2 I'd tell him how my sins arise;
What sorrows I sustain;
How grace decays, and comfort dies
And leaves my heart in pain.

3 He knows what arguments I'd take
To wrestle with my God;
I'd plead for his own mercy's sake,
And for my Saviour's blood.

4 My God will pity my complaints,
And heal my broken bones;
He takes the meaning of his saints,
The language of their groans.

5 Arise, my soul, from deep distress,
And banish ev'ry fear;
He calls thee to his throne of grace,
To spread thy sorrows there.   *Watts.*

REPENTANCE AND CONVERSION.

192   *The Backslider's Prayer.*   C. M.

O FOR a closer walk with God,
    A calm and heavenly frame;
A light to shine upon the road
    That leads me to the Lamb.

2 Where is the blessedness I knew
    When first I saw the Lord?
Where is the soul-refreshing view
    Of Jesus and his word?

3 What peaceful hours I once enjoyed!
    How sweet their mem'ry still!
But they have left an aching void
    The world can never fill.

4 Return, O holy Dove, return,
    Sweet messenger of rest!
I hate the sins that made thee mourn,
    And drove thee from my breast.

5 The dearest idol I have known,
    Whate'er that idol be,
Help me to tear it from thy throne,
    And worship only thee.

6 So shall my walk be close with God,
    Calm and serene my frame;
So purer light shall mark the road
    That leads me to the Lamb.   *Cowper.*

193   *The Backslider's Plea.*   7s.

DEPTH of mercy! can there be
    Mercy still reserved for me?
Can my God his wrath forbear?
Me, the chief of sinners, spare?

2 I have long withstood his grace,
Long provoked him to his face:

REPENTANCE AND CONVERSION.

Would not hearken to his calls;
Grieved him by a thousand falls.

3 Lo! I cumber still the ground:
Lo! an Advocate is found!
"Hasten not to cut him down:
Let this barren soul alone!"

4 Jesus speaks, and pleads his blood:
He disarms the wrath of God!
Now my Father's bowels move;
Justice lingers into love.

5 Kindled his relentings are;
Me he now delights to spare;
Cries, "How shall I give thee up?"
Lets the lifted thunder drop.

6 There for me the Saviour stands,
Shows his wounds, and spreads his hands:
God is love! I know, I feel;
Jesus weeps, and loves me still. *C. Wesley.*

194   *The Backslider's Return.*   S. M.

O JESUS! full of grace,
   To thee I make my moan:
Let me again behold thy face,
   Call home thy banished one.

2 Again my pardon seal,
   Again my soul restore,
And freely my backslidings heal,
   And bid me sin no more.

3 Wilt thou not bid me rise?
   Speak, and my soul shall live:
Forgive, my gasping spirit cries,
   Abundantly forgive.

4 For thine own mercy's sake,
   Relieve my wretchedness:

REPENTANCE AND CONVERSION.

And O, my pardon give me back,
And give me back my peace!
C. Wesley.

195   *The Plea.*   S. M.

JESUS, my Lord, attend
  Thy feeble creature's cry;
And show thyself the sinner's Friend,
  And set me up on high.

2 From hell's oppressive power
   My struggling soul release,
  And to thy Father's grace restore,
   And to thy perfect peace.

3 Rivers of life divine
   From thee, their fountain, flow;
  And all who know that love of thine,
   The joy of angels know.

4 That thou caus't here forgive
   Grant me to testify;
  And justified by faith to live,
   And in that faith to die.   *C. Wesley.*

196   "*Help Thou my Unbelief.*"   C. M.

HOW sad our state by nature is!
  Our sin how deep it stains!
And Satan binds our captive souls
  Fast in his slavish chains.

2 But there's a voice of sovereign grace
   Sounds from the sacred word:
  Ho! ye despairing sinners, come,
   And trust a faithful Lord.

3 My soul obeys the gracious call,
   And runs to this relief;
  I would believe thy promise, Lord,
   O help my unbelief!

REPENTANCE AND CONVERSION.

4 To the blest fountain of thy blood,
  Incarnate God, I fly;
  Here let me wash my spotted soul
  From crimes of deepest dye.

5 A guilty, weak and helpless worm,
  Into thy arms I fall:
  Be thou my strength and righteousness,
  My Jesus and my all.   *Watts.*

197   *Before an inviting Sermon.*   C. M.

JESUS, thou all-redeeming Lord,
  Thy blessings we implore;
Open the door to preach thy word,
  The great effectual door.

2 Gather the outcasts in, and save
  From sin and Satan's power;
  And let them now acceptance have,
  And know their gracious hour.

3 Lover of souls! thou know'st to prize
  What thou hast bought so dear:
  Come, then, and in thy people's eyes,
  With all thy wounds appear!

4 Appear, as when of old confessed,
  The suff"ring Son of God;
  And let them see thee in thy vest,
  But newly dipped in blood.   *C. Wesley.*

198   *Divine Excellence.*   C. M.

WHAT grace, O Lord, and beauty shone
  Around thy steps below;
What patient love was seen in all
  Thy life and death of woe!

REPENTANCE AND CONVERSION.

2 For, ever on thy burdened heart
  A weight of sorrow hung;
  Yet no ungentle, murmuring word
  Escaped thy silent tongue.

3 Thy foes might hate, despise, revile,
  Thy friends unfaithful prove;
  Unwearied in forgiveness still,
  Thy heart could only love.

4 Oh, give us hearts to love like thee!
  Like thee, O Lord, to grieve
  Far more for others' sins than all
  The wrongs that we receive.

5 One with thyself may every eye.
  In us, thy brethren, see
  The gentleness and grace that spring
  From union, Lord, with thee.
  Sir Edw. Denny.

199   *Call to praise.*   C. M.

COME, happy souls, approach your God
  With new melodious songs:
Come, render to Almighty grace
  The tribute of your tongues.

2 So strange, so boundless was the love
  That pitied dying men,
  The Father sent his equal Son
  To give them life again.

3 Thy hands, dear Jesus, were not arm'd
  With a revenging rod,
  No hard commission to perform
  The vengeance of a God.

4 But all was mercy, all was mild,
  And wrath forsook the throne,
  When Christ on the kind errand came,
  And brought salvation down.

5 Here, sinners, you may heal your wounds,
  And wipe your sorrows dry:
  Trust in the mighty Saviour's name,
  And you shall never die.   *Watts.*

200   *The Joyful Sound.*   C. M.

SALVATION! O the joyful sound!
  What pleasure to our ears!
  A sovereign balm for every wound,
  A cordial for our fears.

2 Salvation! let the echo fly
  The spacious earth around,
  While all the armies of the sky
  Conspire to raise the sound.

3 Salvation! O thou bleeding Lamb!
  To thee the praise belongs:
  Salvation shall inspire our hearts,
  And dwell upon our tongues.
                    Isaac Watts.

201   *Refuge in Christ.*   7s.

JESUS, lover of my soul,
   Let me to thy bosom fly,
  While the nearer waters roll,
   While the tempest still is high:
  Hide me, O my Saviour, hide,
   Till the storm of life be past;
  Safe into the haven guide,
   O receive my soul at last!

2 Other refuge have I none,
   Hangs my helpless soul on thee:
  Leave, ah! leave me not alone,
   Still support and comfort me!
  All my trust on thee is stayed,
   All my help from thee I bring,

REPENTANCE AND CONVERSION.

　　Cover my defenceless head
　　　With the shadow of thy wing.

3 Thou, O Christ, art all I want;
　　　More than all in thee I find:
　　Raise the fallen, cheer the faint,
　　　Heal the sick, and lead the blind.
　　Just and holy is thy name;
　　　I am all unrighteousness:
　　False, and full of sin, I am,
　　　Thou art full of truth and grace.

4 Plenteous grace with thee is found,
　　　Grace to cover all my sin:
　　Let the healing streams abound,
　　　Make and keep me pure within:
　　Thou of life the fountain art;
　　　Freely let me take of thee:
　　Spring thou up within my heart.
　　　Rise to all eternity! *C. Wesley.*

202　　　*Vehement Desires.*　　C. M.

I ASK the gift of righteousness,
　　　The sin-subduing power,—
　Power to believe, and go in peace,
　　　And never grieve thee more.

2 I ask the blood-bought pardon sealed,
　　　The liberty from sin,
　　The grace infused, the love revealed,
　　　The kingdom fixed within.

3 Thou hear'st me for salvation pray;
　　　Thou seest my heart's desire:
　　Made ready in thy powerful day,
　　　The fulness I require

REPENTANCE AND CONVERSION.

4 Art thou not able to convert?
Art thou not willing too?
To change this old rebellious heart,
To conquer and renew?   *C. Wesley.*

203   L. M.
An Advocate with the Father.—1 John 2: 1.

JESUS, my Advocate above,
My Friend before the throne of love,
If now for me prevails thy prayer,
If now I find thee pleading there,—

2 If thou the secret wish convey,
And sweetly prompt my heart to pray,
Hear, and my weak petitions join,
Almighty Advocate, to thine.

3 Jesus, my heart's desire obtain;
My earnest suit present, and gain:
My fullness of corruption show;
The knowledge of myself bestow.

4 O sovereign Love, to thee I cry,
Give me thyself, or else I die!
Save me from death, from hell set free;
Death, hell, are but the want of thee.
Charles Wesley.

204   *The Voice of Jesus.*   C. M.

I HEARD the voice of Jesus say,
 "Come unto me and rest;
Lay down, thou weary one, lay down
 Thy head upon my breast!"
I came to Jesus as I was,
 Weary, and worn, and sad;
I found in him a resting-place,
 And he hath made me glad.

REPENTANCE AND CONVERSION.

2 I heard the voice of Jesus say,
"Behold, I freely give
The living water; thirsty one,
Stoop down, and drink, and live!"
I came to Jesus, and I drank
Of that life-giving stream;
My thirst was quenched, my soul revived,
And now I live in him.

3 I heard the voice of Jesus say,
"I am this dark world's Light;
Look unto me thy morn shall rise
And all thy day be bright!"
I looked to Jesus, and I found
In him my Star, my Sun;
And in that light of life I'll walk,
Till all my journey's done. *Horatius Bonar.*

205 *Prayer for conversion.* C. M.

COME, O thou all-victorious Lord,
 Thy power to us make known;
Strike with the hammer of the word,
And break these hearts of stone.

2 O that we all might now begin
Our foolishness to mourn!
And turn at once from every sin,
And to the Saviour turn.

3 Give us ourselves and thee to know
In this our gracious day:
Repentance unto life bestow,
And take our sins away.

4 Convince us first of unbelief,
And freely then release:
Fill every soul with sacred grief,
And then with sacred peace. *C. Wesley*

JUSTIFICATION AND ADOPTION.

SECTION VIII.

Justification and Adoption.

206 *Internal Religion.* 1 John i. 3–11. S. M.

HOW can a sinner know
   His sins on earth forgiven?
How can my gracious Saviour show
   My name inscrib'd in heaven?

2 What we have felt and seen
   With confidence we tell;
And publish to the sons of men
   The signs infallible

3 We who in Christ believe
   That he for us hath died,
We all his unknown peace receive,
   And feel his blood applied.

4 Exults our rising soul,
   Disburden'd of her load,
And swells unutterably full
   Of glory and of God.

5 His love surpassing far
   The love of all beneath,
We find within our hearts, and dare
   The pointless darts of death.

6 Stronger than death or hell
   The sacred power we prove;
And conqu'rors of the world we dwell
   In heaven, who dwell in love.
                        C. Wesley.

207   *Filial trust.*   S. M.

I LIFT my soul to God,
  My trust is in his name;
Let not my foes that seek my blood,
  Still triumph in my shame.

2 From the first dawning light
  Till the dark evening rise,
For thy salvation, Lord! I wait
  With ever-longing eyes.

3 Remember all thy grace,
  And lead me in thy truth;
Forgive the sins of riper days,
  And follies of my youth.

4 The Lord is just and kind;
  The meek shall learn his ways,
And every humble sinner find
  The methods of his grace.

5 For his own goodness' sake
  He saves my soul from shame;
He pardons, though my guilt be great,
  Through my Redeemer's name. *Watts.*

208   *Adoption.*   S. M.

BEHOLD! what wondrous grace
  The Father hath bestowed
On sinners of a mortal race,—
  To call them sons of God!

2 'Tis no surprising thing
  That we should be unknown:
The Jewish world knew not their King,
  God's everlasting Son.

3 Nor does it yet appear.
  How great we must be made;
But when we see our Saviour here,
  We shall be like our Head.

JUSTIFICATION AND ADOPTION.

4 A hope so much divine,
   May trials well endure,
   May purge our souls from sense and sin,
   As Christ, the Lord is pure.
5 If in my Father's love
   I share a filial part,
   Send down thy Spirit, like a dove,
   To rest upon my heart.   *Watts.*

209   *Love and Joy.*   L. M.
[From the German.]

I THIRST, thou wounded Lamb of God,
   To wash me in thy cleansing blood;
To dwell within thy wounds; then pain
Is sweet, and life or death is gain.

2 Take my poor heart, and let it be
Forever closed to all but thee!
Seal thou my breast, and let me wear
That pledge of love forever there.

3 How blest are they who still abide
Close sheltered in thy bleeding side!
Who life and strength from thence derive,
And by thee move, and in thee live.

4 What are our works but sin and death,
Till thou thy quick'ning Spirit breathe?
Thou giv'st the power thy grace to move:
O wondrous grace! O boundless love!
   J. Wesley.

210   *Receiving the Atonement.*   L. M.
[From the German of Zinzendorf.]

JESUS, thy blood and righteousness
   My beauty are, my glorious dress:
'Midst flaming worlds, in these arrayed,
With joy shall I lift up my head.

JUSTIFICATION AND ADOPTION.

2 Bold shall I stand in thy great day,
For who aught to my charge shall lay?
Fully absolved through thee I am,
From sin, and fear, from guilt and shame.

3 The holy, meek, unspotted Lamb,
Who from the Father's bosom came,
Who died for me, e'en me, t' atone,
Now for my Lord and God I own.

4 Lord, I believe thy precious blood,
Which, at the mercy-seat of God,
Forever doth for sinners plead,
For *me*, e'en for *my* soul, was shed.

5 Lord, I believe were sinners more
Than sands upon the ocean shore,
Thou hast for ALL a ransom paid,
For ALL a full atonement made.

J. Wesley.

211   *Ezekiel* xxxvi. 23–25.   L. M.

GOD of all power, and truth, and grace,
   Which shall from age to age endure;
Whose word, when heaven and earth shall pass,
   Remains, and stands forever sure:

2 Calmly to thee my soul looks up,
   And waits thy promises to prove,
The object of my steadfast hope,
   The seal of thy eternal love.

3 That I thy mercy may proclaim,
   That all mankind thy truth may see,
Hallow thy great and glorious name,
   And perfect holiness in me.

4 Thy sanctifying Spirit pour,
   To quench my thirst, and make me clean;

JUSTIFICATION AND ADOPTION.

Now, Father, let the gracious shower
Descend, and make me pure from sin.
C. Wesley.

212   *God the source of Joy.*   C. M.

MY God, the spring of all my joys,
　　The life of my delights,
The glory of my brightest days,
　　And comfort of my nights!

2 In darkest shades if thou appear,
　　My dawning is begun;
Thou art my soul's bright morning star,
　　And thou my rising sun.

3 The opening heavens around me shine
　　With beams of sacred bliss,
If Jesus show his mercy mine,
　　And whisper I am his.

4 My soul would leave this heavy clay
　　At that transporting word,
Run up with joy the shining way,
　　To see and praise my Lord.

5 Fearless of hell and ghastly death,
　　I'd break through every foe;
The wings of love and arms of faith
　　Would bear me conqu'ror through.
Watts.

213   *Looking to Christ.*   C. M.

LOOK unto him, ye nations; own
　　Your God, ye fallen race;
Look, and be saved through faith alone,
　　Be justified by grace.

2 See all your sins on Jesus laid:
　　The Lamb of God was slain;

JUSTIFICATION AND ADOPTION.

 His soul was once an off"ring made
  For every soul of man.
3 Awake from guilty nature's sleep,
  And Christ shall give you light:
 Cast all your sins into the deep,
  And wash the crimson white.
4 With me, your chief, ye then shall know,
  Shall feel, your sins forgiven;
 Anticipate your heaven below,
  And own that love is heaven.   *C. Wesley.*

214   *Bliss.*   7s.

JESUS is our common Lord,
  He our loving Saviour is:
 By his death to life restored,
  Mis'ry we exchange for bliss,—
2 Bliss to carnal minds unknown:
  O 'tis more than tongue can tell!
 Only to believers shown,
  Glorious and unspeakable.
3 Christ, our Brother and our Friend,
  Shows us his eternal love:
 Never shall our triumphs end,
  Till we take our seats above.
4 Let us walk with him in white;
  For our bridal day prepare,
 For our partnership in light,
  For our glorious meeting there!
         C. Wesley.

215   *Forsaking all to follow Christ.*   8s & 7s.

JESUS I my cross have taken,
  All to leave and follow thee;
Naked, poor, despised, forsaken,
  Thou, from hence, my all shalt be:

And whilst thou shalt smile upon me,
  God of wisdom, love, and might,
Foes may hate and friends disown me;
  Show thy face, and all is bright.

2 Man may trouble and distress me;
  'Twill but drive me to thy breast:
Life with trials hard may press me;
  Heaven will bring me sweeter rest:
O, 'tis not in grief to harm me,
  While thy love is left to me;
O, 'twere not in joy to charm me,
  Were that joy unmixed with thee.

Grant.

216 *The Joys of Conversion.* 12, 9.

O HOW happy are they,
    Who the Saviour obey,
And have laid up their treasure above!
  Tongue can never express
  The sweet comfort and peace
Of a soul in its earliest love.

2 That sweet comfort was mine,
    When the favor divine
I received through the blood of the Lamb!
  When my heart first believed,
  What a joy I received,
What a heaven in Jesus's name!

3 'Twas a heaven below
    My Redeemer to know,
And the angels could do nothing more,
  Than to fall at his feet,
  And the story repeat,
And the Lover of sinners adore.

4 Jesus all the day long
   Was my joy and my song:
   O that all his salvation might see!
   " He hath loved me," I cried,
   " He hath suffered and died,
   To redeem even rebels like me."
5 O the rapturous height
   Of that holy delight
   Which I felt in the life-giving blood!
   Of my Saviour possessed,
   I was perfectly blest,
   As if filled with the fullness of God.
                          Charles Wesley.

217 *Just as I am.* L. M.

JUST as I am, without one plea,
   But that thy blood was shed for me,
   And that thou bidst me come to thee,
   O Lamb of God, I come! I come!

2 Just as I am, and waiting not
   To rid my soul of one dark blot,
   To thee, whose blood can cleanse each spot,
   O Lamb of God, I come! I come!

3 Just as I am, though tossed about
   With many a conflict, many a doubt,
   Fightings and fears, within, without,
   O Lamb of God, I come! I come!

4 Just as I am, poor, wretched, blind,
   Sight, riches, healing of the mind,
   Yea, all I need, in thee, to find,
   O Lamb of God, I come! I come!

5 Just as I am, thou wilt receive,
   Wilt, welcome, pardon, cleanse, **relieve;**
   Because thy promise I believe,
   O Lamb of God, I come! I come!

JUSTIFICATION AND ADOPTION.

6 Just as I am, thy love unknown
 Hath broken every barrier down;
 Now to be thine. yea, thine alone,
  O Lamb of God, I come! I come!
                              Miss Elliott.

218   *The Well of Life.*   C. M

FOUNTAIN of life, to all below
  Let thy salvation roll;
Water, replenish, and o'erflow
  Every believing soul.

2 Into that happy number, Lord,
   Us weary sinners take;
 Jesus, fulfill thy gracious word,
   For thine own mercy's sake.

3 Turn back our nature's rapid tide,
   And we shall flow to thee,
 While down the stream of time we glide
   To our eternity.

4 The well of life to us thou art,
   Of joy, the swelling flood;
 Wafted by thee, with willing heart,
   We swift return to God.

5 We soon shall reach the boundless sea;
   Into thy fullness fall;
 Be lost and swallowed up in thee,
   Our God, our all in all.   *Charles Wesley.*

219   *Christ, the Solid Rock.*   L. M. 6 l.

MY hope is built on nothing less
   Than Jesus' blood and righteousness;
 I dare not trust the sweetest frame,
 But wholly lean on Jesus' name:
 On Christ, the solid rock, I stand;
 All other ground is sinking sand.

JUSTIFICATION AND ADOPTION.

2 When darkness seems to veil his face,
   I rest on his unchanging grace;
   In every high and stormy gale,
   My anchor holds within the veil:
   On Christ, the solid rock, I stand;
   All other ground is sinking sand.

3 His oath, his covenant, and blood,
   Support me in the whelming flood:
   When all around my soul gives way,
   He then is all my hope and stay:
   On Christ, the solid rock, I stand;
   All other ground is sinking sand.
Edward Mo.

220   *Salvation by Grace.*   L. M.

WE have no outward righteousness,
   No merits or good works to plead;
We only can be saved by grace:
   Thy grace, O Lord, is free indeed.

2 Save us by grace, through faith alone,
   A faith thou must thyself impart;
   A faith that would by works be shown,
   A faith that purifies the heart:

3 A faith that doth the mountains move,
   A faith that shows our sins forgiven,
   A faith that sweetly works by love,
   And ascertains our claim to heaven.

4 This is the faith we humbly seek,
   The faith in thy all-cleansing blood,
   That blood which doth for sinners speak;
   O let it speak us up to God!
Charles Wesley.

JUSTIFICATION AND ADOPTION.

221 *Following the Saviour.* L. M.

O THOU, to whose all-searching sight
    The darkness shineth as the light,
Search, prove my heart, it pants for thee;
O burst these bonds, and set it free.

2 Wash out its stains, refine its dross,
Nail my affections to the cross;
Hallow each thought; let all within
Be clean, as thou, my Lord, art clean.

3 If in this darksome wild I stray,
Be thou my light, be thou my way:
No foes, no violence I fear,
No fraud, while thou, my God, art near.

4 When rising floods my soul o'erflow,
When sinks my heart in waves of woe,
Jesus, thy timely aid impart,
And raise my head, and cheer my heart.

5 Saviour, where'er thy steps I see,
Dauntless, untired, I follow thee;
O let thy hand support me still,
And lead me to thy holy hill.

6 If rough and thorny be the way,
My strength proportion to my day;
Till toil, and grief, and pain shall cease,
Where all is calm, and joy, and peace
                              Tr. by J. Wesley.

222 *O Happy Day!* L. M.

O HAPPY day that fixed my choice
    On thee, my Saviour and my God!
Well may this glowing heart rejoice,
    And tell its raptures all abroad.

2 O happy bond, that seals my vows
    To him who merits all my love!
Let cheerful anthems fill his house,
    While to that sacred shrine I move.

JUSTIFICATION AND ADOPTION.

3 'Tis done, the great transaction's done;
   I am my Lord's, and he is mine;
   He drew me, and I followed on,
   Charmed to confess the voice divine.
4 Now rest, my long-divided heart;
   Fixed on this blissful center, rest;
   Nor ever from thy Lord depart,
   With him of every good possessed.
5 High Heaven, that heard the solemn vow,
   That vow renewed shall daily hear,
   Till in life's latest hour I bow,
   And bless in death a bond so dear.
                              Philip Doddridge

223   *Amazing grace.*   C. M

AMAZING grace! how sweet the sound
   That saved a wretch like me!
I once was lost, but now am found,
   Was blind, but now I see.
'Twas grace that taught my heart to fear,
   And grace my fears relieved;
How precious did that grace appear
   The hour I first believed!
2 Through many dangers, toils, and snares,
   I have already come;
'Tis grace has brought me safe thus far,
   And grace will lead me home.
The Lord has promised good to me,
   His word my hope secures;
He will my shield and portion be
   As long as life endures.
3 Yes, when this flesh and heart shall fail,
   And mortal life shall cease,
I shall possess, within the veil,
   A life of joy and peace.

The earth shall soon dissolve like snow,
  The sun forbear to shine ;
But God, who called me here below,
  Will be forever mine.   *John Newton.*

224   *Rom.* iv. 16–25.   C. M.

FATHER of Jesus Christ, my Lord,
  My Saviour and my Head,
I trust in thee, whose powerful word
  Hath raised him from the dead.

2 Thou know'st for my offense he died,
  And rose again for me;
Fully and freely justified,
  That I might live to thee.

3 Eternal life to all mankind
  Thou hast in Jesus given ;
And all who seek, in him shall find
  The happiness of heaven.

4 All nations of the earth are blessed
  In him, who would restore,
And take them all into his rest,
  And bid them sin no more.

5 O God, thy record I believe.
  In Abrah'm's footsteps tread ;
And wait, expecting to receive
  The Christ, the promised Seed !
            C. Wesley.

225 "*Purge me—and I shall be clean.*" C. M.
      Psl. li. 7.

MY God, my God, to thee I cry ;
  Thee only would I know ;
Thy purifying blood apply,
  And wash me white as snow.

CONSECRATION AND HOLINESS IMPLORED.

2 Touch me, and make the leper clean;
  Purge my iniquity:
Unless thou wash my soul from sin,
  I have no part in thee.

3 But art thou not already mine?
  Answer, if mine thou art!
Whisper within, thou Love Divine,
  And cheer my drooping heart.

4 Behold for me the Victim bleeds,
  His wounds are open wide;
For me the blood of sprinkling pleads,
  And speaks me justified. *C. Wesley.*

SECTION IX.

Consecration and Holiness Implored.

226   *A perfect heart.*   C. M.

O FOR a heart to praise my God,
  A heart from sin set free!
A heart that always feels thy blood,
  So freely spilt for me!

2 A heart resigned, submissive meek,
  My great Redeemer's throne;
Where only Christ is heard to speak,
  Where Jesus reigns alone.

3 O for a lowly, contrite heart,
  Believing, true and clean,
Which neither life nor death can part
  From him that dwells within!

158

4 A heart in every thought renewed,
    And full of love divine;
Perfect, and right, and pure, and good,
    A copy, Lord, of thine.

5 Thy nature, gracious Lord, impart;
    Come quickly from above;
Write thy new name upon my heart,
    Thy new, best name of Love.
Charles Wesley.

227   *The paradise of love.*   C. M.

O JESUS! at thy feet we wait,
    Till thou shalt bid us rise,
Restored to our unsinning state
    To love's sweet paradise.

2 Saviour from sin, we thee receive;
    From all indwelling sin,
Thy blood, we steadfastly believe,
    Shall make us thoroughly clean.

3 Since thou wouldst have us free from sin
    And pure as those above,
Make haste to bring thy nature in,
    And perfect us in love!

4 The counsel of thy love fulfil;
    Come quickly, gracious Lord!
Be it according to thy will,
    According to thy word.

5 O that the perfect grace were given,
    Thy love diffused abroad!
O that our hearts were all a heaven,
    For ever filled with God!
C. Wesley.

CONSECRATION AND HOLINESS IMPLORED.

228   *Perfect Love.*   C. M.

WHEN Christ doth in my heart appear,
   And love erects its throne,
I then enjoy salvation here,
   And heaven on earth begun.

2 When God is mine, and I am his,
   Of paradise possessed,
I taste unutterable bliss,
   And everlasting rest.

3 The bliss of those that fully dwell,
   Fully in thee believe,
'Tis more than angel-tongues can tell,
   Or angel-minds conceive.

4 Thou only know'st who did obtain,
   And die to make it known:
The great salvation now explain,
   And perfect us in one.

5 May I, may all who humbly wait,
   The glorious joy receive,—
Joy above all conception great,
   Worthy of God to give.
                         C. Wesley

229   *Perfect Purification.*   C. M.

FOREVER here my rest shall be,
   Close to thy bleeding side;
This all my hope, and all my plea,
   For me the Saviour died.

2 My dying Saviour, and my God,
   Fountain for guilt and sin,
Sprinkle me ever with thy blood,
   And cleanse and keep me clean.

3 Wash me, and make me thus thine own;
   Wash me, and mine thou art:

CONSECRATION AND HOLINESS IMPLORED.

Wash me, but not my feet alone,
My hands, my head, my heart.
4 Th' atonement of thy blood apply,
Till faith to sight improve,
Till hope in full fruition die,
And all my soul be love.   *C. Wesley.*

230   *My All-sufficient Good.*   C. M.

I would be thine, thou know'st I would,
And have thee all my own;
Thee, O my all-sufficient Good!
I want, and thee alone.

2 Thy name to me, thy nature grant!
This, only this, be given:
Nothing besides my God I want;
Nothing in earth or heaven.

3 Come, O my Saviour, come away!
Into my soul descend!
No longer from thy creature stay,
My Author and my End!

4 Come, Father, Son and Holy Ghost,
And seal me thine abode:
Let all I am in thee be lost;
Let all be lost in God!   *C. Wesley.*

231   *The Rapture of Love.*   C. M.

I KNOW that my Redeemer lives,
And ever prays for me:
A token of his love he gives,
A pledge of liberty.

2 I find him lifting up my head,
He brings salvation near;
His presence makes me free indeed,
And he will soon appear.

CONSECRATION AND HOLINESS IMPLORED.

3 He wills that I should holy be!
    What can withstand his will?
  The counsel of his grace in me
    He surely shall fulfil.
4 Jesus, I hang upon thy word;
    I steadfastly believe
  Thou wilt return, and claim me, Lord,
    And to thyself receive.
5 Joyful in hope, my spirit soars
    To meet thee from above,
  Thy goodness thankfully adores;
    And sure I taste thy love. *C. Wesley.*

232 *Waiting at the Cross.* S. M.

FATHER, I dare believe
    Thee merciful and true:
  Thou wilt my guilty soul forgive,
    My fallen soul renew.
2 Come then, for Jesus' sake,
    And bid my heart be clean:
  An end of all my troubles make,
    An end of all my sin.
3 I cannot wash my heart,
    But by believing thee,
  And waiting for thy blood t' impart
    The spotless purity.
4 While at thy cross I lie,
    Jesus, the grace bestow;
  Now thy all-cleansing blood apply,
    And I am white as snow. *C. Wesley.*

233 *Depending on Christ.* S. M.

JESUS, my truth, my way,
    My sure, unerring light,
  On thee my feeble steps I stay,
    Which thou wilt guide aright.

162

CONSECRATION AND HOLINESS IMPLORED.

2 My wisdom and my guide,
  My counsellor thou art;
  O never let me leave thy side,
  Or from thy paths depart.

3 I lift mine eyes to thee,
  Thou gracious, bleeding Lamb,
  That I may now enlighten'd be,
  And never put to shame.

4 Never will I remove
  Out of thy hands my cause;
  But rest in thy redeeming love,
  And hang upon thy cross.

5 Teach me the happy art,
  In all things to depend
  On thee: O never, Lord, depart,
  But love me to the end.   *C. Wesley.*

234   *The Act of Consecration.*   L. M.
[From the French.]

COME, Saviour, Jesus, from above!
 Assist me with thy heavenly grace;
Empty my heart of earthly love,
 And for thyself prepare the place.

2 O let thy sacred presence fill,
  And set my longing spirit free,
  Which pants to have no other will,
  But day and night to feast on thee.

3 While in this region here below,
  No other good will I pursue:
  I'll bid this world of noise and show,
  With all its glitt'ring snares, adieu!

4 That path with humble speed I'll seek
  In which my Saviour's footsteps shine,

CONSECRATION AND HOLINESS IMPLORED.

Nor will I hear nor will I speak
Of any other love but thine.
5 Henceforth may no profane delight
Divide this consecrated soul;
Possess it, thou, who hast the right,
As Lord and Master of the whole.
J. Wesley.

235 L. M.
There remaineth therefore a rest to the people of God. Heb. 4: 9.

COME, O Thou greater than our heart,
And make thy faithful mercies known:
The mind which was in thee impart;
Thy constant mind in us be shown.

2 O let us by thy cross abide,
Thee, only thee, resolved to know,
The Lamb for sinners crucified,
A world to save from endless woe.

3 Take us into thy people's rest,
And we from our own works shall cease;
With thy meek Spirit arm our breast,
And keep our minds in perfect peace.

4 Jesus, for this we calmly wait;
O let our eyes behold thee near!
Hasten to make our heaven complete:
Appear, our glorious God, appear!
Charles Wesley.

236 *Christ All in All.* L. M.

HOLY, and true, and righteous Lord,
I wait to prove thy perfect will:
Be mindful of thy gracious word,
And stamp me with thy Spirit's seal.

CONSECRATION AND HOLINESS IMPLORED.

2 Open my faith's interior eye:
  Display thy glory from above;
And all I am shall sink and die,
  Lost in astonishment and love.

3 Confound, o'erpower me by thy grace,
  I would be by myself abhorred;
All might, all majesty, all praise,
  All glory, be to Christ my Lord.

4 Now let me gain perfection's height;
  Now let me into nothing fall,
As less than nothing in thy sight,
  And feel that Christ is all in all.
                              Charles Wesley.

237   *Waiting for the Promise.*   L. M.

O JESUS, full of truth and grace,
    O all-atoning Lamb of God,
I wait to see thy glorious face;
    I seek redemption through thy blood.

2 Thou art the anchor of my hope;
    The faithful promise I receive:
Surely thy death shall raise me up,
    For thou hast died that I might live.

3 Satan, with all his arts, no more
    Me from the gospel hope can move;
I shall receive the gracious power,
    And find the pearl of perfect love.

4 My flesh which cries, "It cannot be,"
    Shall silence keep before the Lord;
And earth, and hell, and sin shall flee
    At Jesus' everlasting word.
                              Charles Wesley.

CONSECRATION AND HOLINESS IMPLORED.

238 *For Lowliness and Purity.* L. M.

JESUS, in whom the Godhead's rays
  Beam forth with mildest majesty;
I see thee full of truth and grace,
And come for all I want to thee.

2 Save me from pride—the plague expel;
  Jesus, thine humble self impart:
O let thy mind within me dwell;
O give me lowliness of heart.

3 Enter thyself, and cast out sin;
  Thy spotless purity bestow:
Touch me, and make the leper clean;
Wash me, and I am white as snow.

4 Sprinkle me, Saviour with thy blood,
  And all thy gentleness is mine;
And plunge me in the purple flood,
Till all I am is lost in thine.

Charles Wesley.

239 *The promised land of perfect love.* L. M.

IF, Lord, I have acceptance found
  With thee, or favor in thy sight,
Still with thy grace and truth surround,
And arm me with thy Spirit's might.

2 O may I hear thy warning voice,
  And timely fly from danger near,
With rev'rence unto thee rejoice,
And love thee with a filial fear!

3 Still hold my soul in second life,
  And suffer not my feet to slide:
Support me in the glorious strife,
And comfort me on every side.

4 O give me faith, and faith's increase;
Finish the work begun in me,
Preserve my soul in perfect peace,
And let me always rest on thee!
C. Wesley.

240   *The Will of God.*   L. M.

HE wills that I should holy be;
That holiness I long to feel;
That full divine conformity
To all my Saviour's righteous will.

2 See, Lord, the travail of thy soul
Accompl'shed in the change of mine;
And plunge me, every whit made whole,
In all the depths of love divine.

3 On thee, O God, my soul is stayed,
And waits to prove thine utmost will;
The promise by thy mercy made,
Thou canst, thou wilt, in me fulfil.

4 No more I stagger at thy power,
Or doubt thy truth, which cannot move:
Hasten the long-expected hour,
And bless me with thy perfect love.
Charles Wesley.

241   *Heavenly Bliss in Prospect.*   L. M.

ARISE, my soul, on wings sublime,
Above the vanities of time;
Let faith now pierce the veil and see
The glories of eternity.

2 Born by a new, celestial birth,
Why should I grovel here on earth?
Why grasp at vain and fleeting toys,
So near to heaven's eternal joys?

3 Shall aught beguile me on the road,
The narrow road that leads to God?
Or can I love this earth so well,
As not to long with God to dwell?

4 To dwell with God, to taste his love,
Is the full heaven enjoyed above:
The glorious expectation now
Is heavenly bliss begun below.
Thomas Gibbons.

242   *The New Covenant.*   L. M.

O GOD, most merciful and true,
  Thy nature to my soul impart;
'Stablish with me the covenant new,
  And stamp thine image on my heart.

2 To real holiness restored,
  O let me gain my Saviour's mind;
And in the knowledge of my Lord,
  Fullness of life eternal find.

3 Remember Lord, my sins no more,
  That them I may no more forget;
But sunk in guiltless shame, adore,
  With speechless wonder at thy feet.

4 O'erwhelmed with thy stupendous grace
  I shall not in thy presence move;
But breathe unutterable praise,
  And rapturous awe and silent love.

5 Then every murmuring thought, and vain,
  Expires, in sweet confusion lost:
I cannot of my cross complain,
  I cannot of my goodness boast.
C. Wesley.

SECTION X.
Christian Perfection.

243   *Rejoice in Hope.*   8s, 6s.

O GLORIOUS hope of perfect love,
  It lifts me up to things above;
  It bears on eagles' wings;
It gives my ravished soul a taste,
And makes me for some moments feast
  With Jesus' priests and kings.

2 Rejoicing now in earnest hope,
I stand, and, from the mountain top,
  See all the land below:
Rivers of milk and honey rise,
And all the fruits of paradise
  In endless plenty grow.

3 A land of corn, and wine, and oil,
Favored with God's peculiar smile,
  With every blessing blessed:
There dwells the Lord our Righteousness,
And keeps his own in perfect peace,
  And everlasting rest.

4 Now, O my Joshua, bring me in!
Cast out thy foes; the inbred sin,
  The carnal mind, remove:
The purchase of thy death divide;
And, O! with all the sanctified,
  Give me a lot of love!   *C. Wesley.*

244   *Panting for fullness of Love.*   8s, 6s.

O LOVE divine, how sweet thou art!
  When shall I find my willing heart
  All taken up by thee?

I thirst, I faint, I die to prove
The greatness of redeeming love,
 The love of Christ to me.
2 Stronger his love than death or hell;
Its riches are unsearchable;
 The first-born sons of light
Desire in vain its depths to see;
They cannot reach the mystery,
 The length, the breadth, the height.
3 God only knows the love of God;
O that it now were shed abroad
 In this poor stony heart!
For love I sigh, for love I pine;
This only portion, Lord, be mine;
 Be mine this better part.
4 O that I could forever sit
With Mary at the Master's feet!
 Be this my happy choice;
My only care, delight, and bliss,
My joy, my heaven on earth, be this,
 To hear the Bridegroom's voice.
5 O that I could, with favored John,
Recline my weary head upon
 The dear Redeemer's breast!
From care, and sin, and sorrow free,
Give me, O Lord, to find in thee
 My everlasting rest. *Charles Wesley.*

245   *The pure in heart shall see God.*   8s, 6s.

SAVIOUR, on me the grace bestow,
 That, with thy children, I may know
  My sins on earth forgiven;
Give me to prove the kingdom mine,
And taste, in holiness divine,
 The happiness of heaven.

CHRISTIAN PERFECTION.

2 Me with that restless thirst inspire,
That sacred, infinite desire,
  And feast my hungry heart;
Less than thyself cannot suffice;
My soul for all thy fullness cries,
  For all thou hast and art.

3 Jesus, the crowning grace impart;
Bless me with purity of heart,
  That, now beholding thee,
I soon may view thy open face,
On all thy glorious beauties gaze,
  And God forever see.
          Charles Wesley.

246   *Power over Temptation.*   8s, 6s.

HELP, Lord, to whom for help I fly,
  And still my tempted soul stand by
    Throughout the evil day;
The sacred watchfulness impart,
And keep the issues of my heart,
  And stir me up to pray.

2 My soul with thy whole armor arm;
In each approach of sin alarm,
  And show the danger near:
Surround, sustain, and strengthen me,
And fill with godly jealousy
  And sanctifying fear.

3 Whene'er my careless hands hang down,
O let me see thy gathering frown,
  And feel thy warning eye;
And, starting, cry from ruin's brink
"Save, Jesus, or I yield, I sink;
  O save me, or I die."

CHRISTIAN PERFECTION.

4 If near the pit I rashly stray,
Before I wholly fall away,
　The keen conviction dart;
Recall me by that pitying look,
That kind, upbraiding glance, which broke
Unfaithful Peter's heart.　　*C. Wesley.*

247　　*Rejoicing in Hope.*　　C. M.

O JOYFUL sound of gospel grace!
　Christ shall in me appear:
I, even I, shall see his face;
　I shall be holy here.

2 The glorious crown of righteousness
　To me reached out I view;
Conqu'ror through him, I soon shall seize,
　And wear it as my due.

3 The promised land from Pisgah's top
　I now exult to see:
My hope is full (O glorious hope!)
　Of immortality.

4 He visits now the house of clay;
　He shakes his future home;
O wouldst thou, Lord, on this glad day,
　Into thy temple come!

5 With me, I know, I feel, thou art;
　But this cannot suffice,
Unless thou plantest in my heart
　A constant paradise.　　*C. Wesley.*

248　　*The heart dissolving in Love.*　　C. M.

JESUS hath died that I might live,
　Might live to God alone;
In him eternal life receive,
　And be in spirit one.

2 Saviour, I thank thee for the grace,
   The gift unspeakable:
   And wait with arms of faith t' embrace,
   And all thy love to feel.
3 My soul breaks out in strong desire
   The perfect bliss to prove:
   My longing heart is all on fire
   To be dissolved in love.
4 Give me thyself; from every boast,
   From every wish set free:
   Let all I am in thee be lost;
   But give thyself to me.
5 Thy gifts alas! cannot suffice,
   Unless thyself be given;
   Thy presence makes my paradise,
   And where thou art is heaven. *C. Wesley.*

49   *The fullness of God.*   C. M.

BEING of beings, God of love,
   To thee our hearts we raise;
Thy all-sustaining power we prove,
   And gladly sing thy praise.
2 Thine, wholly thine, we pant to be;
   Our sacrifice receive:
   Made, and preserved, and saved by thee,
   To thee ourselves we give.
3 Heavenward our every wish aspires
   For all thy mercy's store;
   The sole return thy love requires,
   Is that we ask for more.
4 For more we ask; we open then
   Our hearts to embrace thy will;
   Turn, and revive us, Lord, again;
   With all thy fullness fill.

CHRISTIAN PERFECTION.

5 Come, Holy Ghost. the Saviour's love
   Shed in our hearts abroad;
   So shall we ever live, and move,
   And be, with Christ in God.   *C. Wesley.*

250   *The thought of God.*   C. M.

O HOW the thought of God attracts
   And draws the heart from earth,
And sickens it of passing shows
And dissipating mirth!

2 'Tis not enough to save our souls,
   To shun the eternal fires;
The thought of God will rouse the heart
To more sublime desires.

3 God only is the creature's home,
   Though rough and strait the road;
Yet nothing less can satisfy
The love that longs for God.

4 O utter but the name of God
   Down in your heart of hearts,
And see how from the world at once
All tempting light departs!

5 A trusting heart, a yearning eye,
   Can win their way above;
If mountains can be moved by faith,
Is there less power in love?
                    Frederick W. Faber.

251   *Walk in the light.*   C. M.

WALK in the light! so shalt thou know
   That fellowship of love,
His Spirit only can bestow
Who reigns in light above.

2 Walk in the light! and thou shalt find
   Thy heart made truly his,

Who dwells in cloudless light enshrined,
In whom no darkness is.

3 Walk in the light! and thou shalt own
Thy darkness passed away,
Because that light hath on thee shone
In which is perfect day.

4 Walk in the light! and e'en the tomb
No fearful shade shall wear;
Glory shall chase away its gloom,
For Christ hath conquered there.

5 Walk in the light! thy path shall be
Peaceful, serene, and bright;
For God, by grace, shall dwell in thee,
And God himself is light. *Bernard Barton.*

252 C. M.
Excellence of Christian unanimity and Love.

SPIRIT of peace, celestial Dove,
  How excellent thy praise!
No richer gift than Christian love
Thy gracious power displays.

2 Sweet as the dew on herb and flower,
That silently distills,
At evening's soft and balmy hour,
On Zion's fruitful hills,—

3 So, with mild influence from above,
Shall promis'd grace descend,
Till universal peace and love
O'er all the earth extend.
  Spir. of the Psalms.

253 *"Thy will be done."* C. M.

JESUS, the life, the truth, the way,
  In whom I now believe,

CHRISTIAN PERFECTION.

As taught by thee, in faith I pray,
Expecting to receive.
2 Thy will by me on earth be done,
As by the powers above,
Who always see thee on thy throne,
And glory in thy love.
3 I ask in confidence the grace,
That I may do thy will,
As angels who behold thy face,
And all thy words fulfil.
4 Surely I shall. the sinner I,
Shall serve thee without fear,
If thou my nature sanctify
In answer to my prayer. *C. Wesley.*

254 *A holy heart the Saviour's home.* C. M.

WHAT is our calling's glorious hope
But inward holiness!
For this to Jesus I look up,
I calmly wait for this.
2 I wait, till he shall touch me clean,
Shall life and power impart,
Give me the faith that casts out sin,
And purifies the heart.
3 This is the dear redeeming grace,
For every sinner free;
Surely it shall on me take place,
The chief of sinners, me.
4 From all iniquity, from all,
He shall my soul redeem!
In Jesus I believe, and shall
Believe myself to him.
5 When Jesus makes my heart his home,
My sin shall all depart;

CHRISTIAN PERFECTION.

And, lo he saith: "I quickly come,
To fill and rule thy heart!"

6 Be it according to thy word,
Redeem me from all sin;
My heart would now receive thee, Lord:
Come in, my Lord, come in! *C. Wesley.*

255 *Love to the Saviour.* 7s.

HARK, my soul, it is the Lord!
'Tis thy Saviour, hear his word!
Jesus speaks, he speaks to thee:
"Say, poor sinner, lov'st thou me?

2 "I delivered thee when bound,
And, when bleeding, healed thy wound;
Sought thee wand'ring, set thee right,
Turned thy darkness into light.

3 "Can a mother's tender care
Cease toward the child she bare?
Yes, she may forgetful be,
Yet will I remember thee.

4 "Mine is an unchanging love,
Higher than the heights above,
Deeper than the depths beneath,
Free and faithful, strong as death.

5 "Thou shalt see my glory soon,
When the work of faith is done.
Partner of my throne shalt be:
Say, poor sinner, lov'st thou me?"

6 Lord, it is my chief complaint
That my love is still so faint;
Yet I love thee and adore:
O for grace to love thee more! *Cowper.*

CHRISTIAN PERFECTION.

256. *Humble Aspirations.* 7s

WHEN, my Saviour, shall I be
  Perfectly resigned to thee?
Poor and vile in my own eyes,
  Only in thy wisdom wise?

2 Only thee content to know,
  Ignorant of all below?
Only guided by thy light;
  Only mighty in thy might?

3 So I may thy Spirit know,
  Let him as he listeth blow:
Let the manner be unknown.
  So I may with thee be one.

4 Fully in my life express
  All the heights of holiness;
Sweetly let my spirit prove
  All the depths of humble love.

C. Wesley.

257 *For Entire Consecration.* S. M.

JESUS, my strength, my hope,
  On thee I cast my care;
With humble confidence look up,
  And know thou hear'st my prayer.
Give me on thee to wait,
  Till I can all things do;
On thee, almighty to create,
  Almighty to renew.

2 I want a sober mind,
  A self-renouncing will,
That tramples down, and casts behind,
  The baits of pleasing ill:
A soul inured to pain,
  To hardship, grief, and loss;

CHRISTIAN PERFECTION.

Bold to take up, firm to sustain,
   The consecrated cross.

3 I want a godly fear,
   A quick discerning eye,
That looks to thee when sin is near,
   And sees the tempter fly:
A spirit still prepared,
   And armed with jealous care;
Forever standing on its guard,
   And watching unto prayer. *C. Wesley.*

258   *For Perfect Submission.*   S. M.

I WANT a heart to pray,
   To pray, and never cease;
Never to murmur at thy stay,
   Or wish my sufferings less.
This blessing, above all,
   Always to pray, I want;
Out of the deep on thee to call,
   And never, never faint.

2 I want a true regard,
   A single, steady aim,
Unmoved by threatening or reward,
   To thee and thy great name;
A jealous, just concern
   For thine immortal praise;
A pure desire that all may learn
   And glorify thy grace.

3 I rest upon thy word;
   The promise is for me;
My succor and salvation, Lord,
   Shall surely come from thee:
But let me still abide,
   Nor from my hope remove,

Till thou my patient spirit guide
Into thy perfect love. *Charles Wesley.*

259 *The Solemn Vow.* C. M.

WITNESS, ye men and angels, now,
Before the Lord we speak;
To him we make our solemn vow,
A vow we dare not break:

2 That long as life itself shall last,
Ourselves to Christ we yield;
Nor from his cause will we depart,
Or ever quit the field.

3 We trust not in our native strength,
But on his grace rely,
That, with returning wants, the Lord
Will all our need supply.

4 Lord, guide our doubtful feet aright,
And keep us in thy ways;
And, while we turn our vows to prayers,
Turn thou our prayers to praise.
Benjamin Beddome.

260 *"I will take the cup of salvation."* C. M.
Psalm cxvi. 13.

WHAT shall I render to my God
For all his mercy's store?
I'll take the gifts he hath bestowed,
And humbly ask for more.

2 My vows I will to his great name
Before his people pay,
And all I have, and all I am,
Upon his altar lay.

3 Thy lawful servant, Lord, I owe
To thee whate'er is mine,

CHRISTIAN PERFECTION.

 Born in thy family below.
 And by redemption thine.

4 The God of all-redeeming grace
 My God I will proclaim,
 Offer the sacrifice of praise,
 And call upon his name.

5 Praise him, ye saints, the God of love,
 Who hath my sins forgiven,
 Till, gathered to the Church above,
 We sing the songs of heaven.
      Samuel Wesley

261 *Accept my Heart.* C. M.

MY God, accept my heart this day,
 And make it always thine;
That I from thee no more may stray,
 No more from thee decline.

2 Before the cross of him who died,
 Behold, I prostrate fall;
 Let every sin be crucified,
 Let Christ be all in all.

3 Let every thought, and work, and word,
 To thee be ever given;
 Then life shall be thy service, Lord,
 And death the gate of heaven!
      Matthew Bridges

262 *Soul and body dedicated to the Lord.* C. M.

LET him to whom we now belong,
 His sovereign right assert;
And take up every thankful song,
 And every loving heart.

2 He justly claims us for his own,
 Who bought us with a price:

CHRISTIAN PERFECTION.

The Christian lives to Christ alone;
To Christ alone he dies.
3 Jesus, thine own at last receive:
Fulfil our heart's desire;
And let us to thy glory live,
And in thy cause expire.
4 Our souls and bodies we resign;
With joy we render thee
Our all,—no longer ours, but thine
To all eternity. *Charles Wesley.*

263 *A Living Sacrifice.* L. M. 6 l.

O GOD, what offering shall I give
To thee, the Lord of earth and skies?
My spirit, soul, and flesh receive,
A holy, living sacrifice:
Small as it is, 'tis all my store;
More shouldst thou have, if I had more.
2 Now then, my God, thou hast my soul:
No longer mine, but thine I am:
Guard thou thine own, possess it whole;
Cheer it with hope, with love inflame.
Thou hast my spirit; there display
Thy glory to the perfect day.
3 Thou hast my flesh, thy hallowed shrine,
Devoted solely to thy will:
Here let thy light forever shine:
This house still let thy presence fill:
O Source of life! live, dwell, and move
In me, till all my life be love.
Joachim Lange, tr. by J. Wesley.

264 *The Single Eye.* L. M. 6 L

BEHOLD the servant of the Lord!
I wait thy guiding hand to feel;

To hear and keep thy every word,
  To prove and do thy perfect will:
Joyful from my own works to cease,
  Glad to fulfil all righteousness.

2 My every weak, though good design,
  O'errule or change, as seems thee meet:
Jesus, let all my work be thine!
  Thy work, O Lord is all complete,
And pleasing in thy Father's sight;
  Thou only hast done all things right.

3 Here, then, to thee thine own I leave;
  Mold as thou wilt thy passive clay;
But let me all thy stamp receive,
  But let me all thy words obey;
Serve with a single heart and eye,
  And to thy glory live and die. *Charles Wesley.*

265   *Pressing toward the Mark.*   L. M. 6 *l.*

I THANK thee, uncreated Sun,
  That thy bright beams on me have shined;
I thank thee, who hast overthrown
  My foes, and healed my wounded mind;
I thank thee, whose enlivening voice
Bids my freed heart in thee rejoice.

2 Uphold me in the doubtful race,
  Nor suffer me again to stray;
Strengthen my feet, with steady pace
  Still to press forward in thy way,
My soul and flesh, O Lord of might,
Fill, satiate, with thy heavenly light.

3 Give to mine eyes refreshing tears;
  Give to my heart chaste, hallowed fires;
Give to my soul, with filial fears,
  The love that all heaven's host inspires;

CHRISTIAN PERFECTION.

That all my powers, with all their might,
In thy sole glory may unite.

4 Thee will I love, my joy, my crown;
Thee will I love, my Lord, my God;
Thee will I love, beneath thy frown
Or smile, thy scepter or thy rod.
What though my flesh and heart decay?
Thee shall I love in endless day!
Johann A. Scheffler. Tr. by J. Wesley.

266 *The Prize of our High Calling.* L. M. 6 l.

JESUS, thy boundless love to me
No thought can reach, no tongue declare;
O knit my thankful heart to thee,
And reign without a rival there:
Thine wholly thine alone, I am;
Be thou alone my constant flame.

2 O grant that nothing in my soul
May dwell, but thy pure love alone:
O may thy love possess me whole,
My joy, my treasure, and my crown:
Strange flames far from my heart remove;
My every act, word, thought, be love.

3 Unwearied may I this pursue;
Dauntless to the high prize aspire;
Hourly within my soul renew
This holy flame. this heavenly fire:
And day and night, be all my care
To guard the sacred treasure there.

4 In suffering be thy love my peace;
In weakness be thy love my power;
And when the storms of life shall cease,
Jesus, in that important hour,

THE CHURCH COMFORTED.

In death as life be thou my guide,
And save me, who for me hath died.
Paul Gerhardt. Tr. by J. Wesley.

SECTION XI.

The Church Comforted and Encouraged.

267   L. M.

JESUS, from whom all blessings flow,
   Great Builder of thy Church below,
If now thy Spirit move my breast,
Hear, and fulfil thine own request.

2 The few that truly call thee Lord,
And wait thy sanctifying word,
And thee their utmost Saviour own,—
Unite, and perfect them in one.

3 O let them all thy mind express!
Stand forth thy chosen witnesses;
Thy power unto salvation show,
And perfect holiness below.

4 In them let all mankind behold
How Christians lived in days of old;
Mighty their envious foes to move,
A proverb of reproach – and love.

5 Call them into thy wondrous light,
Worthy to walk with thee in white!
Make up thy jewels, Lord, and show
Thy glorious, spotless Church below.
C. Wesley.

THE CHURCH COMFORTED.

268   *Psalm* lxxxiv. 1-7.   L. M.

HOW pleasant, how divinely fair,
O Lord of hosts, thy dwellings are!
With strong desire my spirit faints
To meet th' assemblies of thy saints.

2 Blest are the saints that sit on high,
Around thy throne of majesty;
Thy brightest glories shine above,
And all their work is praise and love.

3 Blest are the souls that find a place
Within the temple of thy grace:
Here they behold thy gentler rays,
And seek thy face, and learn thy praise.

4 Blest are the men whose hearts are set
To find the way to Zion's gate;
God is their strength, and through the road
They lean upon their helper, God.

5 Cheerful they walk with growing strength,
Till all shall meet in heaven at length,
Till all before thy face appear,
And join in nobler worship there.   *Watts.*

269   *Psalm* lxv. 1-5.   L. M.

THE praise of Zion waits for thee,
My God; and praise becomes thy house;
There shall thy saints thy glory see,
And there perform their public vows.

2 O thou whose mercy bends the skies,
To save when humble sinners pray,
All lands to thee shall lift their eyes,
And grateful isles of every sea.   *Watts.*

THE CHURCH COMFORTED.

270   *Psalm xlvi. 1–5.*   **L. M.**

GOD is the refuge of his saints,
  When storms of sharp distress invade;
Ere we can offer our complaints,
  Behold him present with his aid.

2 Let mountains from their seats be hurled
  Down to the deep, and buried there—
Convulsions shake the solid world—
  Our faith shall never yield to fear.

3 Loud may the troubled ocean roar—
  In sacred peace our souls abide;
While every nation, every shore,
  Trembles and dreads the swelling tide.

4 There is a stream, whose gentle flow
  Supplies the city of our God;
Life, love, and joy, still gliding through,
  And wat'ring our divine abode.

5 That sacred stream, thy holy word,
  Our grief allays, our fear controls.
Sweet peace thy promises afford,
  And give new strength to fainting souls.
                              Watts.

271   *The ministry instituted.*   **L. M.**

THE Saviour, when to heaven he rose,
  In splendid triumph o'er his foes,
Scattered his gifts on men below,
  And still his royal bounties flow.

2 Hence sprang the apostles' honored name,
Sacred beyond heroic fame:
In humbler forms, before our eyes,
Pastors and teachers hence arise.

3 From Christ they all their gifts derive,
And, fed by Christ their graces live;

While guarded by his mighty hand,
'Midst all the rage of hell they stand.
4 So shall the bright succession run
Through all the courses of the sun;
While unborn churches, by their care,
Shall rise and flourish large and fair.
5 Jesus, now teach our hearts to know
The spring whence all these blessings flow,
Pastors and people shout thy praise,
Through the long round of endless days.
Philip Doddridge.

272 *Isaiah* xl. 1–5. L. M.

COMFORT, ye ministers of grace,
Comfort the people of your Lord,
O lift ye up the fallen race,
And cheer them by the gospel word.

2 Go into every nation, go,
Speak to their trembling hearts, and cry
Glad tidings unto all we show:
Jerusalem, thy God is nigh.

3 Hark! in the wilderness a cry,
A voice that loudly calls, Prepare!
Prepare your hearts, for God is nigh,
And means to make his entrance there!

4 The Lord your God shall quickly come;
Sinners, repent, the call obey;
Open your hearts to make him room;
Ye desert souls, prepare his way.

5 The Lord shall clear his way through all:
Whate'er obstructs, obstructs in vain;
The vale shall rise, the mountain fall,
Crooked be straight, and rugged plain.

THE CHURCH COMFORTED.

6 The glory of the Lord displayed
   Shall all mankind together view,
   And what his mouth in truth hath said,
   His own almighty hand shall do.
                                    C. Wesley.

273   *Angels of the Church.*   L. M.

DRAW near, O Son of God, draw near!
   Us with thy flaming eye behold;
Still in thy Church vouchsafe t' appear,
   And let our candlestick be gold.

2 Still hold the stars in thy right hand,
   And let them in thy lustre glow,
The lights of a benighted land,
   The angels of thy Church below.

3 Make good their apostolic boast,
   Their high commission let them prove,
Be temples of the Holy Ghost,
   And filled with faith, and hope, and love.

4 Their hearts from things of earth remove,
   Sprinkle them, Lord, from sin and fear,
Fix their affections all above,
   And lay up all their treasures there.

5 Give them an ear to hear thy word;
   Thou speakest to the Churches now;
And let all tongues confess their Lord,
   Let every knee to Jesus bow.   *C. Wesley.*

274   *Psalm* xlviii. 10-14.   S. M.

FAR as thy name is known
   The world declares thy praise:
Thy saints, O Lord, before thy throne
   Their songs of honor raise.

THE CHURCH COMFORTED.

2 With joy let Judah stand
   On Zion's chosen hill,
Proclaim the wonders of thy hand,
   And counsels of thy will.

3 Let strangers walk around
   The city where we dwell;
Compass and view the holy ground,
   And mark the building well—

4 The order of thy house,
   The worship of thy court,
The cheerful songs, the solemn vows,
   And make a fair report.

5 How decent and how wise!
   How glorious to behold!
Beyond the pomp that charms the eyes,
   And rites adorned with gold. *Watts.*

275   *For an increase of laborers.*   S. M

LORD of the harvest hear
   Thy needy servants' cry;
Answer our faith's effectual prayer,
   And all our wants supply.

2 On thee we humbly wait,
   Our wants are in thy view:
The harvest, truly, Lord, is great,
   The laborers are few.

3 Convert, and send forth more
   Into thy Church abroad,
And let them speak the word of power,
   As workers with their God.

4 O let them spread thy name,
   Their mission fully prove;
Thy universal grace proclaim,
   Thine all-redeeming love! *C. Wesley.*

THE CHURCH COMFORTED.

276   *The Reunion.*   S. M.

O HAPPY, happy place,
   Where saints and angels meet!
There we shall see each other's face,
   And all our brethren greet.

2 With joy we shall behold,
   In yonder blest abode,
The patriarchs and prophets old,
   And all the saints of God.

3 Abrah'm and Isaac there,
   And Jacob shall receive
The foll'wers of their faith and prayer
   Who now in bodies live.

4 We shall our time beneath
   Live out in cheerful hope,
And fearless pass the vale of death,
   And gain the mountain-top.

5 To gather home his own,
   God shall his angels send,
And bid our bliss, on earth begun,
   In glorious triumph end,   *Wesley.*

277   *The minister's theme.*   C. M.

JESUS, the name high over all,
   In hell, or earth, or sky!
Angels and men before it fall,
   And devils fear and fly.

2 Jesus, the name to sinners dear,
   The name to sinners giv'n;
It scatters all their guilty fear;
   It turns their hell to heav'n.

3 Jesus the pris'ner's fetters breaks,
   And bruises Satan's head;

Power into strengthless souls it speaks,
  And life into the dead.
4 O that the world might taste and see
  The riches of his grace;
  The arms of love that compass me
  Would all mankind embrace.
5 His only righteousness I show,
  His saving truth proclaim:
  'Tis all my business here below,
  To cry, "Behold the Lamb!"
6 Happy, if with my latest breath
  I may but gasp his name!
  Preach him to all, and cry in death,
  "Behold, behold the Lamb!" *C. Wesley*

278 C. M.

"*For I am not ashamed of the Gospel of Christ.*" Romans i. 16.

I'M not asham'd to own the Lord,
  Or to defend his cause,
Maintain the honor of his word,
  The glory of his cross.
2 Jesus, my God, I know his name,
  His name is all my trust,
  Nor will he put my soul to shame,
  Nor let my hope be lost.
3 Firm as his throne his promise stands,
  And he can well secure
  What I've committed to his hands
  Till the decisive hour.
4 Then will he own my worthless name
  Before his Father's face,
  And in the New Jerusalem
  Appoint my soul a place. *Watts.*

THE CHURCH COMFORTED.

279 *Let us go into the house of the Lord.* C. M.
Psalm cxxii.

HOW did my heart rejoice to hear
   My friends devoutly say,
"In Zion let us all appear,
   And keep the solemn day!"

2 I love her gates, I love the road!
   The Church adorned with grace,
Stands like a palace built for God,
   To show his milder face.

3 Up to her courts, with joys unknown,
   The holy tribes repair;
The Son of David holds his throne
   And sits in judgment there.

4 He hears our praises and complaints;
   And, while his awful voice
Divides the sinners from the saints,
   We tremble and rejoice!

5 Peace be within this sacred place,
   And joy a constant guest!
With holy gifts and heavenly grace
   Be her attendants blest.

6 My soul shall pray for Zion still,
   While life or breath remains:
There my best friends, my kindred dwell,
   There God, my Saviour, reigns.   *Watts.*

280   *Supplies of the Church.*   8s & 7s.

GLORIOUS things of thee are spoken,
   Zion, city of our God!
He, whose word can ne'er be broken,
   Formed thee for his own abode.

2 On the Rock of ages founded,
   What can shake thy sure repose?

13   193

With salvation's walls surrounded,
  Thou may'st smile at all thy foes.
3 See! the streams of living waters
    Springing from eternal love,
  Well supply thy sons and daughters,
    And all fear of want remove.
4 Who can faint while such a river
    Ever flows their thirst t' assuage?
  Grace which like the Lord, the giver,
    Never fails from age to age.
5 Round each habitation hov'ring,
    See the cloud and fire appear,
  For a glory and a cov'ring—
    Showing that the Lord is near.
6 Glorious things of thee are spoken,
    Zion, city of our God!
  He whose word can ne'er be broken,
    Chose thee for his own abode.   *Newton.*

281 *God her everlasting Light.* 8s & 7s.

HEAR what God the Lord hath spoken:
    O my people, faint and few,
  Comfortless, afflicted, broken,
    Fair abodes I build for you.
  Scenes of heartfelt tribulation
    Shall no more perplex your ways;
  You shall name your walls "Salvation,"
    And your gates shall all be "Praise."

2 There, like streams that feed the garden,
    Pleasures without end shall flow,
  For the Lord, your faith rewarding,
    All his bounty shall bestow.
  Still in undisturbed possession;
    Peace and righteousness shall reign,

THE CHURCH COMFORTED.

 Never shall you feel oppression,
  Hear the voice of war again.
3 Ye, no more your suns descending,
  Waning moons no more shall see;
 But, your griefs forever ending,
  Find eternal noon in me:
 God shall rise, and, shining o'er you,
  Change to day the gloom of night;
 He, the Lord, shall be your glory,
  God your everlasting light.
      William Cowper.

282   *Good news for Zion.* 8, 7, 4.

ON the mountain's top appearing,
  Lo! the sacred herald stands,
Welcome news to Zion bearing,
  Zion, long in hostile lands:
   Mourning captive!
 God himself shall loose thy bands.

2 Has thy night been long and mournful?
  Have thy friends unfaithful proved?
 Have thy foes been proud and scornful,
  By thy sighs and tears unmoved?
   Cease thy mourning;
 Zion still is well beloved.

3 God, thy God, will now restore thee;
  He himself appears thy Friend;
 All thy foes shall flee before thee;
  Here their boasts and triumphs end:
   Great deliverance
 Zion's King will surely send.

4 Peace and joy shall now attend thee;
  All thy warfare now is past·

God thy Saviour will defend thee;
Victory is thine at last:
    All thy conflicts
End in everlasting rest.   *Thomas Kelly.*

283   *Jehovah, the defense of Zion*   8, 7, 4.

ZION stands with hills surrounded,
    Zion, kept by power divine:
All her foes shall be confounded,
    Though the world in arms combine:
        Happy Zion,
    What a favored lot is thine!

2 Every human tie may perish;
    Friend to friend unfaithful prove;
Mothers cease their own to cherish;
    Heaven and earth at last remove;
        But no changes
    Can attend Jehovah's love.

3 In the furnace God may prove thee,
    Thence to bring thee forth more bright,
But can never cease to love thee;
    Thou art precious in his sight:
        God is with thee,
    God, thine everlasting light.
                             Thomas Kelly.

284   *Love for Zion.*   S. M.

I LOVE thy kingdom, Lord,
    The house of thine abode,
The Church our blest Redeemer saved
    With his own precious blood.

2 I love thy Church, O God!
    Her walls before thee stand,

THE CHURCH COMFORTED.

Dear as the apple of thine eye,
  And graven on thy hand.

3 For her my tears shall fall,
    For her my prayers ascend;
  To her my cares and toils be given,
    Till toils and cares shall end.

4 Beyond my highest joy
    I prize her heavenly ways,
  Her sweet communion, solemn vows,
    Her hymns of love and praise.

5 Sure as thy truth shall last,
    To Zion shall be given
  The brightest glories earth can yield,
    And brighter bliss of heaven.
                    Timothy Dwight

285 *The church's confidence and security.* S. M

WHO in the Lord confide,
    And feel his sprinkled blood,
  In storms and hurricanes abide
    Firm as the mount of God:
  Steadfast, and fixed, and sure,
    His Zion cannot move;
  His faithful people stand secure
    In Jesus' guardian love.

2 As round Jerusalem
    The hilly bulwarks rise,
  So God protects and covers them
    From all their enemies.
  On every side he stands,
    And for his Israel cares;
  And safe in his almighty hands
    Their souls forever bears.
                    Charles Wesley.

THE CHURCH COMFORTED.

286   *The Trinity Invoked.*   S. M

O LORD our God! arise,
  The cause of truth maintain,
And wide o'er all the peopled world
  Extend her blessed reign.

2 Thou Prince of life! arise,
    Nor let thy glory cease;
  Far spread the conquests of thy grace,
    And bless the earth with peace.

3 Thou Holy Ghost! arise,
    Extend thy quickening wing,
  And o'er a dark and ruined world
    Let light and order spring.

4 All on the earth arise,
    To God the Saviour sing,
  From shore to shore, from earth to heaven,
    Let echoing anthems ring.
      Ralph Wardlaw from the Presbyterian Coll.

287   *The throne of grace.*   S. M.

BEHOLD the throne of grace;
  The promise calls us near;
There Jesus shows a smiling face,
  And waits to answer prayer.

2 My soul, ask what thou wilt,
    Thou canst not be too bold;
  Since his own blood for thee he spilt,
    What else can he withhold?

3 Thine image, Lord, bestow,
    Thy presence and thy love,
  That we may serve thee here below,
    And reign with thee above.

MINISTERIAL COMMISSION.

4 Teach us to live by faith,
Conform our wills to thine;
Let us victorious be in death,
And then in glory shine.
John Newton.

SECTION XII.
Ministerial Commission.

288 L. M.
Christ's commission to preach the Gospel.
Matt. x. 7–16.

GO forth, ye heralds, in my name,
   Sweetly the gospel trumpet sound;
The glorious jubilee proclaim,
   Where'er the human race is found.

2 The joyful news to all impart,
   And teach them where salvation lies,
With care bind up the broken heart
   And wipe the tears from weeping eyes.

3 Be wise as serpents where you go,
   But harmless as the peaceful dove,
And let your heav'n taught conduct show,
   That ye're commissioned from above.

4 Freely from me ye have received,
   Freely, in love to others give;
Thus shall your doctrines be believ'd,
   And, by your labors, sinners live. *J. Logan.*

289   *Laborers.*   L. M.
[From the German.]

HIGH on his everlasting throne,
   The King of saints his work surveys,

MINISTERIAL COMMISSION.

Marks the dear souls he calls his own,
And smiles on the peculiar race.

2 He rests well pleased their toils to see;
Beneath his easy yoke they move;
With all their heart and strength agree
In the sweet labor of his love.

3 See, where the servants of their God,
A busy multitude, appear:
For Jesus day and night employed,
His heritage they toil to clear.

4 The love of Christ their hearts constrains,
And strengthens their unwearied hands;
They spend their sweat, and blood, and pains
To cultivate Immanuel's lands.

5 O multiply thy sowers' seed,
And fruit we every hour shall bear.
Throughout the world thy gospel spread,
Thine everlasting truth declare! *J. Wesley.*

290 L. M.
"*Go ye into all the world, and preach the gospel to every creature.*" Mark xvi. 15–20.

"GO preach my gospel," saith th' Lord,
"Bid the whole earth my grace receive;
Explain to them my sacred word,
Bid them believe, obey, and live.

2 "I'll make my great commission known,
And ye shall prove my gospel true,
By all the works that I have done,
And all the wonders ye shall do.

3 "Go heal the sick, go raise the dead,
Go cast out devils in my name;

Nor let my prophets be afraid,
  Though Greeks reproach, and Jews blas-
    pheme.
4 " While thus ye follow my commands,
    I'm with you till the world shall end:
  All power is trusted in my hands,
    I can destroy, and can defend."
5 He spake, and light shone round his head;
    On a bright cloud to heav'n he rode;
  They to the farthest nation spread
    The grace of their ascended God. *Watts.*

291   *His universal Effusion.*   L. M.

O SPIRIT of the living God!
  In all the fullness of thy grace,
Where'er the foot of man hath trod,
  Descend on our apostate race.

2 Give tongues of fire and hearts of love
    To preach the reconciling word.
  Give power and unction from above,
    Whene'er the joyful sound is heard.

3 Be darkness, at thy coming, light;
    Confusion, order, in thy path;
  Souls without strength, inspire with might;
    Bid mercy triumph over wrath!

4 Baptize the nations! far and nigh;
    The triumphs of the cross record:
  The name of Jesus glorify,
    Till every kindred call him Lord.

5 God from eternity hath willed
    All flesh shall his salvation see:
  So be the Father's love fulfilled,
    The Saviour's suff'ring crowned through
      thee!   *Montgomery.*

292   *The Church Militant.*   S. M

HARK, how the watchmen cry!
  Attend the trumpet's sound!
Stand to your arms, the foe is nigh;
  The powers of hell surround.

2 Who bow to Christ's command,
  Your arms and hearts prepare:
The day of battle is at hand!
  Go forth to glorious war!

3 See, on the mountain top,
  The standard of your God!
In Jesus' name I lift it up,
  All stained with hallowed blood.

4 His standard-bearer, I
  To all the nations call:
Let all to Jesus' cross draw nigh:
  He bore the cross for all.

5 All power to him is given:
  He ever reigns the same:
Salvation, happiness, and heaven,
  Are all in Jesus' name.   *C. Wesley.*

293   *Isaiah* lii. 7–10.   S. M.

HOW beauteous are their feet
  Who stand on Zion's hill;
Who bring salvation on their tongues,
  And words of peace reveal!

2 How charming is their voice!
  How sweet the tidings are!
"Zion, behold thy Saviour King;
  He reigns and triumphs here!"

3 How happy are our ears
  That hear this joyful sound,

Which kings and prophets waited for,
And sought, but never found!

4 How blessed are our eyes
That see this heavenly light!
Prophets and kings desired it long
But died without the sight.

5 The watchmen join their voice,
And tuneful notes employ;
Jerusalem breaks forth in songs,
And deserts learn the joy.

6 The Lord makes bare his arm
Through all the earth abroad:
Let every nation now behold
Their Saviour and their God. *Watts.*

294 S. M.

YE messengers of Christ!
His sovereign voice obey;
Arise, and follow where he leads,
And peace attend your way.

2 The Master whom you serve
Will needful strength bestow;
Depending on his promised aid,
With sacred courage go—

3 Go, spread the Saviour's fame;
And tell his matchless grace
To the most guilty and depraved
Of Adam's numerous race.

4 Mountains shall sink to plains,
And hell in vain oppose;
The cause is God's, and must prevail,
In spite of all his foes.
Mrs. Voke, from the Presbyterian Coll.

MINISTERIAL COMMISSION.

295 *Opening Conference.* S. M.

AND are we yet alive,
 And see each other's face?
Glory and praise to Jesus give
 For his redeeming grace!
Preserved by power Divine
 To full salvation here,
Again in Jesus' praise we join,
 And in his sight appear.

2 What troubles have we seen,
 What conflicts have we passed,
Fightings without, and fears within,
 Since we assembled last;
But out of all the Lord
 Hath brought us by his love;
And still he doth his help afford,
 And hides our life above.

3 Then let us make our boast
 Of his redeeming power,
Which saves us to the uttermost,
 Till we can sin no more:
Let us take up the cross,
 Till we the crown obtain;
And gladly reckon all things loss,
 So we may Jesus gain. *C. Wesley.*

296 *Closing Conference.* S. M.

AND let our bodies part,
 To diff'rent climes repair;
Inseparably joined in heart
 The friends of Jesus are.

2 Jesus the Corner-stone
 Did first our hearts unite,
And still he keeps our spirits one,
 Who walk with him in white.

3 O let us still proceed
   In Jesus' work below,
And, foll'wing our triumphant Head,
   To further conquests go.

4 The vineyard of the Lord
   Before his lab'rers lies;
And lo! we see the vast reward
   Which waits us in the skies.

5 O let our heart and mind
   Continually ascend,
That heaven of repose to find,
   Where all our labors end! *C. Wesley*

297 *Zion's Watchmen.* C. M

LET Zion's watchmen all awake,
   And take th' alarm they give;
Now let them from the mouth of God
   Their awful charge receive.

2 'Tis not a cause of small import
   The pastor's care demands;
But what might fill an angel's heart,
   And filled a Saviour's hands.

3 They watch for souls, for which the Lord
   Did heavenly bliss forego!
For souls which must forever live
   In raptures, or in woe.

4 May they that Jesus whom they preach,
   Their own Redeemer see,
And watch thou daily o'er their souls,
   That they may watch for thee.
                              C. Wesley

298 *Christ, the Conqueror.* **C. M**

JESUS, immortal King, arise;
　Assert thy rightful sway,
Till earth, subdued, its tribute brings,
　And distant lands obey.

2 Ride forth, victorious Conqueror, ride,
　Till all thy foes submit,
And all the powers of hell resign
　Their trophies at thy feet.

3 Send forth thy word, and let it fly
　The spacious earth around,
Till every soul beneath the sun
　Shall hear the joyful sound.

4 O may the great Redeemer's name
　Through every clime be known,
And heathen gods forsaken, fall,
　And Jesus reign alone.

5 From sea to sea, from shore to shore,
　Be thou, O Christ, adored,
And earth, with all her millions, shout
　Hosannas to the Lord.
　　　　　　　A. C. Hobart Seymour.

299 *The Gospel for all Nations.* **C. M.**

GREAT God, the nations of the earth
　Are by creation thine;
And in thy works, by all beheld,
　Thy radiant glories shine.

2 But, Lord, thy greater love has sent
　Thy gospel to mankind,
Unveiling what rich stores of grace
　Are treasured in thy mind.

MINISTERIAL COMMISSION.

3 Lord, when shall these glad tidings spread
   The spacious earth around,
Till every tribe and every soul
   Shall hear the joyful sound?

4 Smile, Lord, on each divine attempt
   To spread the gospel's rays,
And build on sin's demolished throne
   The temples of thy praise.
                        Thomas Gibbons.

300   *Let all the angels of God worship him.* C. M.

HOW great the wisdom, power and grace
   Which in redemption shine!
The heavenly host with joy confess
   The work is all divine.

2 Before his feet they cast their crowns,—
   Those crowns which Jesus gave,—
And, with ten thousand thousand tongues,
   Proclaim his power to save.

3 They tell the triumphs of his cross,
   The suff'rings which he bore.—
How low he stooped, how high he rose,
   And rose to stoop no more.

4 O let them still their voices raise,
   And still their songs renew:
Salvation well deserves the praise
   Of men and angels too.   *Beddome.*

301   *Full and Free.*   C. M.

O WHAT amazing words of grace
   Are in the gospel found!
Suited to every sinner's case,
   Who knows the joyful sound.

2 Poor, sinful, thirsty, fainting souls
Are freely welcome here;
Salvation, like a river, rolls
Abundant, free and clear.

3 Come then, with all your wants and wounds,
Your every burden bring:
Here love, unchanging love, abounds,
A deep, celestial spring.

4 Whoever will—O gracious word!
May of this stream partake;
Come. thirsty souls, and bless the Lord,
And drink, for Jesus' sake.

5 Millions of sinners, vile as you,
Have here found life and peace;
Come, then, and prove its virtues too,
And drink, adore, and bless.
Samuel Medley

SECTION XIII.

Christian Ordinances.

BAPTISM

302   L. M.

COME, Father, Son, and Holy Ghost,
Honor the means ordained by thee;
Make good our apostolic boast,
And own thy glorious ministry.

2 We now thy promised presence claim:
Sent to disciple all mankind—

BAPTISM.

Sent to baptize into thy name—
We now thy promised presence find.
3 Father, in these reveal thy Son—
In these, for whom we seek thy face,
The hidden mystery make known,
The inward, pure, baptizing grace.
4 Jesus, with us thou always art;
Effectuate now the sacred sign,
The gift unspeakable impart,
And bless the ordinance divine.
5 Eternal Spirit come from high,
Baptizer of our spirits thou!
The sacramental seal apply,
And witness with the water now!
C. Wesley.

303   *The Commission.*   L. M.

'TWAS the commission of our Lord,
"Go, teach the nations, and baptize;"
The nations have received the word
Since he ascended to the skies.

2 "Repent and be baptized," he saith,
"For the remission of your sins;"
And thus our sense assists our faith,
And shows us what his gospel means.

3 Our souls he washes in his blood,
As water makes the body clean;
And the good Spirit from our God
Descends, like purifying rain.

4 Thus we engage ourselves to thee,
And seal our cov'nant with the Lord:
O may the great Eternal Three
In heaven our solemn vows record! *Watts.*

CHRISTIAN ORDINANCES.

304   *Significance of Baptism.*   C. M.

O LORD, while we confess the worth
  Of this the outward seal,
Do thou the truth herein set forth
  To every heart reveal.

2 Death to the world we here avow,
  Death to each fleshly lust;
Newness of life our calling now,
  A risen Lord our trust.

3 And we, O Lord, who now partake
  Of resurrection life,
With every sin, for thy dear sake,
  Would be at constant strife.

4 Baptized into the Father's name
  We'd walk as sons of God;
Baptized in thine, we own thy claim
  As ransomed by thy blood.

5 Baptized into the Holy Ghost,
  We'd keep his temple pure,
And make thy grace our only boast,
  And by thy strength endure.
                    Mary P. Bowly.

305   *Children in the arms of Jesus.*   C. M.

BEHOLD what condescending love
  Jesus on earth displays!
To little children he extends
  The riches of his grace.

2 He still the ancient promise keeps,
  To our forefathers given;
Our infants in his arms he takes,
  And calls them heirs of heaven.

210

BAPTISM.

3 Forbid them not, whom Jesus calls,
   Nor dare the claim resist,
Since his own lips to us declare
   Of such will heaven consist.
4 With flowing tears, and thankful hearts,
   We give them up to thee;
Receive them, Lord, into thine arms;
   Thine may they ever be.
                Augustus M. Toplady.

306   *Infant.*   C. M.

HOW large the promise, how Divine,
   To Abrah'm and his seed!
"I am a God to thee and thine,
   Supplying all their need."
2 The words of his extensive love
   From age to age endure;
The angel of the cov'nant proves
   And seals the blessing sure.
3 Jesus the ancient faith confirms,
   To our great father given;
He takes our children to his arms,
   And calls them heirs of heaven.
4 O God, how faithful are thy ways!
   Thy love endures the same;
Nor from the promise of thy grace
   Blots out our children's name. *Watts.*

307   *Infant.* Mark x. 13–16. C. M.

SEE Israel's gentle Shepherd stands
   With all-engaging charms:
Hark how he calls the tender lambs,
   And folds them in his arms!
2 "Permit them to approach," he cries,
   "Nor scorn their humble name:

CHRISTIAN ORDINANCES.

For 'twas to bless such souls as these
The Lord of angels came."

3 We bring them, Lord, in thankful hands,
And yield them up to thee:
Joyful that we ourselves are thine,
Thine let our offspring be. *Doddridge.*

308 S. M.
Christ a Fountain. Acts xxii. 16.

MY Saviour's pierced side,
Pour'd out a double flood;
By water we are purified,
And pardon'd by the blood.

2 Call'd from above, I rise,
And wash away my sin;
The stream to which my spirit flies,
Can make the foulest clean.

3 It runs divinely clear,
A fountain deep and wide;
'Twas opened by the soldier's spear,
In my Redeemer's side! *Stafford.*

THE LORD'S SUPPER.

309 S. M.
Communion with Christ and with Saints.

JESUS invites his saints
To meet around his board;
Here pardoned rebels sit, and hold
Communion with their Lord.

2 For food he gives his flesh:
He bids us drink his blood;
Amazing favor, matchless grace
Of our descending God.

THE LORD'S SUPPER.

2 This holy bread and wine
 Maintain our fainting breath,
By union with our living Lord,
 And interest in his death.

4 Our heavenly Father calls
 Christ and his members one:
We the young children of his love,
 And he the first-born Son.

5 Let all our powers be joined
 His glorious name to raise:
Pleasure and love fill every mind,
 And every voice be praise. *Watts.*

310   *The Triumph.*   S. M.

1 "THE good fight have fought,"
 O when shall I declare!
The vict'ry by my Saviour got
 I long with Paul to share.

2 O may I triumph so,
 When all my warfare's past;
And, dying, find my latest foe
 Under my feet at last!

3 This bl-ssed word be mine,
 Just as the port is gained,
"Kept by the power of grace Divine,
 I have the faith maintained."

4 Th' apostles of my Lord,
 To whom it first was given,—
They could not speak a greater word,
 Nor all the saints in heaven. *C. Wesley.*

311   *The Invitation.*   C. M.

THE King of heaven his table spreads,
 And blessings crown the board

Not paradise, with all its joys,
  Could such delight afford.

2 Pardon and peace to dying men,
  And endless life are given,
Through the rich blood that Jesus shed
  To raise our souls to heaven.

3 Millions of souls, in glory now,
  Were fed and feasted here;
And millions more, still on the way,
  Around the board appear.

4 All things are ready: come away,
  Nor weak excuses frame;
Crowd to your places at the feast,
  And bless the Founder's name.
                              Doddridge.

312   *Heb.* iv. 14–16.   C. M.

WITH joy we meditate the grace
    Of our High Priest above:
His heart is made of tenderness,
  His bowels melt with love.

2 Touched with a sympathy within,
  He knows our feeble frame:
He knows what sore temptations mean,
  For he hath felt the same.

3 He in the days of feeble flesh
    Poured out strong cries and tears,
And in his measure feels afresh
    What every member bears.

4 He'll never quench the smoking flax,
    But raise it to a flame:
The bruised reed he never breaks,
  Nor scorns the meanest name.

THE LORD'S SUPPER.

5 Then let our humble faith address
His mercy and his power:
We shall obtain deliv'ring grace
In the distressing hour. *Watts.*

313 *The Institution.* C. M.

THAT doleful night before his death,
  The Lamb for sinners slain,
Did, almost with his dying breath,
  This solemn feast ordain.

2 To keep the feast, Lord, we have met,
  And to remember thee:
Help each poor trembler to repeat,
  "For me, he died for me!"

3 Thy suff'rings, Lord, each sacred sign
  To our remembrance brings:
We eat the bread, and drink the wine,
  But think on nobler things.

4 O tune our tongues, and set in frame
  Each heart that pants for thee,
To sing, "Hosanna to the Lamb!"
  The Lamb that died for me! *Hart.*

314 *Rich gifts of Gospel Grace.* C. M.

O LOVE divine! O matchless grace!
  Which in this sacred rite
Shines forth so full, so free, in rays
  Of purest living light.

2 O wondrous death! O precious blood!
  For us so freely spilt,
To cleanse our sin-polluted souls
  From every stain of guilt.

3 O covenant of life and peace,
   By blood and suffering sealed!
All the rich gifts of gospel grace
   Are here to faith revealed.

4 Jesus, we bow our souls to thee,
   Our life, our hope, our all,
While we, with thankful, contrite hearts,
   Thy dying love recall.

5 O may thy pure and perfect love
   Be written on our minds;
Nor earth, nor self, nor sin obscure
   The ever-radiant lines. *Edward Turney.*

315   *Grateful Remembrance.*   C. M.

ACCORDING to thy gracious word,
   In meek humility,
This will I do, my dying Lord,
   I will remember thee!

2 Thy body, broken for my sake,
   My bread from heaven shall be;
Thy testamental cup I take,
   And thus remember thee!

3 Gethsemane can I forget?
   Or there thy conflict see,
Thine agony and bloody sweat,
   And not remember thee?

4 When to the cross I turn mine eyes,
   And rest on Calvary,
O Lamb of God, my Sacrifice,
   I must remember thee!

5 Remember thee, and all thy pains,
   And all thy love to me;
Yea, while a breath, a pulse remains,
   Will I remember thee!

THE LORD'S SUPPER.

6 And when these failing lips grow dumb,
And mind and memory flee,
When thou shalt in thy kingdom come,
Jesus, remember me! *James Montgomery.*

316 *Approaching the Table.* C. M.

JESUS, at whose supreme command,
  We now approach to God,
Before us in thy vesture stand,
  Thy vesture dipped in blood.

2 The tokens of thy dying love
  O let us all receive,
And feel the quickening Spirit move,
  And sensibly believe.

3 The cup of blessing, blest by thee,
  Let it thy blood impart;
The bread thy mystic body be,
  To cheer each languid heart.

4 The living bread sent down from heaven,
  In us vouchsafe to be:
Thy flesh for all the world is given,
  And all may live by thee.
          Charles Wesley.

317 *A foretaste of Glory.* S. M.

O WHAT delight is this,
  Which now in Christ we know,
An earnest of our glorious bliss,
  Our heaven begun below!

2 When he the table spreads,
  How royal is the cheer!
With rapture we lift up our heads,
  And own that God is here.

CHRISTIAN ORDINANCES.

3 The Lamb for sinners slain,
  Who died to die no more,
  Let all the ransomed sons of men,
  With all his hosts, adore.

4 Let earth and heaven be joined,
  His glories to display,
  And hymn the Saviour of mankind
  In one eternal day.   *Charles Wesley.*

318   *Universal Gladness.*   S. M.

GLORY to God on high.
  Our peace is made with Heaven;
The Son of God came down to die,
  That we might be forgiven.

2 His precious blood was shed,
  His body bruised, for sin:
Remember this in eating bread,
  And this in drinking wine.

3 Approach his royal board,
  In his rich garments clad;
Join every tongue to praise the Lord,
  And every heart be glad

4 The Father gives the Son;
  The Son, his flesh and blood;
The Spirit seals; and faith puts on
  The righteousness of God.   *Joseph Hart*

319   *Gratitude and Love.*   C. M

IF human kindness meets return,
  And owns the grateful tie;
If tender thoughts within us burn
  To feel a friend is nigh;

2 O shall not warmer accents tell
  The gratitude we owe

THE LORD'S SUPPER.

To him who died our fears to quell,
And save from endless woe?

3 While yet in anguish he surveyed
Those pangs he would not flee,
What love his latest words displayed!
"Meet, and remember me."

4 Remember thee! thy death, thy shame,
The griefs which thou didst bear!
O memory, leave no other name
So deeply graven there. *Gerard T. Noel.*

320 *The Passion realized.* C. M.

COME, Holy Ghost, set to thy seal,
Thine inward witness give,
To all our waiting souls reveal
The death by which we live.

2 Spectators of the pangs Divine
O that we now may be,
Discerning in the sacred sign
His passion on the tree!

3 Give us to hear the dreadful sound
Which told his mortal pain,
Tore up the graves, and shook the ground,
And rent the rocks in twain.

4 Repeat the Saviour's dying cry,
In every heart so loud,
That every heart may now reply,
"This was the Son of God!" *C. Wesley.*

321 *Discerning the Lord's Body.* 7s.

JESUS, all-redeeming Lord,
Magnify thy dying word;
In thine ordinance appear;
Come, and meet thy followers here.

2 In the rite thou hast enjoined,
Let us now our Saviour find;
Drink thy blood for sinners shed,
Taste thee in the broken bread.

3 Thou our faithful hearts prepare;
Thou thy pardoning grace declare;
Thou that hast for sinners died,
Show thyself the Crucified!

4 All the power of sin remove;
Fill us with thy perfect love;
Stamp us with the stamp divine;
Seal our souls forever thine.

Charles Wesley

322   *Praise to our Victorious King.*   7s

AT the Lamb's high feast we sing
  Praise to our victorious King,
Who hath washed us in the tide
Flowing from his pierced side;

2 Praise we him, whose love divine
Gives his sacred blood for wine,
Gives his body for the feast,
Christ the Victim, Christ the Priest.

3 Where the paschal blood is poured,
Death's dark angel sheaths his sword;
Israel's hosts triumphant go
Through the wave that drowns the foe.

4 Praise we Christ, whose blood was shed,
Paschal Victim, paschal Bread;
With sincerity and love
Eat we manna from above.

5 Mighty Victim from the sky!
Hell's fierce powers beneath thee lie;

THE LORD'S SUPPER.

Thou hast conquered in the fight,
Thou hast brought us life and light:

6 Now no more can death appall,
Now no more the grave enthrall;
Thou hast opened paradise,
And in thee thy saints shall rise.
Roman Breviary. Tr. by R. Campbell.

323 *Our Paschal Lamb.* S. M.

LET all who truly bear
The bleeding Saviour's name,
Their faithful hearts with us prepare,
And eat the Paschal Lamb.

2 This eucharistic feast
Our every want supplies,
And still we by his death are blest,
And share his sacrifice.

3 Who thus our faith employ,
His sufferings to record,
E'en now we mournfully enjoy
Communion with our Lord.

4 We too with him are dead,
And shall, with him arise;
The cross on which he bows his head
Shall lift us to the skies.
Charles Wesley.

324 S. M.
Partaking of the Lord's Supper. Luke xxi. 19–20.

JESUS, we thus obey
Thy last and kindest word,
Here in thine own appointed way,
We come to meet thee, Lord.

221

CHRISTIAN WARFARE AND FAITH.

2 The way thou hast enjoin'd,
  Thou wilt therein appear;
We come with confidence to find
  Thy special presence here.

3 Whate'er the Almighty can
  To pardon'd sinners give,
The fulness of our God made man,
  We here with Christ receive.
                          C. Wesley

SECTION XIV.

Christian Warfare and Faith under Trials.

325   *Isaiah* xxxv. 10.   C. M.

SING, O ye ransom'd of the Lord,
  Your great Deliv'rer sing;
Pilgrims, for Zion's city bound,
  Be joyful in your King.

2 A hand Divine shall lead you on,
  Through all the blissful road,
Till to the sacred mount you rise,
  And see your smiling God.

3 There garlands of immortal joy
  Shall bloom on every head;
While sorrow, sighing, and distress,
  Like shadows, all are fled.

4 March on in your Redeemer's strength;
  Pursue his footsteps still;
And let the prospect cheer your eye,
  While lab'ring up the hill.   *Doddridge.*

CHRISTIAN WARFARE AND FAITH.

326 *Talking with God.* C. M.

TALK with us, Lord, thyself reveal,
   While here o'er earth we rove;
Speak to our hearts, and let us feel
   The kindling of thy love.

2 With thee conversing, we forget
   All time, and toil, and care;
Labor is rest, and pain is sweet,
   If thou, my God, art here.

3 Here, then, my God, vouchsafe to stay,
   And bid my heart rejoice;
My bounding heart shall own thy sway,
   And echo to thy voice.

4 Thou callest me to seek thy face —
   'Tis all I wish to seek;
To attend the whispers of thy grace,
   And hear thee inly speak.

5 Let this my every hour employ,
   Till I thy glory see;
Enter into my Master's joy,
   And find my heaven in thee.
                        Charles Wesley.

327 *For Victorious Faith.* C. M.

O FOR a faith that will not shrink,
   Though pressed by every foe,
That will not tremble on the brink
   Of any earthly woe!

2 That will not murmur nor complain
   Beneath the chastening rod,
But, in the hour of grief or pain,
   Will lean upon its God;

CHRISTIAN WARFARE AND FAITH.

3 A faith that shines more bright and clear
   When tempests rage without;
   That when in danger knows no fear,
   In darkness feels no doubt;

4 That bears, unmoved, the world's dread frown,
   Nor heeds its scornful smile;
   That seas of trouble cannot drown,
   Nor Satan's arts beguile.

5 A faith that keeps the narrow way
   Till life's last hour is fled,
   And with a pure and heavenly ray
   Illumes a dying bed.

6 Lord, give us such a faith as this,
   And then whate'er may come,
   We'll taste e'en here, the hallowed bliss
   Of an eternal home.   *William H. Bathurst.*

328   C. M.
Strength renewed in waiting upon the Lord

LORD, I believe thy every word,
   Thy every promise true;
And lo! I wait on thee, my Lord,
   Till I my strength renew.

2 If in this feeble flesh I may
   Awhile show forth thy praise,
   Jesus, support the tottering clay,
   And lengthen out my days.

3 If such a worm as I can spread
   The common Saviour's name,
   Let him who raised thee from the dead,
   Quicken my mortal frame.

CHRISTIAN WARFARE AND FAITH.

4 Still let me live thy blood to show,
  Which purges every stain;
And gladly linger out below
  A few more years in pain.
Charles Wesley (when old and worn by sickness).

329   C. M.
To live is Christ, and to die is Gain.—Phil. 1: 21.

LORD, it belongs not to my care
  Whether I die or live;
To love and serve thee is my share,
  And this thy grace must give.

2 If life be long, I will be glad
  That I may long obey;
If short, yet why should I be sad
  To soar to endless day?

3 Christ leads me through no darker rooms
  Than he went through before;
He that unto God's kingdom comes
  Must enter by his door.

4 Come, Lord, when grace hath made me meet
  Thy blessed face to see;
For, if thy work on earth be sweet,
  What will thy glory be?

5 Then I shall end my sad complaints,
  And weary, sinful days
And join with the triumphant saints
  Who sing Jehovah's praise.
                          Richard Baxter.

330   *The Christian Race.*   C. M.

AWAKE, my soul! stretch every nerve,
  And press with vigor on:
A heav'nly race demands thy zeal,
  And an immortal crown.

CHRISTIAN WARFARE AND FAITH.

2 A cloud of witnesses around
  Hold thee in full survey;
  Forget the steps already trod,
  And onward urge thy way.
3 'Tis God's all-animating voice
  That calls thee from on high;
  'Tis his own hand presents the prize
  To thine aspiring eye:
4 That prize, with peerless glories bright,
  Which shall new lustre boast,
  When victors' wreaths and monarchs' gems
  Shall blend in common dust.
5 Blest Saviour! introduced by thee,
  Have I my race begun;
  And crown'd with vict'ry, at thy feet
  I'll lay my honors down. *Doddridge*

331 *Taking the Cross.* C. M.

MUST Jesus bear the cross alone,
  And all the world go free?
No; there's a cross for every one,
  And there's a cross for me.
2 The consecrated cross I'll bear
  Till death shall set me free,
  And then go home my crown to wear,
  For there's a crown for me.
3 Upon the crystal pavement, down
  At Jesus' piercéd feet,
  Joyful, I'll cast my golden crown,
  And his dear name repeat.
4 And palms shall wave and harps shall ring
  Beneath heaven's arches high;
  The Lord that lives, the ransomed sing,
  That lives no more to die.

5 Oh, precious cross! oh, glorious crown!
   Oh, resurrection day!
Ye angels, from the stars come down,
   And bear my soul away.   *G. N. Allen*

332   *Psalm* lxxi. 15.   C. M.

MY Saviour, my almighty friend,
   When I begin thy praise,
Where will the growing numbers end,
   The numbers of thy grace?

2 Thou art my everlasting trust:
   Thy goodness I adore:
Send down thy grace, O blessed Lord,
   That I may love thee more.

3 My feet shall travel all the length
   Of the celestial road:
And march with courage in thy strength,
   To see the Lord my God.

4 Awake! awake! my tuneful powers:
   With this delightful song
I'll entertain the darkest hours,
   Nor think the season long.   *Watts.*

333   *He Leadeth Me.*   L. M.

HE leadeth me! O blessed thought!
   O words with heavenly comfort fraught!
Whate'er I do, where'er I be,
Still 'tis God's hand that leadeth me.
   He leadeth me, he leadeth me,
   By his own hand he leadeth me:
   His faithful follower I would be,
   For by his hand he leadeth me.

2 Sometimes 'mid scenes of deepest gloom,
   Sometimes where Eden's bowers bloom,

By waters calm, or troubled sea,—
Still 'tis his hand that leadeth me!

3 Lord, I would clasp thy hand in mine,
Nor ever murmur or repine,
Content, whatever lot I see,
Since 'tis my God that leadeth me!

4 And when my task on earth is done,
When, by thy grace, the victory's won,
E'en death's cold wave I will not flee,
Since God through Jordan leadeth me.
J. H. Gilmore.

334 *Patient Thankfulness and Trust.* L. M.

ETERNAL Beam of light divine,
Fountain of unexhausted love,
In whom the Father's glories shine,
Through earth beneath, and heaven above;

2 Jesus, the weary wanderer's rest,
Give me thy easy yoke to bear;
With steadfast patience arm my breast,
With spotless love and lowly fear.

3 Thankful I take the cup from thee,
Prepared and mingled by thy skill;
Though bitter to the taste it be,
Powerful the wounded soul to heal.

4 Be thou, O Rock of ages, nigh!
So shall each murmuring thought be gone,
And grief, and fear, and care shall fly,
As clouds before the midday sun.

5 Speak to my warring passions, "Peace;"
Say to my trembling heart, "Be still;"
Thy power my strength and fortress is,
For all things serve thy sovereign will.

CHRISTIAN WARFARE AND FAITH.

6 O Death! where is thy sting? Where now
Thy boasted victory, O Grave?
Who shall contend with God? or who
Can hurt whom God delights to save?
Charles Wesley.

335 *In hope, believing against hope.* L. M.

AWAY, my unbelieving fear!
　Fear shall in me no more have place;
My Saviour doth not yet appear,
　He hides the brightness of his face;
But shall I therefore let him go,
　And basely to the tempter yield?
No, in the strength of Jesus no,
　I never will give up my shield.

2 Although the vine its fruits deny,
　Although the olives yield no oil,
The withering fig-trees droop and die,
　The fields elude the tiller's toil,
The empty stall no herd afford,
　And perish all the bleating race,
Yet will I triumph in the Lord,—
　The God of my salvation praise.

3 In hope believing against hope,
　Jesus, my Lord, my God, I claim;
Jesus my strength shall lift me up,
　Salvation is in Jesus' name;
To me he soon shall bring it nigh,
　My soul shall then outstrip the wind,
On wings of love mount up on high,
　And leave the world and sin behind.
Charles Wesley.

CHRISTIAN WARFARE AND FAITH.

336   *Resignation.*   L. M.

THY will be done! I will not fear
   The fate provided by thy love;
Though clouds and darkness shroud me here,
   I know that all is bright above.

2 The stars of heaven are shining on,
   Though these frail eyes are dimmed with tears;
The hopes of earth indeed are gone,
   But are not ours the immortal years?

3 Father, forgive the heart that clings,
   Thus trembling, to the things of time·
And bid my soul, on angel wings,
   Ascend into a purer clime.

4 There shall no doubts disturb its trust,
   No sorrows dim celestial love;
But these afflictions of the dust,
   Like shadows of the night, remove.

5 E'en now, above, there's radiant day,
   While clouds and darkness brood below;
Then, Father, joyful on my way
   To drink the bitter cup I go.   *J. Roscoe.*

337   *Sympathetic Love.*   L. M.

O LOVE divine, that stooped to share
   Our sharpest pang, our bitterest tear!
On thee we cast each earthborn care;
   We smile at pain while thou art near.

2 Though long the weary way we tread,
   And sorrow crown each lingering year,
No path we shun, no darkness dread,
   Our hearts still whispering, "Thou art near!"

CHRISTIAN WARFARE AND FAITH.

3 When drooping pleasure turns to grief,
   And trembling faith is changed to fear,
The murmuring wind, the quivering leaf,
   Shall softly tell us, "Thou art near!"

4 On thee we fling our burdening woe,
   O Love divine, forever dear;
Content to suffer while we know,
   Living and dying, thou art near!
                  Oliver W. Holmes.

338   *Meekness and Patience.*   L. M.

THOU Lamb of God, thou Prince of peace,
   For thee my thirsty soul doth pine;
My longing heart implores thy grace;
   O make me in thy likeness shine.

2 When pain o'er my weak flesh prevails,
   With lamb-like patience arm my breast;
When grief my wounded soul assails
   In lowly meekness may I rest.

3 Close by thy side still may I keep,
   Howe'er life's various currents flow;
With steadfast eye mark every step,
   And follow thee where'er thou go.

4 Thou, Lord, the dreadful fight hast won;
   Alone thou hast the wine-press trod;
In me thy strengthening grace be shown:
   O may I conquer through thy blood.

5 So, when on Zion thou shalt stand,
   And all heaven's host adore their King,
Shall I be found at thy right hand,
   And, free from pain, thy glories sing.
            C. F. Richter. Tr. by J. Wesley.

CHRISTIAN WARFARE AND FAITH.

339 *The Pilgrim's Song.* 7s.

CHILDREN of the heavenly King,
As we journey let us sing;
Sing our Saviour's worthy praise,
Glorious in his works and ways.

2 We are trav'ling home to God
In the way our fathers trod;
They are happy now, and we
Soon their happiness shall see.

3 O ye banished seed, be glad!
Christ our Advocate is made:
Us to save, our flesh assumes,
Brother to our souls becomes.

4 Fear not, brethren, joyful stand
On the borders of our land;
Jesus Christ, our Father's Son,
Bids us undismay'd go on.

5 Lord! obediently we'll go,
Gladly leaving all below:
Only thou our leader be,
And we still will follow thee. *Cennick.*

340 *With Christ.* S. M.

JESUS, one word from thee
Fills my sad soul with peace:
My griefs are like a tossing sea;
They hear thy voice and cease.

2 Soon as thy pitying face
Shone through my stormy fears,
The storm swept by, nor left a trace,
Save the sweet dew of tears.

3 And when thou call'st me, Lord,
Where thickest dangers be,

Even the waves a path afford;
I walk the waves with thee.

4 With thee within my bark
I'll dare death's threatening tide,
Nor count the passage strange or dark
With Jesus by my side.

5 Dear Lord, thy faithful grace
I know and I adore:
What shall it be to see thy face
In heaven forevermore!
Hervey D. Ganse.

341 *In the Saviour's Care.* S. M.

MY spirit on thy care,
 Blest Saviour, I recline;
Thou wilt not leave me to despair,
 For thou art Love divine.

2 In thee I place my trust,
 On thee I calmly rest;
I know thee good, I know thee just,
 And count thy choice the best.

3 Whate'er events betide,
 Thy will they all perform;
Safe in thy breast my head I hide,
 Nor fear the coming storm.

4 Let good or ill befall,
 It must be good for me;
Secure of having thee in all,
 Of having all in thee. *Henry F. Lyte.*

342 S. M.
My times are in thy hand. Ps. xxxi. 15.

" MY times are in thy hand:"
 My God, I wish them there;

My life, my friends, my soul, I leave
 Entirely to thy care.
2 "My times are in thy hand,"
 Whatever they may be;
 Pleasing or painful, dark or bright,
 As best may seem to thee.
3 "My times are in thy hand;"
 Why should I doubt or fear?
 My Father's hand will never cause
 His child a needless tear.
4 "My times are in thy hand,"
 Jesus, the crucified!
 The hand my cruel sins had pierced
 Is now my guard and guide.
5 "My times are in thy hand;"
 I'll always trust in thee;
 And, after death, at thy right hand
 I shall forever be.   *W. F. Lloyd.*

343   *Believers Encouraged.*   S M.

YOUR harps, ye trembling saints,
 Down from the willows take;
 Loud to the praise of love divine
 Bid every string awake.
2 Though in a foreign land,
 We are not far from home;
 And nearer to our house above
 We every moment come.
3 His grace will to the end
 Stronger and brighter shine;
 Nor present things, nor things to come
 Shall quench the spark divine.
4 When we in darkness walk,
 Nor feel the heavenly flame,

Then is the time to trust our God,
And rest upon his name.

5 Soon shall our doubts and fears
Subside at his control;
His loving-kindness shall break through
The midnight of the soul.

6 Blest is the man, O God,
That stays himself on thee;
Who wait for thy salvation, Lord,
Shall thy salvation see.
Toplady, alt. by B. W. Noel.

344   *Longing for Heaven.*   7s & 6s.

O WHEN shall I see Jesus,
And reign with him above,
And from that flowing fountain
Drink everlasting love?
When shall I be deliver'd
From this vain world of sin,
And with my blessed Jesus
Drink endless pleasures in?

2 But now I am a soldier;
My Captain's gone before,
He's given me my orders,
And bids me not give o'er:
And, if I hold out faithful,
A crown of life he'll give;
And all his valiant soldiers
Shall ever with him live.

3 O do not be discouraged,
For Jesus is your friend;
And, if you lack for knowledge,
He'll not refuse to lend:

CHRISTIAN WARFARE AND FAITH.

Neither will he upbraid you,
Though often you request:
He'll give you grace to conquer,
And take you home to rest. *Unknown.*

345   *Peace and Joy.*   7s & 6s.

SOMETIMES a light surprises
   The Christian while he sings;
It is the Lord who rises
   With healing on his wings;
When comforts are declining,
   He grants the soul again
A season of clear shining,
   To cheer it after rain.

2 In holy contemplation,
   We sweetly then pursue
The theme of God's salvation,
   And find it ever new:
Set free from present sorrow,
   We cheerfully can say,
Let the unknown to morrow
   Bring with it what it may.

3 It can bring with it nothing
   But he will bear us through;
Who gives the lilies clothing,
   Will clothe his people too:
Beneath the spreading heavens
   No creature but is fed;
And he who feeds the ravens
   Will give his children bread.

4 Though vine nor fig-tree neither
   Their wonted fruit should bear,
Though all the fields should wither,
   Nor flocks nor herds be there;

Yet God the same abiding,
  His praise shall tune my voice;
For while in him confiding,
  I cannot but rejoice.   *Wm. Cowper.*

346   *A Watchful Spirit.*   L. M.

JESUS, my Saviour, Brother, Friend,
  On whom I cast my every care,—
On whom for all things I depend,—
  Inspire, and then accept my prayer.

2 If I have tasted of thy grace,
  The grace that sure salvation brings,
If with me now thy Spirit stays,
  And hov'ring, hides me in his wings:

3 Still let him with my weakness stay,
  Nor for a moment's space depart;
Evil and danger turn away,
  And keep till he renews my heart.

4 When to the right or left I stray,
  His voice behind me may I hear,
"Return, and walk in Christ thy way;
  Fly back to Christ, for sin is near!"

5 Jesus, I fain would walk in thee,
  From nature's every path retreat:
Thou art my way; my leader be,
  And set upon the rock my feet.
                      C. Wesley.

347   *Watchful dependence on Christ.*   L. M.

UPHOLD me, Saviour or I fall;
  O reach me out thy gracious hand!
Only on thee for help I call;
  Only by thee in faith I stand.

2 Pierce, fill me, with an humble fear;
  My utter helplessness reveal!

CHRISTIAN WARFARE AND FAITH.

   Satan and sin are always near,
     Thee may I always nearer feel.
3 O that to thee my constant mind
    Might with an even flame aspire!
   Pride in its earliest motions find,
    And mark the risings of desire!
4 O that my tender soul might fly
    The first abhorr'd approach of ill:
   Quick, as the apple of an eye,
    The slightest touch of sin to feel!
5 Till thou anew my soul create,
    Still may I strive, and watch, and pray,—
   Humbly and confidently wait,
    And long to see the perfect day.
                           C. *Wesley.*

348   "*All in All.*"   L. M. 6l.

THOU hidden source of calm repose,
    Thou all-sufficient Love Divine,
My help and refuge from my foes,
    Secure I am if thou art mine!
And lo! from sin, and grief, and shame
   I hide me, Jesus, in thy name.
2 Thy mighty name salvation is,
    And keeps my happy soul above:
   Comfort it brings, and power, and peac
    And joy, and everlasting love:
   To me, with thy great name, are given
    Pardon, and holiness, and heaven.
3 Jesus, my All in all thou art,
    My rest in toil; my ease in pain;
   The med'cine of my broken heart;
    In war, my peace; in loss, my gain;
   My smile beneath the tyrant's frown;
    In shame, my glory and my crown;

4 In want, my plentiful supply;
In weakness, my almighty power;
In bonds, my perfect liberty;
My light, in Satan's darkest hour;
In grief my joy unspeakable;
My life in death—my All in all.
C. Wesley.

349 *General Redemption.* L. M. 6*l.*

WOULD Jesus have the sinner die?
Why hangs he then on yonder tree?
What means that strange expiring cry?
(Sinners, he prays for you and me:)
"Forgive them, Father, O forgive,
They know not that by me they live!"

2 Jesus, descended from above,
Our loss of Eden to retrieve,
Great God of universal love,
If all the world through thee may live,
In us a quick'ning spirit be,
And witness thou hast died for me.

3 Thou loving, all-atoning Lamb,
Thee—by thy painful agony,
Thy bloody sweat, thy grief and shame,
Thy cross and passion on the tree,
Thy precious death and life—I pray,
Take all, take all my sins away. *C. Wesley.*

350 *Praise to the Redeemer.* 8s-7s.

MIGHTY God, while angels bless thee,
May a mortal lisp thy name?
Lord of men, as well as angels,
Thou art every creature's theme.

2 Lord of every land and nation,
Ancient of eternal days!

Sounded through the wide creation
Be thy just and lawful praise.

3 For the grandeur of thy nature—
Grand beyond a seraph's thought—
For created works of power,
Works with skill and kindness wrought:

4 For thy providence that governs
Through thine empire's wide domain,
Wings an angel—guides a sparrow—
Blessed be thy gentle reign.

5 But thy rich, thy free redemption,
Dark through brightness all along!
Thought is poor, and poor expression:
Who dare sing that awful song?

6 Brightness of the Father's glory,
Shall thy praise unuttered lie?
Fiy, my tongue, such guilty silence!
Sing the Lord who came to die. *Robinson.*

351   8's, 7's *double.*
Praise to Christ for his Divine Grace.   Rev. v. 9.

COME, thou fount of ev'ry blessing,
   Tune my heart to sing thy grace;
Streams of mercy never ceasing,
   Call for songs of loudest praise:
Teach me some melodious sonnet,
   Sung by flaming tongues above;
Praise the mount!—I'm fixed upon it,
   Mount of thy redeeming love!

2 Here I'll raise my Ebenezer;
   Hither by thy help I'm come,
And I hope, by thy good pleasure,
   Safely to arrive at home;

Jesus sought me when a stranger,
  Wand'ring from the fold of God:
He, to rescue me from danger,
  Interpos'd his precious blood!

3 O! to grace how great a debtor
  Daily I'm constrain'd to be!
Let thy goodness, like a fetter,
  Bind my wand'ring heart to thee
Prone to wander, Lord, I feel it;
  Prone to leave the God I love—
Here's my heart, O take and seal it,
  Seal it for thy c urts above. *Huntingdon.*

352 *Invoking Divine Love.* 8s-7s.

LOVE Divine, all loves excelling,
  Joy of heaven, to earth come down,
Fix in us thy humble dwelling,
  All thy faithful mercies crown!
Jesus, thou art all compassion,
  Pure unbounded love thou art;
Visit us with thy salvation;
  Enter every trembling heart.

2 Breathe, O breathe thy loving Spirit
  Into every troubled breast!
Let us all in thee inherit,
  Let us find that second rest.
Take away our bent to sinning,
  Alpha and Omega be,
End of faith, as its beginning,
  Set our hearts at liberty.

3 Come, almighty to deliver,
  Let us all thy life receive,
Suddenly return, and never,
  Never more thy temples leave:

Thee we would be always blessing;
　Serve thee as thy hosts above;
Pray, and praise thee, without ceasing,
　Glory in thy perfect love.　　*C. Wesley.*

353　　　*Delight in Christ.*　　　8s.

HOW tedious and tasteless the hours
　　When Jesus no longer I see!
Sweet prospects, sweet birds, and sweet flowers,
　Have all lost their sweetness to me:
The midsummer sun shines but dim,
　The fields strive in vain to look gay;
But when I am happy in him,
　December's as pleasant as May.

2 His name yields the richest perfume,
　And sweeter than music his voice;
His presence disperses my gloom,
　And makes all within me rejoice:
I should, were he always thus nigh,
　Have nothing to wish or to fear,
No mortal so happy as I,
　My summer would last all the year.

3 Content with beholding his face,
　My all to his pleasure resign'd,
No changes of season or place
　Would make any change in my mind:
While bless'd with a sense of his love,
　A palace a toy would appear;
And prisons would palaces prove,
　If Jesus would dwell with me there.

4 Dear Lord, if indeed I am thine,
　If thou art my sun and my song,
Say why do I languish and pine?
　And why are my winters so long?

O drive these dark clouds from my sky,—
Thy soul-cheering presence restore;
Or take me to thee up on high,
Where winters and clouds are no more.
Newton.

354   *Full assurance of hope.*   8, 8, 6.

COME on, my partners in distress,
My comrades through the wilderness,
Who still your bodies feel:
Awhile forget your griefs and fears,
And look beyond this vale of tears
To that celestial hill.

2 Beyond the bounds of time and space
Look forward to that heavenly place,
The saints' secure abode:
On faith's strong eagle-pinions rise,
And force your passage to the skies,
And scale the mount of God.

3 Who suffer with our Master here,
We shall before his face appear,
And by his side sit down:
To patient faith the prize is sure;
And all that to the end endure
The cross, shall wear the crown.

4 Thrice-blessed, bliss inspiring hope!
It lifts the fainting spirits up,
It brings to life the dead:
Our conflicts here shall soon be past,
And you and I ascend at last,
Triumphant with our Head. *C. Wesley.*

355   *Gently lead us.*   8, 7, 4.

GENTLY, Lord, O gently lead us
Through this gloomy vale of tears;

CHRISTIAN WARFARE AND FAITH.

And O Lord, in mercy give us
Thy rich grace in all our fears.
O refresh us,
Traveling through this wilderness.
2 When temptation's darts assail us,
When in devious paths we stray,
Let thy goodness never fail us,
Lead us in thy perfect way.
3 In the hour of pain and anguish,
In the hour when death draws near,
Suffer not our hearts to languish,
Suffer not our souls to fear.
4 When this mortal life is ended,
Bid us in thine arms to rest,
Till, by angel-bands attended,
We awake among the blest.
Thomas Hastings.

356 *In deep Affliction.* 8s, 7s.

FULL of trembling expectation,
Feeling much, and fearing more,
Mighty God of my salvation,
I thy timely aid implore
2 Suffering Son of man, be near me,
In my sufferings to sustain;
By thy sorer griefs to cheer me,
By thy more than mortal pain.
3 By thy most severe temptation
In that dark Satanic hour,
By thy last mysterious passion,
Screen me from the adverse power.
4 By thy fainting in the garden,
By thy dreadful death, I pray,
Write upon my heart the pardon;
Take my sins and fears away. *C. Wesley.*

CHRISTIAN WARFARE AND FAITH.

357 *The Precious Name.* 8s, 7s.

TAKE the name of Jesus with you,
  Child of sorrow and of woe;
It will joy and comfort give you;
  Take it, then, where'er you go.
    Precious name, O how sweet!
    Hope of earth and joy of heaven.

2 Take the name of Jesus ever,
  As a shield from every snare;
If temptations round you gather,
  Breathe that holy name in prayer.

3 O the precious name of Jesus!
  How it thrills our souls with joy,
When his loving arms receive us,
  And his songs our tongues employ!

4 At the name of Jesus bowing,
  Falling prostrate at his feet.
King of kings in heaven we'll crown him,
  When our journey is complete.
            Mrs. Lydia Baxter.

358 *Waiting in the Sanctuary.* C. M.

FATHER, behold with gracious eyes
  The souls before thy throne,
Who now present their sacrifice,
  And seek thee in thy Son.
Well pleased in him thyself declare,
  Thy pard'ning love reveal,
The peaceful answer of our prayer
  To every conscience seal.

2 Meanest of all thy servants, I
  Those happier spirits meet,
And mix with theirs my feeble cry,
  And worship at thy feet.

On me, on all, some gift bestow,
  Some blessing now impart;
The seed of life eternal sow
  In every mournful heart.

3 Thy loving, powerful Spirit shed,
  And speak our sins forgiven,
Or haste throughout the lump to spread
  The sanctifying leaven.
Refresh us with a ceaseless shower
  Of graces from above
Till all receive the perfect power
  Of everlasting love.   *C. Wesley.*

359   *The Rest of Faith.*   C. M.

LORD, I believe a rest remains,
  To all thy people known;
A rest where pure enjoyment reigns,
  And thou art loved alone:

2 A rest where all our soul's desire
  Is fixed on things above;
Where fear, and sin, and grief expire,
  Cast out by perfect love.

3 O that I now the rest might know,
  Believe, and enter in!
Now, Saviour, now the power bestow,
  And let me cease from sin!

4 Remove this hardness from my heart,
  This unbelief remove:
To me the rest of faith impart,
  The Sabbath of thy love.   *C. Wesley.*

360   *God, my Sufficient Portion.*   C. M.

MY God, my Portion, and my Love,
  My everlasting All,

CHRISTIAN WARFARE AND FAITH.

I've none but thee in heaven above,
  Or on this earthly ball.
2 What empty things are all the skies,
    And this inferior clod!
  There's nothing here deserves my joys,
    There's nothing like my God.

3 To thee I owe my wealth, and friends,
    And health, and safe abode:
  Thanks to thy name for meaner things;
    But they are not my God.

4 How vain a toy is glittering wealth,
    If once compared to thee!
  Or what's my safety, or my health,
    Or all my friends to me?

5 Were I possessor of the earth,
    And called the stars my own,
  Without thy graces and thyself,
    I were a wretch undone.

6 Let others stretch their arms like seas,
    And grasp in all the shore;
  Grant me the visits of thy grace,
    And I desire no more.   *Isaac Watts.*

361   *"Our Rejoicing is This"—*   L. M.

LORD, how secure and blest are they
    Who feel the joys of pardoned sin!
Should storms of wrath shake earth and sea,
    Their minds have heaven and peace within.

2 The day glides sweetly o'er their heads,
    Made up of innocence and love:
  And soft and silent as the shades
    Their nightly minutes gently move.

3 Quick as their thoughts their joys come on,
 But fly not half so fast away:
Their souls are ever bright as noon,
 And calm as summer evenings be.

4 They scorn to seek our golden toys,
 But spend the day and share the night
In numbering o'er the richer joys
 That heaven prepares for their delight.
Watts.

362   . *Friend of the friendless.*   L. M.

GOD of my life, to thee I call,
 Afflicted at thy feet I fall;
When the great water-floods prevail,
Leave not my trembling heart to fail.

2 Friend of the friendless and the faint,
Where should I lodge my deep complaint?
Where, but with thee, whose open door
Invites the helpless and the poor?

3 Did ever mourner plead with thee,
And thou refuse that mourner's plea?
Does not the promise still remain,
That none shall seek thy face in vain?

4 Poor I may be, despised, forgot,
Yet God, my God, forgets me not;
And he is safe, and must succeed,
For whom the Saviour deigns to plead.
William Cowper.

363   *Psalm* lxviii. 17, 18.   L. M.

LORD, when thou didst ascend on high,
 Ten thousand angels filled the sky:
Those heavenly guards around thee wait,
Like chariots that attend thy state.

CHRISTIAN WARFARE AND FAITH.

2 Not Sinai's mountain could appear
More glorious, when the Lord was there:
While he pronounced his dreadful law,
And struck the chosen tribes with awe.

3 How bright the triumph none can tell,
When the rebellious powers of hell,
That thousand souls had captives made,
Were all in chains, like captives, led,

4 Raised by his Father to the throne,
He sent the promised Spirit down,
With gifts and grace for rebel men,
That God might dwell on earth again.
Watts.

364 *Sweet hour of prayer.* L. M.

SWEET hour of prayer, sweet hour of prayer
That calls me from a world of care,
And bids me, at my Father's throne,
Make all my wants and wishes known!
In seasons of distress and grief,
My soul has often found relief,
And oft escaped the tempter's snare,
By thy return, sweet hour of prayer.

2 Sweet hour of prayer, sweet hour of prayer,
Thy wings shall my petition bear
To him, whose truth and faithfulness
Engage the waiting soul to bless:
And since he bids me seek his face,
Believe his word and trust his grace,
I'll cast on him my every care,
And wait for thee, sweet hour of prayer.

3 Sweet hour of prayer, sweet hour of prayer,
May I thy consolation share,

CHRISTIAN WARFARE AND FAITH.

Till, from Mount Pisgah's lofty height,
I view my home, and take my flight:
This robe of flesh I'll drop, and rise,
To seize the everlasting prize;
And shout while passing through the air,
Farewell, farewell, sweet hour of prayer!
William W. Walford.

365 *The joy of loving hearts.* L. M.

JESUS, thou Joy of loving hearts!
Thou Fount of life! thou Light of men!
From the best bliss that earth imparts,
We turn unfilled to thee again.

2 Thy truth unchanged hath ever stood;
Thou savest those that on thee call;
To them that seek thee, thou art good,
To them that find thee, all in all.

3 We taste thee, O thou Living Bread.
And long to feast upon thee still;
We drink of thee, the Fountain Head,
And thirst our souls from thee to fill!

4 Our restless spirits yearn for thee,
Where'er our changeful lot is cast;
Glad, when thy gracious smile we see,
Blest, when our faith can hold thee fast.

5 O Jesus, ever with us stay;
Make all our moments calm and bright;
Chase the dark night of sin away,
Shed o'er the world thy holy light!
Bernard of Clairvaux. Tr. by R. Palmer.

366 *His loving-kindness better than life.* L. M.

O GOD, thou art my God alone;
Early to thee my soul shall cry:

A pilgrim in a land unknown,
A thirsty land, whose springs are dry.
2 Thee in the watches of the night,
When I remember on my bed,
Thy presence makes the darkness light;
Thy guardian wings are round my head.
3 Better than life itself, thy love;
Dearer than all beside to me;
For whom have I in heaven above,
Or what on earth, compared with thee?
4 Praise with my heart, my mind, my voice,
For all thy mercy I will give;
My soul shall still in God rejoice,
My tongue shall bless thee while I live.
                           James Montgomery.

367   *At home with God anywhere.*   L. M.

MY Lord, how full of sweet content
I pass my years of banishment!
Where'er I dwell, I dwell with thee,
In heaven, in earth or on the sea.
To me remains nor place nor time;
My country is in every clime:
I can be calm and free from care
On any shore, since God is there.

2 While place we seek, or place we shun,
The soul finds happiness in none;
But with a God to guide our way,
'Tis equal joy to go or stay.
Could I be cast where thou art not,
That were indeed a dreadful lot;
But regions none remote I call,
Secure of finding God in all.
              Mad. J. M. B. De La Motte Guyon.
                 [*Tr. by Wm. Cowper.*]

868 *Watchfulness.* **S. M.**

GRACIOUS Redeemer, shake
  This slumber from my soul!
Say to me now, "Awake, awake!
  And Christ shall make thee whole."

2 Lay to thy mighty hand;
  Alarm me in this hour;
And make me fully understand
  The thunder of thy power!

3 Give me on thee to call,
  Always to watch and pray,
Lest I into temptation fall,
  And cast my shield away.

4 For each assault prepar'd
  And ready may I be;
For ever standing on my guard,
  And looking up to thee.

5 O do thou always warn
  My soul of evil near!
When to the right or left I turn,
  Thy voice still let me hear:

6 "Come back! this is the way!
  Come back! and walk herein!"
O may I hearken and obey,
  And shun the paths of sin! *C. Wesley.*

869 *The mind that was in Christ.* **S. M.**

EQUIP me for the war,
  And teach my hands to fight;
My simple, upright heart prepare
  And guide my words aright.

2 Control my every thought,
  My whole of sin remove;

CHRISTIAN WARFARE AND FAITH.

Let all my works in thee be wrought,
Let all be wrought in love.
3 O arm me with the mind,
Meek Lamb, that was in thee;
And let my knowing zeal be joined
With perfect charity.
4 With calm and tempered zeal
Let me enforce thy call;
And vindicate thy gracious will,
Which offers life to all. *C. Wesley.*

870 *Watch and pray.* Matt. xxiv. 41. S. M.

MY soul, be on thy guard,
Ten thousand foes arise;
And hosts of sins are pressing hard,
To draw thee from the skies.
2 O watch, and fight, and pray,
The battle ne'er give o'er;
Renew it boldly every day,
And help divine implore.
3 Ne'er think the victory won,
Nor once at ease sit down;
Thy arduous work will not be done
Till thou hast got the crown.
4 Fight on, my soul, till death
Shall bring thee to thy God;
He'll take thee, at thy parting breath,
Up to his blest abode. *Heath.*

371 *Make haste to live.* S. M.

MAKE haste, O man, to live,
For thou so soon must die;
Time hurries past thee like the breeze:
How swift its moments fly!

2 Make haste, O man, to do
   Whatever must be done;
 Thou hast no time to lose in sloth,
   Thy day will soon be gone.

3 Up, then, with speed, and work;
   Fling ease and self away;
 This is no time for thee to sleep,
   Up, watch, and work, and pray!

4 Make haste, O man, to live,
   Thy time is almost o'er;
 O sleep not, dream not, but arise,
   The Judge is at the door.
                    Horatius Bonar.

SECTION XV.

Church Activities.

PRAYER.

372　　*Prevailing Prayer.*　　L. M.

PRAYER is appointed to convey
   The blessings God designs to give:
 Long as they live should Christians pray,
   They learn to pray when first they live.

2 If pain afflict, or wrongs oppress;
   If cares distract, or fears dismay;
 If guilt deject; if sin distress;—
   In every case, still watch and pray.

3 'Tis prayer supports the soul that's weak:
   Though thought be broken, language lame,
 Pray if thou canst, or canst not speak;
   But pray with faith in Jesus' name.

4 Depend on him, thou canst not fail;
  Make all thy wants and wishes known:
  Fear not; his merits must prevail;
  Ask but in faith, it shall be done.   *Hart.*

373   *A Morning Prayer.*   L. M.

AWAKE, my soul, and with the sun
  Thy daily stage of duty run;
Shake off dull sloth, and early rise
To pay thy morning sacrifice.

2 Wake, and lift up thyself, my heart,
  And with the angels bear thy part;
  Who all night long unwearied sing
  High praises to th' eternal King.

3 Glory to thee, who safe hast kept,
  And hast refreshed me while I slept:
  Grant, Lord when I from death shall wake,
  I may of endless life partake.

4 Direct, control, suggest this day,
  All I design, or do, or say,
  That all my powers, with all their might,
  In thy sole glory may unite.   *T. Ken.*

374   *Early Vows.*   L. M.

MY God, accept my early vows,
  Like morning incense in thy house,
And let my nightly worship rise
Sweet as the evening sacrifice.

2 Watch o'er my lips, and guard them, Lord,
  From every rash and heedless word;
  Nor let my feet incline to tread
  The guilty path where sinners lead.

3 O, may the righteous, when I stray,
Smite, and reprove my wand'ring way?
Their gentle words, like ointment shed,
Shall never bruise, but cheer my head.

4 When I behold them pressed with grief,
I'll cry to heaven for their relief;
And by my warm petitions prove
How much I prize their faithful love. *Watts.*

375   *Evening song.*   L. M.

HOW do thy mercies close me round!
   Forever be thy name ador'd:
I blush in all things to abound;
   The servant is above his Lord!

2 Inur'd to poverty and pain,
   A suff'ring life my Master led;
The Son of God, the Son of man,
   He had not where to lay his head.

3 But, lo! a place he hath prepar'd
   For me, whom watchful angels keep;
Yea, he himself becomes my guard;
   He smooths my bed, and gives me sleep.

4 Jesus protects; my fears, begone!
   What can the rock of ages move!
Safe in thy arms I lay me down,
   Thy everlasting arms of love. *C. Wesley.*

376   *How frail I am.* Psalm xxxix.   C. M.

TEACH me the measure of my days,
   Thou Maker of my frame:
I would survey life's narrow space,
   And learn how frail I am.

PRAYER.

2 A span is all that we can boast,
   An inch or two of time:
   Man is but vanity and dust,
   In all his flower and prime.

3 What should I wish, or wait for, then,
   From creatures, earth, and dust?
   They make our expectations vain
   And disappoint our trust.

4 Now I forbid my carnal hope,
   My fond desires recall;
   I give my mortal interest up,
   And make my God my all.   *Watts.*

377   *The Lord our help.*   Psalm xc.   C. M.

O GOD, our help in ages past,
   Our hope for years to come,
Our shelter from the stormy blast,
   And our eternal home:

2 Under the shadow of thy throne,
   Still may we dwell secure;
   Sufficient is thine arm alone,
   And our defense is sure.

3 Before the hills in order stood,
   Or earth receiv'd her frame,
   From everlasting thou art God,
   To endless years the same.

4 A thousand ages, in thy sight,
   Are like an evening gone:
   Short as the watch that ends the night
   Before the rising sun.

5 Time, like an ever-rolling stream,
   Bears all its sons away;

They fly, forgotten, as a dream
  Dies at the op'ning day.
6 O God, our help in ages past,
  Our hope for years to come,
  Be thou our guard while life shall last,
  And our perpetual home! *Watts.*

378   *A Morning meditation.*   C. M.

ONCE more, my soul, the rising day,
  Salutes thy waking eyes;
Once more, my voice, thy tribute pay
  To him that rules the skies.

2 Night unto night his name repeats,
  The day renews the sound,—
Wide as the heavens on which he sits,
  To turn the seasons round.

3 'Tis he supports my mortal frame;
  My tongue shall speak his praise:
My sins might rouse his wrath to flame,
  But yet his wrath delays.

4 O God, let all my hours be thine,
  While I enjoy the light!
Then shall my sun in smiles decline,
  And bring a pleasant night. *Watts.*

379   *Awake, my soul.*   C. M.

AWAKE, my soul, to meet the day,
  Unfold thy drowsy eyes,
And burst the pond'rous chain that loads
  Thine active faculties.

2 God's guardian shield was round me spread
  In my defenseless sleep:
Let him have all my waking hours
  Who doth my slumbers keep.

PRAYER.

3 Pardon, O God, my former sloth,
  And arm my soul with grace;
  As rising now, I seal my vows
  To prosecute thy ways.

4 Bright Sun of righteousness, arise;
  Thy radiant beams display,
  And guide my dark, bewilder'd soul
  To everlasting day. *Doddridge.*

380 *Meditation.* C. M.

GIVER and guardian of my sleep,
  To praise thy name I wake:
Still, Lord, thy helpless servant keep,
  For thine own mercy's sake.

2 The blessing of another day
  I thankfully receive:
  O may I only thee obey,
  And to thy glory live!

3 Upon me lay thy mighty hand,
  My words and thoughts restrain:
  Bow my whole soul to thy command,
  Nor let my faith be vain.

4 Pris'ner of hope, I wait the hour
  Which shall salvation bring;
  When all I am shall own thy power,
  And call my Jesus King. *C. Wesley.*

381 C. M.
A Sabbath morning carol. Psalm v. 1-8.

LORD, in the morning thou shalt hear
  My voice ascending high;
To thee will I direct my prayer,
  To thee lift up mine eye:

CHURCH ACTIVITIES.

2 Up to the hills where Christ is gone,
To plead for all his saints,
Presenting at his Father's throne
Our songs and our complaints.

3 Thou art a God before whose sight
The wicked shall not stand;
Sinners shall ne'er be thy delight,
Nor dwell at thy right hand.

4 But to thy house will I resort,
To taste thy mercies there;
I will frequent thy holy court,
And worship in thy fear.

5 O may thy Spirit guide my feet
In ways of righteousness,
Make ev'ry path of duty straight
And plain before my face. *Watts*

382 *Morning Hymn.* 7s.

NOW the shades of night are gone;
Now the morning light is come;
Lord, may we be thine to-day,
Drive the shades of sin away.

2 Fill our souls with heav'nly light,
Banish doubt and clear our sight;
In thy service, Lord, to-day,
May we labor, watch, and pray.

3 Keep our haughty passions bound;
Save us from our foes around;
Going out and coming in
Keep us safe from ev'ry sin.

4 When our work of life is past,
O receive us then at last;

PRAYER.

Night and sin will be no more,
When we reach the heav'nly shore.
Unknown.

383   *Evening.*   7s.

OMNIPRESENT God! whose aid
   No one ever asked in vain,
Be this night about my bed,
   Every evil thought restrain:
Lay thy hand upon my soul,
   God of my unguarded hours!
All my enemies control,
   Hell, and earth and nature's powers.

2 O thou jealous God! come down,
   God of spotless purity;
Claim and seize me for thine own,
   Consecrate my heart to thee:
Under thy protection take;
   Songs in the night season give;
Let me sleep to thee, and wake;
   Let me die to thee, and live.

3 Let me of thy life partake,
   Thy own holiness impart;
O that I may sweetly wake,
   With my Saviour in my heart!
O that I may know thee mine!
   O that I may thee receive!
Only live the life Divine!
   Only to thy glory live!   *C. W'ley*

384   *For reviving grace.*   7s.

LIGHT of life, seraphic fire,
   Love Divine, thyself impart;
Every fainting soul inspire;
   Shine in every drooping heart:

Every mournful sinner cheer;
　Scatter all our guilty gloom;
　Son of God, appear! appear!
　To thy human temples come.
2 Come in this accepted hour;
　Bring thy heavenly kingdom in;
　Fill us with thy glorious power,
　　Rooting out the seeds of sin:
　Nothing more can we require,
　　We will covet nothing less;
　Be thou all our hearts' desire,
　　All our joy, and all our peace.

C. Wesley.

385　　*New Year's Day.*　　10, 5, 11.

COME, let us anew our journey pursue,
　Roll round with the year,
And never stand still till the Master appear!
His adorable will let us gladly fulfil,
　And our talents improve,
By the patience of hope, and the labor of love.

2 Our life is a dream;—our time, as a stream,
　Glides swiftly away;
And the fugitive moment refuses to stay.
The arrow is flown, the moment is gone,
　The millennial year
Rushes on to our view, and eternity's here.

3 O that each in the day of his coming may say,
　"I have fought my way through;
I have finished the work thou didst give me to do!"

O that each from his Lord may receive the
    glad word,
" Well and faithfully done!
Enter into my joy, and sit down on my
    throne."   *C. Wesley.*

386   *The opening year.*   **H. M.**

THE Lord of earth and sky,
    The God of ages praise!
Who reigns enthroned on high,
    Ancient of endless days!
Who lengthens out our trials here,
And spares us yet another year.

2 Barren and wither'd trees,
    We cumber'd long the ground!
No fruit of holiness
    On our dead souls was found;
Yet doth he us in mercy spare
Another and another year.

3 When justice gave the word,
    To cut the fig-tree down,
The pity of the Lord
    Cried, " Let it still alone!"
The Father mild inclines his ear,
And spares us yet another year.

4 Jesus, thy speaking blood
    From God obtain'd the grace;
Who therefore hath bestow'd
    On us a longer space:
Thou didst in our behalf appear,
And lo! we see another year!

5 Then dig about the root,
    Break up our fallow ground,

CHURCH ACTIVITIES.

And let our gracious fruit
To thy great praise abound:
O let us all thy praise declare,
And fruit unto perfection bear! *C. Wesley.*

387   *Lo, I am with you alway.*   **8, 7.**

ALWAYS with us, always with us ;—
  Words of cheer and words of love;
Thus the risen Saviour whispers,
  From his dwelling-place above.
With us when we toil in sadness,
  Sowing much, and reaping none;
Telling us that in the future
  Golden harvests shall be won.

2 With us when the storm is sweeping
  O'er our pathway dark and drear;
Waking hope within our bosoms,
  Stilling every anxious fear.
With us in the lonely valley,
  When we cross the chilling stream;
Lighting up the steps to glory
  With salvation's radiant beam.
                      Edwin H. Nevin.

388   *A holy life.*   **S. M.**

GOD of almighty love,—
  By whose sufficient grace
I lift my heart to things above,
  And humbly seek thy face,—
Through Jesus Christ, the just,
  My faint desires receive,
And let me in thy goodness trust,
  And to thy glory live.

PRAYER.

2 Whate'er I say or do,
    Thy glory be my aim;
  My off'rings all be offer'd through
    The ever-blessed name.
  Jesus, my single eye
    Be fix'd on thee alone:
  Thy name be prais'd on earth, on high,
    Thy will by all be done!

3 Spirit of faith, inspire
    My consecrated heart:
  Fill me with pure, celestial fire,
    With all thou hast and art.
  My feeble mind transform,
    And, perfectly renew'd,
  Into a saint exalt a worm—
    A worm exalt to God! *C. Wesley.*

289 *Trust in old age.* S. M.

THOU seest my feebleness;
    Jesus, be thou my power,
  My help and refuge in distress,
    My fortress and my tower.

2 Give me to trust in thee;
    Be thou my sure abode:
  My horn, and rock, and buckler be,
    My Saviour and my God.

3 Myself I cannot save,
    Myself I cannot keep;
  But strength in thee I surely have,
    Whose eyelids never sleep,

4 My soul to thee alone,
    Now, therefore, I commend:
  Thou, Jesus, love me as thine own,
    And love me to the end! *C. Wesley*

265

CHURCH ACTIVITIES.

390   "*Praying always, with all prayer.*"   S. M.

TO God your every want
    In instant prayer display:
Pray always; pray, and never faint:
    Pray without ceasing, pray.

2 In fellowship,—alone—
    To God with faith draw near:
Approach his courts, besiege his throne,
    With all the power of prayer:

3 Go to his temple, go,
    Nor from his altar move:
Let every house his worship know,
    And every heart his love.

4 To God your spirits dart;
    Your souls in words declare;
Or groan, to him who reads the heart,
    Th' unutterable prayer:

5 His mercy now implore;
    And now show forth his praise;
In shouts, or silent awe, adore
    His miracles of grace.

6 Pour out your souls to God,
    And bow them with your knees;
And spread your hearts and hands abroad,
    And pray for Zion's peace.   *C. Wesley.*

391   *Thyself the way.*   S. M.

O THOU that would-t not have
    One wretched sinner die;
Who diedst thyself, my soul to save
    From endless misery!
Show me the way to shun
    Thy dreadful wrath severe;

PRAYER.

 That when thou comest on thy throne,
  I may with joy appear!
2 Thou art thyself the way,
  Thyself in me reveal;
 So shall I spend my life's short day
  Obedient to thy will:
 So shall I love my God,
  Because he first lov'd me;
 And praise thee in thy bright abode
  To all eternity.   *C. Wesley.*

392   *Intercession.*   S. M.

WE lift our hearts to thee,
  O Day-Star from on high!
 The sun itself is but thy shade,
  Yet cheers both earth and sky.

2 O let thy orient beams
  The night of sin disperse,
 The mists of error and of vice
  Which shade the universe!

3 How beauteous nature now!
  How dark and sad before!
 With joy we view the pleasing change,
  And nature's God adore.

4 May we this life improve,
  To mourn for errors past,—
 And live this short revolving day
  As if it were our last.

5 To God, the Father, Son,
  And Spirit,—One in Three,—
 Be glory, as it was, is now,
  And shall forever be.   *John Wesley.*

CHURCH ACTIVITIES.

393   *Not ashamed of Christ.*   L. M.

JESUS! and shall it ever be,
   A mortal man ashamed of thee!
Ashamed of thee, whom angels praise,
Whose glories shine through endless days.

2 Ashamed of Jesus! sooner far
Let evening blush to own a star;
He sheds the beams of light divine
O'er this benighted soul of mine.

3 Ashamed of Jesus! just as soon
Let midnight be ashamed of noon;
'Tis midnight with my soul, till he,
Bright morning star, bid darkness flee.

4 Ashamed of Jesus! that dear friend
On whom my hopes of heaven depend·
No, when I blush, be this my shame,
That I no more revere his name.

5 Ashamed of Jesus! yes, I may,
When I've no guilt to wash away,
No tear to wipe, no good to crave,
No fears to quell, no soul to save.

6 Till then—nor is my boasting vain—
Till then I boast a Saviour slain!
And O, may this my glory be,
That Christ is not ashamed of me!   *Gregg.*

394   *Evening: Memorials of his Grace.*   I. M.

THUS far the Lord hath led me on,—
   Thus far his pow'r prolongs my days;
And every ev'ning shall make known
Some fresh memorial of his grace.

2 Much of my time has run to waste,
   And I, perhaps, am near my home:

But he forgives my follies past,
And gives me strength for days to come.

3 I lay my body down to sleep;
Peace is the pillow for my head:
While well-appointed angels keep
Their watchful stations round my bed.

4 Thus, when the night of death shall come
My flesh shall rest beneath the ground,
And wait thy voice to rouse my tomb,
With sweet salvation in the sound. *Watts.*

395 L. M.
"*Thou crownest the Year with thy Goodness.*"

ETERNAL Source of every joy,
Well may thy praise our lips employ,
While in thy temple we appear,
Whose goodness crowns the circling year.

2 The flow'ry spring, at thy command,
Embalms the air, and paints the land;
The summer rays with vigor shine,
To raise the corn and cheer the vine.

3 Thy hand in autumn richly pours,
Through all our coasts, redundant stores;
And winters, soften'd by thy care,
No more a face of horror wear.

4 Seasons, and months, and weeks, and days
Demand successive songs of praise:
Still be the cheerful homage paid
With op'ning light and ev'ning shade.

5 Here in thy house shall incense rise,
As circling Sabbaths bless our eyes;
Still we will make thy mercies known
Around thy board, and round our own.

6 O may our more harmonious tongue
In worlds unknown pursue the song;
And in those brighter courts adore,
Where days and years revolve no more!
Doddridge

396 *A Song for the opening year.* L. M.

GREAT God, we sing that mighty hand,
By which supported still we stand:
The opening year thy mercy shows;
Let mercy crown it till it close.

2 By day, by night, at home, abroad,
Still we are guarded by our God;
By his incessant bounty fed,
By his unerring counsel led.

3 With grateful hearts the past we own.
The future—all to us unknown—
We to thy guardian care commit,
And peaceful leave before thy feet.

4 In scenes exalted or depress'd,
Be thou our joy, and thou our rest;
Thy goodness all our hopes shall raise,
Ador'd through all our changing days.

5 When death shall close our earthly songs
And seal in silence mortal tongues,
Our Helper, God, in whom we trust,
In brighter worlds our souls shall boast
Doddridge.

397 *Worth of prayer.* L. M.

WHAT various hind'rances we meet
In coming to a mercy-seat!
Yet who that knows the worth of prayer
But wishes to be often there?

2 Prayer makes the darkened cloud withdraw;
Prayer climbs the ladder Jacob saw;
Gives exercise to faith and love;
Brings every blessing from above.

3 Restraining prayer, we cease to fight:
Prayer makes the Christian's armor bright;
And Satan trembles when he sees
The weakest saint upon his knees.

4 Have you no words? Ah! think again,
Words flow apace when you complain,
And fill your fellow-creature's ear
With the sad tale of all your care.

5 Were half the breath thus vainly spent,
To heaven in supplication sent,
Your cheerful song would oft'ner be,
" Hear what the Lord has done for me."
Cowper.

398   *The Lord's Prayer.*   S. M.

OUR Heavenly Father, hear
   The prayer we offer now:
Thy name be hallowed far and near;
   To thee all nations bow.

2 Thy kingdom come; thy will
   On earth be done in love,
As saints and seraphim fulfil
   Thy perfect law above.

3 Our daily bread supply
   While by the word we live;
The guilt of our iniquity
   Forgive, as we forgive.

4 From dark temptation's power,
   From Satan's wiles defend;

Deliver in the evil hour,
And guide us to the end.

5 Thine shall forever be
Glory and power Divine;
The sceptre, throne, and majesty,
Of heaven and earth, are thine.
Montgomery.

399 *Evening.* S. M.

THE day is past and gone,
The evening shades appear:
O may we all remember well,
The night of death draws near!

2 We lay our garments by,
Upon our beds to rest;
So death will soon disrobe us all
Of what is here possess'd.

3 Lord, keep us safe this night,
Secure from all our fears;
May angels guard us while we sleep,
Till morning light appears.

4 And when we early rise,
And view th' unwearied sun,
May we set out to win the prize,
And after glory run.

5 And when our days are past,
And we from time remove,
O may we in thy bosom rest,
The bosom of thy love. *J Leland.*

400 *Dedication to God, our Preserver.* S. M.
Psalm iii. 5.

SERENE I laid me down
Beneath his guardian care;

PRAYER.

I slept, and I awoke, and found
  My kind preserver near!

2 Thus does thine arm support
  This weak, defenseless frame:
  But whence these favors, Lord, to me,
  All worthless as I am?

3 O! how shall I repay
  The bounties of my God?
  This feeble spirit pants beneath
  The pleasing, painful load.

4 Dear Saviour, to thy cross
  I bring my sacrifice;
  Ting'd with thy blood, it shall ascend
  With fragrance to the skies.

5 My life I would anew
  Devote, O Lord, to thee;
  And in thy service I would spend
  A long eternity.   *Dwight.*

401 *Whoso putteth his trust in the Lord* S. M.
         shall be safe.

COMMIT thou all thy griefs
  And ways into his hands,
To his sure trust and tender care
  Who earth and heaven commands.

2 Who points the clouds their course,
  Whom winds and seas obey,
  He shall direct thy wandering feet,
  He shall prepare thy way.

3 Thou on the Lord rely,
  So, safe, shalt thou go on;
  Fix on his work thy steadfast eye,
  So shall thy work be done.

4 No profit canst thou gain
By self-consuming care;
To him commend thy cause; his ear
Attends the softest prayer.

5 Thy everlasting truth,
Father, thy ceaseless love.
Sees all thy children's wants, and knows
What best for each will prove.

Tr. by J. Wesley.

402 *An Evening Prayer.* Psalm iv. C. M

LORD, thou wilt hear me when I pray;
I am forever thine:
I fear before thee all the day,
Nor would I dare to sin.

2 And while I rest my weary head,
From cares and business free,
'Tis sweet conversing on my bed
With my own heart and thee.

3 I pay this ev'ning sacrifice;
And when my work is done,
Great God, my faith, my hope, relies
Upon thy grace alone.

4 Thus, with my thoughts compos'd to peace,
I'll give mine eyes to sleep:
Thy hand in safety keeps my days,
And will my slumbers keep. *Watts.*

403 C. M.
"And is a discerner of the thoughts and intents of the heart." Heb. iv. 12, 13.

ALL praise to him who dwells in bliss,
Who made both day and night:

PRAYER.

Whose throne is darkness in th' abyss
Of uncreated light.

2 Each thought and deed his piercing eyes,
With strictest search survey;
The deepest shades no more disguise,
Than the full blaze of day.

3 Whom thou dost guard, O King of kings,
No evil shall molest:
Under the shadow of thy wings
Shall they securely rest.

4 Thy angels shall around their beds
Their constant stations keep;
Thy faith and truth shall shield their heads,
For thou dost never sleep.

5 May we, with calm and sweet repose
And heavenly thoughts refresh'd,
Our eyelids with the morn unclose,
And bless thee, ever bless'd. *C. Wesley.*

404 *Twilight Meditation.* C. M.

I LOVE to steal awhile away
From every cumbering care;
And spend the hours of setting day
In humble, grateful pray'r.

2 I love in solitude to shed
The penitential tear,
And all his promises to plead,
Where none but God can hear.

3 I love to think on mercies past,
And future good implore,
And all my cares and sorrows cast
On him whom I adore.

4 I love by faith to take a view
  Of brighter scenes in heav'n;
  The prospect does my strength renew,
  While here by tempest driv'n.
5 Thus, when life's toilsome day is o'er,
  May its departing ray
  Be calm as this impressive hour,
  And lead to endless day. *Mrs. Browne.*

405 *Evening Hymn.* Ps. cxli. 2. C. M.

DREAD Sovereign, let my ev'ning song
  Like holy incense rise;
  Assist the off'ring of my tongue
  To reach the lofty skies.
2 Through all the dangers of the day
  Thy hand was still my guard;
  And still to drive my wants away
  Thy mercy stood prepared.
3 Perpetual blessings from above
  Encompass me around;
  But, O, how few returns of love
  Hath my Creator found!
4 What have I done for him who died
  To save my guilty soul?
  Alas! my sins are multiplied,
  Fast as my minutes roll.
5 Lord, with this guilty heart of mine,
  To thy dear cross I flee,
  And to thy grace my soul resign,
  To be renew'd by thee. *Watts.*

406 *The greatness and goodness of God.* L. M.
  Psalm lxiii. 1–4.

GREAT God, indulge my humble claim,
  Be thou my hope, my joy, my rest;

PRAYER.

The glories that compose thy name
Stand all engaged to make me blest.

2 Thou great and good, thou just and wise,
Thou art my Father and my God!
And I am thine by sacred ties,
Thy son, thy servant bought with blood.

3 With heart, and eyes, and lifted hands,
For thee I long, to thee I look,
As travelers in thirsty lands
Pant for the cooling water-brook.

4 E'en life itself, without thy love,
No lasting pleasure can afford;
Yea, 'twould a tiresome burden prove,
If I were banished from thee, Lord!

5 I'll lift my hands, I'll raise my voice,
While I have breath to pray or praise:
This work shall make my heart rejoice,
And spend the remnant of my days.
Watts.

407 *For the lambs of the flock.* L. M.

AUTHOR of faith, we seek thy face,
For all who feel thy work begun;
Confirm, and strengthen them in grace,
And bring thy feeblest children on.

2 Thou seest their wants, thou know'st their names.
Be mindful of thy youngest care;
Be tender of the new-born lambs,
And gently in thy bosom bear.

3 The lion roaring for his prey,
With rav'ning wolves on every side,
Watch over them to tear and slay,
If found one moment from their Guide.

4 In safety lead thy little flock!
  From hell, the world, and sin, secure:
  And set their feet upon the rock,
  And make in thee their goings sure.
                                    C. Wesley.

408   L. M.
Praise on Earth, in Heaven. Rev. i. 5, 6.

NOW to the Lord, who makes us know
  The wonders of his dying love,
Be humble honors paid below,
  And strains of nobler praise above.

2 'Twas he who cleansed our foulest sins,
  And washed us in his richest blood:
'Tis he who makes us priests and kings,
  And brings us rebels near to God.

3 To Jesus, our atoning Priest.
  To Jesus, our superior King,
Be everlasting power confest—
  Let every tongue his glory sing.   *Watts.*

409 *The Mercy-seat.* Exod. xxv. 22. L. M.

FROM every stormy wind that blows,
  From every swelling tide of woes,
There is a calm, a sure retreat;
  'Tis found before the mercy-seat.

2 There is a place where Jesus sheds
  The oil of gladness on our heads—
A place of all on earth most sweet;
  It is the blood-bought mercy-seat.

3 There is a scene where spirits blend,
  Where friend holds fellowship with friend;
Though sunder'd far, by faith they meet
  Around one common mercy-seat.

PRAYER.

4 There, there, on eagle wings we soar,
And sin and sense molest no more;
And heaven comes down our souls to greet,
And glory crowns the mercy-seat. *Stowell.*

410   *United—though separate*   C. M.

BLEST be the dear uniting love,
  That will not let us part:
Our bodies may far off remove,
  We still are one in heart

2 Joined in one spirit to our Head,
  Where he appoints we go;
And still in Jesus' footsteps tread,
  And show his praise below.

3 O may we ever walk in him,
  And nothing know beside;
Nothing desire, nothing esteem,
  But Jesus crucified.

4 Closer and closer let us cleave
  To his beloved embrace;
Expect his fullness to receive,
  And grace to answer grace.

5 Partakers of the Saviour's grace,
  The same in mind and heart,
Nor joy, nor grief, nor time, nor place,
  Nor life, nor death can part. *C. Wesley.*

411   C. M.
"*Thy Will be done.*" Matt. vi. 10.

THY presence, Lord, the place shall fill,
  My heart shall be thy throne;
Thy holy, just, and perfect will,
  Shall in my flesh be done.

CHURCH ACTIVITIES.

2 I thank thee for the present grace,
   And now in hope rejoice,
In confidence to see thy face,
   And always hear thy voice.
3 I have the things I ask of thee,
   What shall I more require?
That still my soul may restless be,
   And only thee desire.
4 Thy only will be done not mine,
   But make me, Lord, thy home;
Come as thou wilt, I that resign,
   But O, my Jesus, come!   *C. Wesley.*

412   *Lord teach us to pray.* Luke xi. 1. C. M.

LORD, teach thy servants how to pray
   With reverence and with fear:
Though dust and ashes, yet we may,
   We must to thee draw near.
2 We come, then, God of grace, to thee;
   Give broken, contrite hearts;
Give—what thine eyes delight to see—
   Truth in the inward parts.
3 Give deep humility; the sense
   Of godly sorrow give;
A strong, desiring confidence
   To see thy face and live.
4 Give faith in that one sacrifice
   Which can for sin atone;
To cast our hopes, to fix our eyes,
   On Christ, and Christ alone. *Montgomery.*

413   *New Year's Day.*   C. M.

SING to the great Jehovah's praise!
   All praise to him belongs,

PRAYER.

Who kindly lengthens out our days,
  Demands our choicest songs:
His providence hath brought us through
  Another various year;
We all with vows and anthems new
  Before our God appear.

2 Father, thy mercies past we own,
  Thy still continued care:
To thee presenting, through thy Son,
  Whate'er we have or are:
Our lips and lives shall gladly show
  The wonders of thy love,
While on in Jesus' steps we go
  To seek thy face above.

3 Our residue of days or hours,
  Thine, wholly thine, shall be;
And all our consecrated powers
  A sacrifice to thee;
Till Jesus in the clouds appear
  To saints on earth forgiv'n,
And bring the grand sabbatic year,
  The jubilee of heav'n.   *C. Wesley.*

414   *Winter.*   Psalm cxlvii.   C. M.

WITH songs and honors sounding loud,
  Address the Lord on high:
Over the heavens he spreads his cloud,
  And waters veil the sky.

2 His steady counsels change the face
  Of the declining year:
He bids the sun cut short his race,
  And wintry days appear.

3 His hoary frost, his fleecy snow,
  Descend and clothe the ground;

281

The liquid streams forbear to flow,
In icy fetters bound.

4 When, from his dreadful stores on high,
He pours the sounding hail,
The wretch that dares his God defy
Shall find his courage fail.

5 The changing wind, the flying cloud,
Obey his mighty word;
With songs and honors sounding loud,
Praise ye the sov'reign Lord. *Watts.*

115 *End of the year.* C. M.

AND now, my soul, another year
Of thy short life is past;
I cannot long continue here,
And this may be my last.

2 Awake, my soul! with utmost care
Thy true condition learn:
What are thy hopes? how sure? how fair?
What is thy great concern?

3 Behold, another year begins!
Set out afresh for heaven;
Seek pardon for thy former sins,
In Christ so freely given.

4 Devoutly yield thyself to God,
And on his grace depend;
With zeal pursue the heav'nly road,
Nor doubt a happy end. *Browne.*

416 *Close of the year.* C. M.

AWAKE, ye saints, and raise your eyes,
And raise your voices high:

PRAYER.

Awake, and praise that sov'reign love
That shows salvation nigh.

2 On all the wings of time it flies,
Each moment brings it near,
Then welcome, each declining day!
Welcome, each closing year!

3 Ye wheels of nature, speed your course;
Ye mortal powers, decay;
Fast as ye bring the night of death,
Ye bring eternal day. *Doddridge.*

417 *Morning: Confident security.* C. M.

ON thee, each morning, O my God,
My waking thoughts attend;
In thee are founded all my hopes,—
In thee my wishes end.

2 My soul, in pleasing wonder lost,
Thy boundless love surveys;
And, fired with grateful zeal, prepares
A sacrifice of praise.

3 God leads me through the maze of sleep,
And brings me safe to light;
And, with the same paternal care,
Conducts my steps till night.

4 When ev'ning slumbers press mine eyes,
With his protection blest,
In peace and safety I commit
My wearied limbs to rest.

5 My spirit, in his hand secure,
Fears no approaching ill;
For, whether waking or asleep,
The Lord is with me still. *Knapp.*

SECTION XV.—Continued.

Christian Activities.

ERECTION AND CONSECRATION OF CHURCHES

418   *Dedication.*   L. M.

AND will the great, eternal God,
 On earth establish his abode?
And will he, from his radiant throne,
Avow our temple for his own?

2 We bring the tribute of our praise;
And sing that condescending grace,
Which to our notes will lend an ear,
And call us sinful mortals near.

3 These walls we to thy honor raise,
Long may they echo to thy praise,
And thou, descending, fill the place
With choicest tokens of thy grace.

4 And in the great, decisive day,
When God the nations shall survey,
May it before the world appear
That crowds were born to glory here!
                              Doddridge.

419   *A House for God.*   L. M.

WHERE shall I go to seek and find
 A habitation for our God?
A dwelling for th' Eternal Mind
Among the sons of flesh and blood?

2 The God of Jacob chose the hill
Of Zion for his ancient rest;

And Zion is his dwelling still;
His church is with his presence blest.

3 Here will he meet the hungry poor,
And fill their souls with living bread;
Here sinners, waiting at his door,
With sweet provision shall be fed.

4 "Here will I fix my gracious throne,
And reign forever," saith the Lord;
"Here shall my power and love be known,
And blessings shall attend my word."

Watts.

420 *Dedication.* L. M.

BEHOLD thy temple, God of grace,
The house that we have rear'd for thee,
Regard it as thy resting-place,
And fill it with thy majesty.

2 When from its altars shall arise
Joint supplications to thy name,
Deign to accept the sacrifice.
Thyself our answ'ring God proclaim.

3 And when from hence the voice of praise
Shall lift its triumphs to thy throne,
Show thy acceptance of our lays,
By making all thy glory known.

4 When here thy ministers shall stand,
To speak what thou shalt bid them say,
Maintain thy cause with thine own hand,
And give thy truth a winning way

5 Now, therefore, O our God, arise!
In this thy resting-place appear,
And let thy people's longing eyes
Behold thee fix thy dwelling here. *Palmer.*

421 L. M.
God's Earthly House. 1 Kings viii. 13.

HERE, in thy name, eternal God,
    We build this earthly house for thee,
O, choose it for thy fix'd abode,
    And guard it long from error free.

2 Here, when thy people seek thy face,
    And dying sinners pray to live,
Hear thou, in heaven, thy dwelling-place,
    And when thou hearest, Lord, forgive.

3 Here, when thy messengers proclaim
    The blessed gospel of thy Son,
Still by the pow'r of his great name
    Be mighty signs and wonders done.

4 But will, indeed, Jehovah deign
    Here to abide, no transient guest?
Here will our great Redeemer reign,
    And here the Holy Spirit rest?

5 Thy glory never hence depart:
    Yet choose not, Lord, this house alone;
Thy kingdom come to every heart;
    In every bosom fix thy throne. *Montgomery.*

422 8s, 7s.

GOD of thunder and the lightning
    Cloth'd in majesty divine,
To thy feet we bring this tribute
    Lord accept this house as thine.

2 To thy name, O Lord Jehovah,
    We this temple dedicate;
Lord receive this humble tribute,
    Sanctify it. 'arly, late.

3 Send thy Spirit, Lord from heav'n.
    Consecrate its sacred halls;

ERECTION AND CONSECRATION.

   Let thy ever biding presence
     Dwell within these humble walls.
4 Here may thousands hear thy gospel,
     Preach'd in love and power divine,
   While the glitt'ring choirs of heav'n
     Swell thy upper courts sublime.
5 Here may sinners be converted,
     While we sing our Saviour's praise;
   May the deaf, the halt, the blinded,
     Now their Ebenezer raise. *H. M. Turner.*

423   *Dedication.*   H. M.

GOD of thine Israel true,
    Their pillar, shield, and rock,
Who, all the desert through,
    Didst lead them like a flock;
In this our sanctuary dwell,
Thou glorious, felt, invisible!

2 That holy peace shed down,
    The world can never give;
Thy truth with triumph crown,
    Command the dead to live;
And fill this consecrated place
With living trophies of thy grace.

3 Great Shepherd of thy flock,
    Our glorious leader be;
Our pillar, shield, and rock,
    Till the fair land we see:
Ruler of heaven's eternal sphere,
Be thou the guardian glory here!
             G. Robinson.

424   *Invoking God's Presence.*   H. M.

GREAT King of glory, come,
    And with thy favor crown

This temple as thy home,
This people as thine own
Beneath this roof, O deign to show
How God can dwell with men below

2   Here may thine ears attend
   Our interceding cries,
And grateful praise ascend,
   Like incense, to the skies:
Here may thy word melodious sound,
And spread celestial joys around.

3   Here may our unborn sons
   And daughters sound thy praise,
And shine, like polished stones
   Through long-succeeding days:
Here, Lord, display thy saving power,
While temples stand and men adore.

4   Here may the listening throng
   Receive thy truth in love:
Here Christians join the song
   Of seraphim above;
Till all, who humbly seek thy face,
Rejoice in thy abounding grace.
                    Benjamin Francis

425   *I have put my name there forever.*   7s,
         1 Kings ix. 3.

LORD of hosts, to thee we raise
   Here a house of prayer and praise,
Thou thy people's hearts prepare
Here to meet for praise and prayer.

2 Let the living here be fed
With thy word, the heavenly bread:
Here, in hope of glory blest,
May the dead be laid to rest;—

3 Here to thee a temple stand,
  While the sea shall gird the land;
  Here reveal thy mercy sure,
  While the sun and moon endure.
4 Hallelujah!—earth and sky
  To the joyful sound reply;
  Hallelujah!—hence ascend
  Prayer and praise till time shall end.
  Montgomery.

426   *Sinai Tabor, Calvary.*   7s.

WHEN on Sinai's top I see
  God descend, in majesty,
To proclaim his holy law,
All my spirit sinks with awe.

2 When, in ecstasy sublime,
  Tabor's glorious steep I climb,
  At the too transporting light,
  Darkness rushes o'er my sight.

3 When on Calvary I rest,
  God, in flesh made manifest,
  Shines in my Redeemer's face,
  Full of beauty, truth, and grace.

4 Here I would forever stay,
  Weep and gaze my soul away;
  Thou art heaven on earth to me,
  Lovely, mournful Calvary.   *Montgomery.*

427   *Psalm cxxxii. 8, 15.*   C. M.

ARISE, O King of grace, arise,
  And enter to thy rest!
Lo! thy church waits, with longing eyes,
  Thus to be own'd and bless'd.

2 Enter, with all thy glorious train,
  Thy Spirit and thy word:

CHRISTIAN ACTIVITIES.

All that the ark did once contain
Could no such grace afford.

3 Here, mighty God, accept our vows;
Here let thy praise be spread:
Bless the provisions of thy house,
And fill thy poor with bread. *Watts*

428   *God dwelling among men.*   C. M.
(2 Chron. vi. 18.)

WILL God in very deed descend,
And dwell with men below?
An ear to mortal worship lend?
To us his glory show?

2 While heaven's exalted spheres resound
With hymns which angels sing,
Will God in mercy so abound,
T' accept the praise we bring?

3 Allow'd within thy courts to meet,
Thy presence we implore;
Smile on us from thy mercy-seat,
And we desire no more.

4 Here let thy gospel be declar'd;
Here make thy power be known;
May every heart, by grace prepar'd,
Be the Redeemer's throne.

5 Here make thyself a glorious name,
And form us for thy praise;
Thy promis'd presence, Lord, we claim,
And supplicate thy grace. *Shepherd's Col.*

429   *Divine blessing solicited.*   C. M.

TO thee this temple we devote,
Our Father and our God;
Accept it thine, and seal it now
Thy Spirit's blest abode.

ERECTION AND CONSECRATION.

2 Here may the prayer of faith ascend,
    The voice of praise arise;
    O, may each lowly service prove
    Accepted sacrifice.

3 Here may the sinner learn his guilt,
    And weep before his Lord;
    Here, pardoned, sing a Saviour's love,
    And here his vows record.

4 Here may affliction dry the tear,
    And learn to trust in God,
    Convinced it is a Father smites,
    And love that guides the rod.

5 Peace be within these sacred walls;
    Prosperity be here;
    Long smile upon thy people, Lord,
    And evermore be near.   *J. R. Scott.*

430   S. M.
Hymn for the Consecration of Churches.

FATHER of life, descend!
    Within this sacred fane,
Before thy throne our spirits bend,
    O here come down and reign!

2 Thou Son of God, descend!
    And consecrate this place,
O make it Lord, till time shall end,
    The temple of thy grace!

3 Spirit of light, descend!
    And shed thy glory here,
Thine unction with our worship blend,
    And waft to heaven our prayer.

4 There let the gospel sound
    Its tones of peace and love;

Spread holiness and life around,
And lift our hopes above.

5 Give to the blind their sight,
Bind up the broken heart,
The erring spirit guide aright,
And strength to all impart.
Bishop Payne.

431   *Psalm* xlviii.   S. M.

GREAT is the Lord our God,
And let his praise be great:
He makes his churches his abode,
His most delightful seat.

2 These temples of his grace,
How beautiful they stand!
The honors of our native place
And bulwarks of our land.

3 In Sion God is known
A refuge in distress:
How bright has his salvation shone
Through all her palaces.

4 In every new distress
We'll to his house repair;
We'll think upon his wondrous grace,
And seek deliv'rance there.   *Watts.*

MISSIONS.

432   *"Come over—and help us."*   7, 6, 7, 6.

FROM Greenland's icy mountains,
From India's coral strand;
Where Afric's sunny fountains
Roll down their golden sand;

MISSIONS.

From many an ancient river,
  From many a palmy plain,
They call us to deliver
  Their land from error's chain.

2 What though the spicy breezes
  Blow soft o'er Ceylon's isle,
Though every prospect pleases,
  And only man is vile:
In vain with lavish kindness
  The gifts of God are strown;
The heathen in his blindness
  Bows down to wood and stone.

3 Shall we, whose souls are lighted
  With wisdom from on high,
Shall we to men benighted
  The lamp of life deny?
Salvation! O salvation!
  The joyful sound proclaim,
Till earth's remotest nation
  Has learned Messiah's name.

4 Waft, waft, ye winds, his story,
  And you, ye waters, roll,
Till, like a sea of glory,
  It spreads from pole to pole:
Till o'er our ransom'd nature,
  The Lamb for sinners slain,
Redeemer, King, Creator,
  In bliss returns to reign. *Bishop Heber.*

135. *Success.* 7s.

SEE how great a flame aspires,
  Kindled by a spark of grace!
Jesus' love the nations fires,
  Sets the kingdoms on a blaze.

To bring fire on earth he came;
Kindled in some hearts it is:
O that all might catch the flame,
All partake the glorious bliss!

2 When he first the work begun,
Small and feeble was his day:
Now the word doth swiftly run,
Now it wins its wid'ning way:
More and more it spreads and grows
Ever mighty to prevail;
Sin's strongholds it now o'erthrows,
Shakes the trembling gates of hell.

3 Saw ye not the cloud arise,
Little as a human hand?
Now it spreads along the skies,
Hangs o'er all the thirsty land;
Lo! the promise of a shower
Drops already from above;
But the Lord will shortly pour
All the Spirit of his love. *C. Wesley.*

434 *The Song of Jubilee.* 7s

HARK! the song of Jubilee,
Loud—as mighty thunders roar:
Or the fullness of the sea,
When it breaks upon the shore.—

2 Hallelujah! for the Lord,
God Omnipotent, shall reign:
Hallelujah! let the word
Echo round the earth and main.

3 Hallelujah! hark! the sound,
From the centre to the skies,
Wakes, above, beneath, around,
All creation's harmonies!

MISSIONS.

4 See Jehovah's banners furl'd,
    Sheath'd his sword! he speaks—'tis done,
And the kingdoms of this world
    Are the kingdoms of his Son.

5 He shall reign from pole to pole
    With illimitable sway:
He shall reign, when, like a scroll,
    Yonder heav'ns have pass'd away!

6 Then the end—beneath his rod,
    Man's last enemy shall fall:
Hallelujah! Christ in God,
    God in Christ, is All in All. *Montgomery.*

435   *Missions.*   7's.

HASTEN, Lord, the glorious time,
    When, beneath Messiah's sway,
Every nation, every clime,
    Shall the gospel call obey.

2 Mightiest kings his power shall own,
    Heathen tribes his name adore:
Satan and his host, o'erthrown,
    Bound in chains, shall hurt no more.

3 Then shall wars and tumults cease,
    Then be banish'd grief and pain;
Righteousness, and joy, and peace,
    Undisturb'd shall ever reign.

4 Bless we, then, our gracious Lord,
    Ever praise his glorious name;
All his mighty acts record,
    All his wondrous love proclaim.
    Lincoln.

CHRISTIAN ACTIVITIES.

436 6s & 4s, or 10s.
They call beyond the Sea.

OVER the ocean wave,
    Far, far away,
There the poor heathen live,
    Waiting for day;
Groping in ignorance,
    Dark as the night,
No blessed Bible to
    Give them the light.

Pity them, pity them,
    Christians at home,
Haste with the bread of life,
    Hasten and come.

2 Here in this happy land
    We have the light
Shining from God's own word,
    Free, pure, and bright;
Shall we not send to them
    Bibles to read,
Teachers, and preachers, and
    All that they need?

3 Then, while the mission ships
    Glad tidings bring,
List! as the heathen band
    Joyfully sing,
"Over the ocean wave,
    O see them come,
Bringing the bread of life,
    Guiding us home."

Unknown.

MISSIONS.

437 *Who will go to-day?* 8s & 7s.

HARK! the voice of Jesus crying—
"Who will go and work to-day?
Fields are white, and harvest waiting;
Who will bear the sheaves away?"
Loud and strong the Master calleth,
Rich reward he offers thee;
Who will answer, gladly saying,
"Here am I; send me, send me!"

2 If you cannot cross the ocean,
And the heathen lands explore,
You can find the heathen nearer,
You can help them at your door.
If you cannot give your thousands,
You can give the widow's mite;
And the least you do for Jesus,
Will be precious in his sight.

3 If you cannot be the watchman
Standing high on Zion's wall,
Pointing out the path to heaven,
Offering life and peace to all;—
With your prayers and with your bounties
You can do what heaven demands;
You can be like faithful Aaron,
Holding up the prophet's hands.

4 Let none hear you idly saying,
"There is nothing I can do,"
While the souls of men are dying,
And the Master calls for you.
Take the task he gives you gladly,
Let his work your pleasure be;
Answer quickly when he calleth,
"Here am I; send me, send me!"

Dan'l March.

438   *Dawn of the Millennium.*   11s & 10s.

HAIL to the brightness of Zion's glad morning;
Joy to the lands that in darkness have lain;
Hush'd be the accents of sorrow and mourning;
Zion in triumph begins her mild reign.

2 Hail to the brightness of Zion's glad morning;
Long by the prophets of Isr'el foretold;
Hail to the millions from bondage returning;
Gentiles and Jews the blest vision behold.

3 Lo, in the desert rich flowers are springing;
Streams ever copious are gliding along;
Loud from the mountain tops echoes are ringing;
Wastes rise in verdure, and mingle in song.

4 See from all lands, from the isles of the ocean,
Praise to Jehovah ascending on high;
Fall'n are the engines of war and commotion,
Shouts of salvation are rending the sky.
Spir. Songs.

439   *Responding to the Appeal.*   C. M.

THE nations call! from sea to sea
Extends the thrilling cry,
"Come over, Christians, if there be,
And help us, ere we die."

2 Our hearts, O Lord, the summons feel
Let hand with heart combine,
And answer to the world's appeal
By giving "that is thine."

3 Say to thy gifted servants, "Speed!
Behold the world your field;"

MISSIONS.

Say to the gold, "The Lord hath need,"
Till hoarded treasures yield.

4 Say to the slumb'ring soul, "Awake!
Ere wanes thy noon away;
Lo! soon I come th' account to take,
Ye stewards of a day."

5 Saviour, forgive; asham'd we lie,
Thy gracious will we know:
Behold, while we delay, they die!
Bid, bid us send, or go. *Gilbert.*

440 *Glory of the latter days.* Isa. ii. 1–5. C. M.

BEHOLD, the mountain of the Lord
In latter days shall rise
Above the mountains and the hills,
And draw the wond'ring eyes.

2 To this the joyful nations round,
All tribes and tongues, shall flow:
"Up to the hill of God," they say,
"And to his house, we'll go."

3 The beam that shines on Zion's hill
Shall lighten every land:
The King who reigns in Zion's towers
Shall all the world command.

4 Among the nations he shall judge;
His judgments truth shall guide;
His sceptre shall protect the just,
And quell the sinner's pride.

5 Come, then, O house of Jacob! come
To worship at his shrine;
And, walking in the light of God,
With holy beauties shine. *Logan.*

441 *Missions to the Heathen.* L. M.

BEHOLD, the heathen waits to know
    The joy the gospel will bestow;
The exiled captive to receive
The freedom Jesus has to give.

2 " Come, let us, with a grateful heart,
In this blest labor share a part;
Our prayers and offerings gladly bring
To aid the triumphs of our King."

3 Our hearts exult in songs of praise,
That we have seen these latter days,
When our Redeemer shall be known
Where Satan long hath held his throne.

4 Where'er his hand hath spread the skies,
Sweet incense to his name shall rise,
And slave and freeman, Greek and Jew,
By sovereign grace be formed anew. *Voke.*

442 *Missionaries encouraged.* L. M.

YE Christian heralds, go, proclaim
    Salvation in Immanuel's name;
To distant climes the tidings bear,
And plant the rose of Sharon there.

2 He'll shield you with a wall of fire,
With holy zeal your hearts inspire,
Bid raging winds their fury cease,
And calm the savage breast to peace.

3 And when our labors all are o'er,
Then we shall meet to part no more—
Meet, wi h the blood-bought throng to fall,
And crown the Saviour, Lord of all.

Winchell's Sel.

MISSIONS.

443   *Hebrew Missionaries.*   S. M.

ALMIGHTY God of love,
    Set up th' attracting sign,
And summon whom thou dost approve
    For messengers Divine.

2 From favor'd Abrah'm's seed
    The new apostles choose,
In isles and continents to spread
    The dead-reviving news.

3 O send thy servants forth,
    To call the Hebrews home!
From East, and West, and South, and North,
    Let all the wand'rers come:

4 With Israel's myriads seal'd,
    Let all the nations meet,
And show the mystery fulfill'd,
    The family complete!   *C. Wesley.*

444   *God giveth the Increase.*   S. M.

LORD, if at thy command
    The word of life we sow,
Watered by thy almighty hand,
    The seed shall surely grow.

2 The virtue of thy grace
    A large increase shall give,
And multiply the faithful race,
    Who to thy glory live.

3 Now, then, the ceaseless shower
    Of gospel-blessings send,
And let the soul-converting power
    Thy ministers attend.

4 On multitudes confer
　The heart-renewing love,
　And by the joy of grace prepare
　For fuller joys above.　　*C. Wesley.*

445　　*The acceptable year.*　　8s, 7s, & 4s.

O'ER the gloomy hills of darkness,
　　Look, my soul, be still and gaze;
See the promises advancing
　To a glorious day of grace;
　　Blessed jubilee,
　Let thy glorious morning dawn.

2 Let the dark, benighted pagan,
　　Let the rude barbarian, see
That divine and glorious conquest,
　Once obtain'd on Calvary:
　　Let the gospel,
　Loud resound, from pole to pole.

3 Kingdoms wide, that sit in darkness,
　　Grant them, Lord, the glorious light;
Now, from eastern coast to western,
　May the morning chase the night:
　　Let redemption,
　Freely purchas'd, win the day.

4 Fly abroad, thou mighty gospel,
　　Win and conquer—never cease:
May thy lasting, wide dominions,
　Multiply and still increase:
　　Sway thy sceptre,
　Saviour, all the world around.　*P. Williams.*

446　　　　　　　　　　　　8 & 7.
Collection for the spread of the Gospel.

WITH my substance I will honor
　　My Redeemer and my Lord;

MISSIONS.

Were ten thousand worlds my manor,
All were nothing to his word.
2 While the heralds of salvation
His abounding grace proclaim;
Let his friends of every station,
Gladly join to spread his fame.
3 May his kingdom be promoted;
May the world the Saviour know:
Be my all to him devoted;
To my Lord my all I owe.

4 Praise the Saviour, all ye nations;
Praise him, all ye hosts above;
Shout, with joyful acclamations,
His divine—victorious love. *Francis.*

447 *Fields white to the harvest.* 8, 7, & 4.

WHO but thou, almighty Spirit,
Can the heathen world reclaim?
Men may preach, but till thou favor,
Heathens will be still the same:
Mighty Spirit!
Witness to the Saviour's name.
2 Thou hast promised by thy prophets
Glorious light in latter days:
Come, and bless bewildered nations,
Change our prayers and tears to praise:
Promised Spirit!
Round the world diffuse thy rays.
3 All our hopes, and prayers, and labors
Must be vain without thine aid:
But thou wilt not disappoint us,
All is true that thou hast said:
Faithful Spirit!
O'er the world thine influence shed
Unknown.

CHRISTIAN ACTIVITIES.

448   8, 7.
So shall he sprinkle many Nations.—Isa. lii. 15.

SAVIOUR, sprinkle many nations,
   Fruitful let thy sorrows be;
By thy pains and consolations,
   Draw the Gentiles unto thee:
Of thy cross the wondrous story,
   Be it to the nations told;
Let them see thee in thy glory,
   And thy mercy manifold.

2 Far and wide, though all unknowing,
   Pants for thee each mortal breast;
Human tears for thee are flowing,
   Human hearts in thee would rest;
Thirsting, as for dews of even,
   As the new-mown grass for rain,
Thee they seek, as God of heaven,
   Thee, as Man for sinners slain.

3 Saviour, lo! the isles are waiting,
   Stretched the hand, and strained the sight,
For thy Spirit, new creating
   Love's pure flame and wisdom's light;
Give the word, and of the preacher
   Speed the foot, and touch the tongue,
Till on earth by every creature
   Glory to the Lamb be sung.
                       A. Cleveland Coxe.

449   L. M.
The missionary charged and encouraged.

GO, messenger of peace and love,
   To peop'e plunged in shades of night,
Like angels sent from fields above,
   Be thine to shed celestial light.

MISSIONS.

2 On barren rock and desert isle,
　Go, bid the rose of Sharon bloom;
Till arid wastes around thee smile,
　And bear to heaven a sweet perfume.

3 Go to the hungry—food impart;
　To paths of peace the wanderer guide;
And lead the thirsty, panting heart
　Where streams of living water glide.

4 Go, bid the bright and morning star
　From Bethlehem's plains resplendent shine,
And, piercing through the gloom afar,
　Shed heav'nly light and love divine.

5 O, faint not in the day of toil,
　When harvest waits the reaper's hand;
Go, gather in the glorious spoil,
　And joyous in his presence stand.

6 Thy love a rich reward sha'l find
　From him who sits enthron'd on high;
For they who turn the erring mind
　Shall shine like stars above the sky.
　　　　　　　　　　A. Balfour.

450　*Approaching Millennium.*　L. M.

BEHOLD the expected time draw near,
　The shades disperse, the dawn appear;
Behold the wilderness assume
The beauteous tints of Eden's bloom.

2 The untaught heathen waits to know
The joy the gospel will bestow;
The exiled captive, to receive
The freedom Jesus has to give.

3 Come, let us with a grateful heart,
In the blest labor share a part;

Our pray'rs and off'rings gladly bring
To aid the triumphs of our King.

3 Invite the world to come and prove
A Saviour's condescending love;
And humbly fall before His feet,
Assured they shall acceptance meet. *Coxe.*

451   "*Watchman, what of the night?*"   7s.

WATCHMAN, tell us of the night,
    What its signs of promise are:
Trav'ller, o'er yon mountain height,
    See that glory-beaming star.
Watchman, does its beauteous ray
    Aught of hope or joy foretell?
Trav'ller, yes; it brings the day,
    Promis'd day of Israel.

2 Watchman, tell us of the night:
    Higher yet that star ascends.
Trav'ller, blessedness and light,
    Peace and truth, its course portends.
Watchman, will its beams alone
    Gild the spot that gave them birth?
Trav'ller, ages are its own,
    See! it bursts o'er all the earth.

3 Watchman, tell us of the night,
    For the morning seems to dawn,
Trav'ller, darkness takes its flight,
    Doubt and terror are withdrawn.
Watchman, let thy wand'rings cease;
    Hie thee to thy quiet home.
Trav'ller, lo! the Prince of peace,
    Lo! the Son of God is come. *Bowring*

MISSIONS.

452 *Praying for the Kingdom of God.* S. M.
Phil. ii. 10, 11.

O THOU whom we adore!
   To bless our earth again,
Assume thine own almighty power,
   And o'er the nations reign.

2 The world's Desire and Hope,
   All power to thee is given;
Now set the last great empire up,
   Eternal Lord of heaven!

3 A gracious Saviour, thou
   Wilt all thy creatures bless;
And every knee to thee shall bow,
   And every tongue confess.

4 According to thy word,
   Now be thy grace revealed;
And with the knowledge of the Lord,
   Let all the earth be filled. *C. Wesley.*

453 *Make all things new.* Rev. xxii. 20. S. M.

COME, Lord, and tarry not!
   Bring the long-looked for day;
Oh, why these years of waiting here,
   These ages of delay?

2 Come for thy saints still wait;
   Daily ascends their sigh;
The Spirit and the Bride say, Come!
   Dost thou not hear the cry?

3 Come, for creation groans,
   Impatient of thy stay,
Worn out with these long years of ill,
   These ages of delay.

4 Come, and make all things new,
   Build up this ruined earth,

Restore our faded paradise,—
Creation's second birth.

5 Come and begin thy reign
Of everlasting peace;
Come, take the kingdom to thyself,
Great King of Righteousness. *Bonar.*

454 *"Revive thy work."* Hab. iii. 2. S. M.

O LORD, thy work revive,
In Zion's gloomy hour,
And make her dying graces live
By thy restoring power.

2 Awake thy chosen few
To fervent, earnest prayer;
Again may they their vows renew,
Thy blessèd presence share.

3 Thy Spirit then will speak
Through lips of feeble clay,
And hearts of adamant will break,
And rebels will obey.

4 Lord, lend thy gracious ear;
Oh, listen to our cry;
Oh, come and bring salvation here,
Our hopes on thee rely. *Mrs. Brown.*

455 *Oh, for the happy hour.* Lam. i. 4. S. M.

OH, for the happy hour
When God will hear our cry,
And send, with a reviving power,
His Spirit from on high.

2 We meet, we sing, we pray,
We listen to the word,
In vain:—we see no cheering ray,
No cheering voice is heard.

LOVE FEASTS.

3 While many crowd thy house,
How few, around thy board,
Meet to recount their solemn vows,
And bless thee as their Lord!

4 Thou, thou alone, canst give
Thy gospel sure success;
Canst bid the dying sinner live
Anew in holiness.

5 Come, then, with power divine,
Spirit of life and love!
Then shall this people all be thine,
This church like that above. *Bethune.*

LOVE FEASTS.

456   *With one accord.*   - 7s.

COME, and let us sweetly join,
Christ to praise in hymns divine!
Give we all, with one accord,
Glory to our common Lord;
Hands, and hearts, and voices, raise;
Sing as in the ancient days;
Antedate the joys above;
Celebrate the feast of love.

2 Strive we, in affection strive.
Let the purer flame revive,
Such as in the martyrs glow'd,
Dying champions for their God.
We for Christ, our Master, stand,
Lights in a benighted land:
We our dying Lord confess,
We are Jesus' witnesses.

CHRISTIAN ACTIVITIES.

3 Witnesses that Christ hath died:
We with him are crucified:
Christ hath burst the bands of death,
We his quick'ning Spirit breathe:
Christ is now gone up on high;
Thither all our wishes fly:
Sits at God's right hand above;
There with him we reign in love.
C. Wesley

457 *Unity, peace.* 7s.

COME, thou high and lofty Lord!
Lowly, meek incarnate Word:
Humbly stoop to earth again:
Come and visit abject man!
Jesus, dear expected guest,
Thou art bidden to the feast:
For thyself our hearts prepare:
Come, and sit, and banquet there!

2 Jesus, we thy promise claim:
We are met in thy great name:
In the midst do thou appear,
Manifest thy presence here!
Sanctify us, Lord, and bless!
Breathe thy Spirit, give thy peace!
Thou thyself within us move:
Make our feast a feast of love.

3 Make us all in thee complete;
Make us all for glory meet—
Meet t' appear before thy sight,
Partners with the saints in light.
Call, O call us each by name,
To the marriage of the Lamb:
Let us lean upon thy breast;
Love be there our endless feast. *C. Wesley.*

LOVE FEASTS.

458   *Fitly joined together.*   7s.

LET us join, ('tis God commands,)
   Let us join our hearts and hands;
Help to gain our calling's hope,
Build we each the other up:
Still forget the things behind,
Follow Christ in heart and mind;
Toward the mark unwearied press,
Seize the crown of righteousness.

2 Plead we thus for faith alone,
Faith which by our works is shown:
God it is who justifies,
Only faith the grace applies;
Active faith that lives within;
Conquers earth, and hell, and sin;
Sanctifies and makes us whole;
Forms the Saviour in the soul.

3 Let us for this faith contend;
Sure salvation is its end:
Heav'n already is begun,
Everlasting life is won:
Only let us persevere,
Till we see our Lord appear;
Never from the Rock remove,
Saved by faith, which works by love.
                          C. Wesley.

459   *Of one heart and mind.*   7s.

JESUS, Lord, we look to thee;
   Let us in thy name agree;
Show thyself the Prince of peace;
Bid our jars forever cease.

2 By thy reconciling love,
Every stumbling-block remove;

CHRISTIAN ACTIVITIES.

Each to each unite, endear,
Come, and spread thy banner here.

3 Make us of one heart and mind,
Courteous, pitiful, and kind,
Lowly, meek, in thought and word,
Altogether like our Lord.

4 Let us for each other care,
Each the other's burden bear;
To thy Church the pattern give,
Show how true believers live.

5 Free from anger and from pride,
Let us thus in God abide;
All the depths of love express,
All the heights of holiness.

6 Let us then with joy remove
To the family above;
On the wings of angels fly;
Show how true believers die.
Charles Wesley.

460 *Brotherly Love.* C. M.

HOW sweet and heav'nly is the sight,
When those who love the Lord
In one another's peace delight,
And so fulfil his word!

2 Oh! may we feel each brother's sigh,
And with him bear a part;
May sorrows flow from eye to eye,
And joy from heart to heart.

3 Let love, in one delightful stream,
Through every bosom flow;
Let union sweet, and dear esteem,
In every action, glow.

LOVE FEASTS.

4 Love is the golden chain that binds
   The happy souls above;
And he's an heir of heaven, who finds
   His bosom glow with love.   *Swain.*

461   *Love to Christ's Disciples.*   C. M.

LORD, thou on earth didst love thine own;
   Didst love them to the end;
Oh! still from thy celestial throne,
   Let gifts of love descend.

2 As thou for us didst stoop so low,
   Warm'd by love's holy flame,
So let our deeds of kindness flow
   To all who bear thy name.

3 One blessed fellowship in love
   Thy living church should stand,
Till, faultless, she at last above
   Shall shine at thy right hand.

4 Oh! glorious day when she the bride,
   With her dear Lord appears;
When robed in beauty at his side,
   She shall forget her tears.   *Ray Palmer.*

462   *Mutual aid.*   C. M.

TRY us, O God, and search the ground
   Of every sinful heart:
Whate'er of sin in us is found,
   O bid it all depart!

2 When to the right or left we stray,
   Leave us not comfortless;
But guide our feet into the way
   Of everlasting peace.

3 Help us to help each other, Lord,
   Each other's cross to bear:

CHRISTIAN ACTIVITIES.

Let each his friendly aid afford,
And feel his brother's care.

4 Help us to build each other up,
Our little stock improve:
Increase our faith, confirm our hope,
And perfect us in love.

5 Up into thee, our living Head,
Let us in all things grow;
Till thou hast made us free indeed,
And spotless here below.

6 Then, when the mighty work is wrought,
Receive thy ready bride:
Give us in heaven a happy lot
With all the sanctified.   *C. Wesley.*

463 *Christians drawn with cords of Love.* C. M.

MY God, what gentle cords are thine,
How soft and yet how strong!
While pow'r, and truth, and love combine
To draw our souls along.

2 Thou saw'st us crush'd beneath the yoke
Of Satan and of sin;
Thy hand the iron bondage broke,
Our sinful hearts to win.

3 The guilt of twice ten thousand sins
One offering takes away;
And grace, when first the war begins,
Secures the crowning day.   *Doddridge.*

464   *Christian Love.*   C. M.

HAPPY the heart where graces reign,
Where love inspires the breast;
Love is the brightest of the train,
And strengthens all the rest.

LOVE FEASTS.

2 Knowledge, alas! 'tis all in vain,
  And all in vain our fear;
Our stubborn sins will fight and reign,
  If love be absent there.

3 'Tis love that makes our cheerful feet
  In swift obedience move;
The devils know and tremble too,
  But devils cannot love.

4 This is the grace that lives and sings,
  When faith and hope shall cease;
'Tis this shall strike our joyful strings,
  In the sweet realms of bliss. *Watts.*

465 — *Safety in Union.* C. M.

JESUS, great Shepherd of the sheep,
  To thee for help we fly;
Thy little flock in safety keep,
  For O, the wolf is nigh!

2 He comes, of hellish malice full,
  To scatter, tear, and slay;
He seizes every straggling soul
  As his own lawful prey.

3 Us into thy protection take,
  And gather with thine arm;
Unless the fold we first forsake,
  The wolf can never harm.

4 We laugh to scorn his cruel power
  While by our Shepherd's side;
The sheep he never can devour,
  Unless he first divide.

5 O do not suffer him to part
  The souls that here agree;

But make us of one mind and heart,
And keep us one in thee.

6 Together let us sweetly live,
Together let us die;
And each a starry crown receive,
And reign above the sky. *Charles Wesley.*

SECTION XVI.

Funerals and other Occasions.

DEATH—THE JUDGMENT—HEAVEN.

466   *Brevity of Life.*   C. M.

THEE we adore, eternal Name!
   And humbly own to thee
How feeble is our mortal frame,
   What dying worms we be!

2 The year rolls round, and steals away
   The breath that first it gave:
Whate'er we do, where'er we be,
   We're trav'ling to the grave.

3 Dangers stand thick through all the ground,
   To push us to the tomb;
And fierce diseases wait around
   To hurry mortals home.

4 Great God! on what a slender thread,
   Hang everlasting things!
Th' eternal states of all the dead
   Upon life's feeble strings.

DEATH—THE JUDGMENT—HEAVEN.

5 Infinite joy, or endless woe,
    Attends on every breath;
And yet how unconcern'd we go
    Upon the brink of death!

6 Waken, O Lord, our drowsy sense,
    To walk this dang'rous road;
And if our souls be hurried hence
    May they be found with God! *Watts.*

467   *A Voice from the Tombs.*   C. M.

HARK! from the tombs a doleful sound,
    My ears attend the cry:
"Ye living men, come view the ground
    Where you must shortly lie.

2 "Princes, this clay must be your bed,
    In spite of all your towers:
The tall, the wise, the rev'rend head,
    Must lie as low as ours."

3 Great God! is this our certain doom!
    And are we still secure!
Still walking downward to the tomb,
    And yet prepar'd no more!

4 Grant us the power of quick'ning grace,
    To fit our souls to fly;
Then, when we drop this dying flesh,
    We'll rise above the sky. *Watts.*

468   *The day of Judgment.*   C M.

AND must I be to judgment brought
    And answer in that day
For every vain and idle thought,
    And every word I say?

2 Yes, every secret of my heart
    Shall shortly be made known,

FUNERALS AND OTHER OCCASIONS.

And I receive my just desert
For all that I have done.

3 How careful, then, ought I to live!
With what religious fear!
Who such a strict account must give
For my behavior here!

4 Thou awful Judge of quick and dead,
The watchful power bestow;
So shall I to my ways take heed,
To all I speak or do.

5 If now thou standest at the door,
O let me feel thee near!
And make my peace with God, before
I at thy bar appear. *C. Wesley.*

469 *The vain man warned.* C. M.

VAIN man, thy fond pursuits forbear;
Repent, thy end is nigh:
Death, at the farthest, can't be far:
O! think before thou die.

2 Reflect: thou hast a soul to save;
Thy sins, how high they mount!
What are thy hopes beyond the grave?
How stands that dark account?

3 Death enters, and there's no defense,
His time there's none can tell;
He'll in a moment call thee hence,
To heaven, or down to hell.

4 Thy flesh, perhaps thy greatest care,
Shall crawling worms consume:
But ah! destruction stops not there;
Sin kills beyond the tomb. *Joseph Hart.*

DEATH—THE JUDGMENT—HEAVEN.

470   *Eternal Death.*   C. M.

THAT awful day will surely come,
   Th' appointed hour makes haste,
When I must stand before my Judge
   And pass the solemn test.

2 Jesus, thou Source of all my joys,
   Thou Ruler of my heart,
How could I bear to hear thy voice
   Pronounce the sound, " Depart!"

3 The thunder of that awful word,
   Would so torment my ear,
'Twould tear my soul asunder, Lord,
   With most tormenting fear.

4 What, to be banished from my Lord,
   And yet forbid to die!
To linger in eternal pain,
   And death forever fly!

5 O wretched state of deep despair,
   To see my God remove,
And fix my doleful station where
   I must not taste his love!   *Watts.*

471 *The whole family in heaven and earth.* C. M.

COME, let us join our friends above,
   That have obtain'd the prize;
And on the eagle wings of love
   To joys celestial rise:
Let all the saints terrestrial sing,
   With those to glory gone;
For all the servants of our King,
   In earth and heaven, are one.

2 One family we dwell in him,
   One Church above, beneath,

Though now divided by the stream,
　The narrow stream of death.
One army of the living God,
　To his command we bow;
Part of his host have cross'd the flood,
　And part are crossing now.

3 Our spirits too shall quickly join,
　Like theirs with glory crown'd,
And shout to see our Captain's sign,
　To hear his trumpet sound.
O that we now might grasp our Guide!
　O that the word were given!
Come, Lord of hosts, the waves divide,
　And land us all in heaven!　*C. Wesley.*

472　　*The seat of Judgment.*　　S. M.

THOU Judge of quick and dead,
　Before whose bar severe,
With holy joy, or guilty dread,
　We all shall soon appear;
　Our caution'd souls prepare
　　For that tremendous day.
And fill us now with watchful care,
　And stir us up to pray:

2 To pray, and wait the hour,
　That awful hour unknown,
When, robed in majesty and power,
　Thou shalt from heaven come down,
　Th' immortal Son of man,
　　To judge the human race,
With all thy Father's dazzling train,
　With all thy glorious grace.

3 O may we thus be found,
　Obedient to his word;

Attentive to the trumpet's sound,
And looking for our Lord!
O may we thus insure
A lot among the blest;
And watch a moment to secure
An everlasting rest! *C. Wesley.*

473 *A house not made with hands.* S. M..
2 Cor. v. 1-9.

WE know, by faith we know,
If this vile house of clay,
This tabernacle, sink below,
In ruinous decay,
We have a house above,
Not made with mortal hands;
And firm as our Redeemer's love
That heavenly fabric stands.

2 It stands securely high,
Indissolubly sure;
Our glorious mansion in the sky
Shall evermore endure:
O were we enter'd there!
To perfect heaven restor'd!
O were we all caught up to share
The triumph of our Lord!

3 For this in faith we call;
For this we weep and pray:
O might the tabernacle fall!
O might we 'scape away!
Full of immortal hope,
We urge the restless strife,
And hasten to be swallow'd up
Of everlasting life. *C. Wesley.*

474   *The momentous question.*   S. M.

AND must this body die,
   This well-wrought frame decay?
And must these active limbs of mine
   Lie mould'ring in the clay!

2 Corruption, earth, and worms,
   Shall but refine this flesh,
Till my triumphant spirit comes
   To put it on afresh.

3 God my Redeemer lives,
   And ever from the skies
Looks down, and watches all my dust,
   Till he shall bid it rise.

4 Array'd in glorious grace
   Shall these vile bodies shine,
And every shape, and every face,
   Be heavenly and divine.

5 These lively hopes we owe,
   Lord, to thy dying love:
O may we bless thy grace below,
   And sing thy grace above!   *Watts.*

475   *The end of Life.*   S. M.

AND am I born to die?
   To lay this body down?
And must my trembling spirit fly
   Into a world unknown?
A land of deepest shade,
   Unpierced by human thought;
The dreary regions of the dead,
   Where all things are forgot!

2 Soon as from earth I go,
   What will become of me?

Eternal happiness or woe
  Must then my portion be!
Waked by the trumpet's sound,
  I from my grave shall rise;
And see the Judge with glory crown'd,
  And see the flaming skies.

3 How shall I leave my tomb—
  With triumph or regret?
A fearful or a joyful doom,
  A curse or blessing, meet?
Will angel bands convey
  Their brother to the bar?
Or devils drag my soul away
  To meet its sentence there? *C. Wesley.*

476 *Always rejoicing.* 8s and 6s.

HOW happy, gracious Lord, are we,
  Divinely drawn to follow thee!
Whose hours divided are
Betwixt the mount and multitude;
Our day is spent in doing good,
  Our night in praise and prayer.

2 With us no melancholy void,
No moment lingers unemployed,
  Or unimproved, below:
Our weariness of life is gone,
Who live to serve our God alone,
  And only thee to know.

3 The winter's night, the summer's day,
Glide imperceptibly away,
  Too short to sing thy praise;
Too few we find the happy hours,
And haste to join those heavenly powers
  In everlasting lays.

4 With all who chant thy name on high,
And, " Holy, holy, holy," cry,—
A bright, harmonious throng!
We long thy praises to repeat,
And ceaseless sing around thy seat
The new, eternal song. *Charles Wesley.*

477 *To be with Christ is far better.* 8s

O WHEN shall we sweetly remove,
O when shall we enter our rest,
Return to the Zion above,
The mother of spirits distressed!
That city of God the great King,
Where sorrow and death are no more,
But saints our Immanuel sing,
And cherub and seraph adore.

2 Not all the archangels can tell
The joys of that holiest place,
Where Jesus is pleased to reveal
The light of his heavenly face:
When, caught in the rapturous flame,
The sight beatific they prove,
And walk in the light of the Lamb,
Enjoying the beams of his love.

3 Thou know'st in the spirit of prayer
We long thy appearing to see,
Resigned to the burden we bear,
But longing to triumph with thee:
'Tis good at thy word to be here:
'Tis better in thee to be gone,
And see thee in glory appear,
And rise to a share in thy throne.
Charles Wesley.

DEATH—THE JUDGMENT—HEAVEN.

478 *Desiring to depart.* 8s.

I LONG to behold him arrayed
  With glory and light from above;
The King in his beauty displayed,
  His beauty of holiest love:
I languish and sigh to be there,
  Where Jesus hath fixed his abode;
O when shall we meet in the air,
  And fly to the mountain of God!

2 With him I on Zion shall stand,
  For Jesus hath spoken the word;
The breadth of Immanuel's land
  Survey by the light of my Lord:
But when, on thy bosom reclined,
  Thy face I am strengthened to see,
My fullness of rapture I find,
  My heaven of heavens in thee.

3 How happy the people that dwell
  Secure in the city above!
No pain the inhabitants feel,
  No sickness or sorrow shall prove.
Physician of souls, unto me
  Forgiveness and holiness give;
And then from the body set free,
  And then to the city receive.
                    Charles Wesley.

479 *Saints and angels round the throne.* 7s.

LIFT your eyes of faith, and see
  Saints and angels joined in one:
What a countless company
  Stand before yon dazzling throne!
Each before his Saviour stands,
  All in whitest robes arrayed;

Palms they carry in their hands,
 Crowns of glory on their head.

2 Saints begin the endless song,
  Cry aloud in heavenly lays,
 Glory doth to God belong,
  God, the glorious Saviour, praise:
 All salvation from him came,
  Him, who reigns enthroned on high:
 Glory to the bleeding Lamb,
  Let the morning stars reply.

3 Angel powers the throne surround,
  Next the saints in glory they;
 Lulled with the transporting sound,
  They their silent homage pay:
 Prostrate on their face, before
  God and his Messiah fall;
 Then in hymns of praise adore,
  Shout the Lamb that died for all.

Charles Wesley.

480 *Make his praise glorious.* 8s & 6s.

O COULD I speak the matchless worth,
  O could I sound the glories forth,
   Which in my Saviour shine,
 I'd soar and touch the heavenly strings,
 And vie with Gabriel while he sings
   In notes almost divine.

2 I'd sing the precious blood he spilt,
 My ransom from the dreadful guilt
   Of sin, and wrath divine;
 I'd sing his glorious righteousness,
 In which all-perfect, heavenly dress
   My soul shall ever shine.

3 I'd sing the characters he bears,
And all the forms of love he wears,
   Exalted on his throne ;
In loftiest songs of sweetest praise
I would to everlasting days
   Make all his glories known.

4 Well, the delightful day will come
When my dear Lord will bring me home,
   And I shall see his face ;
Then with my Saviour, Brother, Friend,
A blest eternity I'll spend,
   Triumphant in his grace.
                              Samuel Medley.

481   *The heavenly Canaan.*   C. M.

THERE is a land of pure delight,
   Where saints immortal reign ;
Infinite day excludes the night,
   And pleasures banish pain.

2 There everlasting spring abides,
   And never-with'ring flowers:
Death, like a narrow sea, divides
   This heavenly land from ours.

3 Sweet fields beyond the swelling flood
   Stand dress'd in living green ;
So to the Jews old Canaan stood,
   While Jordan rolled between,

4 But tim'rous mortals start and shrink,
   To cross this narrow sea ;
And linger, trembling, on the brink,
   And fear to launch away.

5 Could we but climb where Moses stood,
   And view the landscape o'er,
Not Jordan's stream, nor death's cold flood,
   Should fright us from the shore.   *Watts.*

482 *Visions of Heaven.* C. M.

AND let this feeble body fail,
  And let it droop or die:
My soul shall quit the mournful vale,
  And soar to worlds on high,—
Shall join the disembodied saints,
  And find its long-sought rest,
That only bliss for which it pants,
  In my Redeemer's breast.

2 In hope of that immortal crown,
  I now the cross sustain;
And gladly wander up and down,
  And smile at toil and pain:
I suffer out my threescore years,
  Till my Deliv'rer come,
And wipe away his servant's tears,
  And take his exile home.

3 O what are all my suff'rings here,
  If, Lord, thou count me meet
With that enraptur'd host t' appear,
  And worship at thy feet!
Give joy or grief, give ease or pain:—
  Take life or friends away,
I come to find them all again
  In that eternal day. *Charles Wesley.*

483 *We have our conversation in Heaven.* C. M.

MY thoughts surmount these lower skies,
  And look within the veil;
There springs of endless pleasure rise,
  The waters never fail.

2 There I behold with sweet delight
  The blessed Three in One,

And strong affections fix my sight
On God's incarnate Son.

3 His promise stands forever firm,
His grace shall ne'er depart;
He binds my name upon his arm,
And seals it on his heart.

4 I would not be a stranger still
To that celestial place,
Where I forever hope to dwell
Near my Redeemer's face.   *Watts.*

184   *Vision of Heaven.*   C. M.

GIVE me the wings of faith to rise
Within the veil, and see
The saints above, how great their joys,
How bright their glories be.

2 Once they were mourning here below,
And wet their couch with tears;
They wrestled hard, as we do now,
With sins and doubts and fears.

3 I asked from whence their vict'ry came;
They, with united breath,
Ascribe their conquest to the Lamb,
Their triumph to his death.

4 They marked the footsteps that he trod,
His zeal inspired their breast,
And following their incarnate God,
Possess the promised rest.

5 Our glorious Leader claims our praise
For his own pattern given,
While the long cloud of witnesses
Show the same path to heaven.   *Watts.*

485   *Resting in hope.*   S. M.

REST for the toiling hand,
  Rest for the anxious brow,
Rest for the weary, way-sore feet,
  Rest from all labor now.

2 Rest for the fevered brain,
  Rest for the throbbing eye;
Through these parched lips of thine no more
  Shall pass the moan or sigh.

3 Soon shall the trump of God
  Give out the welcome sound,
That shakes thy silent chamber-walls,
  And breaks the turf-sealed ground.

4 Ye dwellers in the dust,
  Awake, come forth and sing!
Sharp has your frost of winter been,
  But bright shall be your spring.   *H. Bonar.*

486   *Funeral of an aged Minister.*   S. M.

"SERVANT of God, well done!
  Rest from thy loved employ;
The battle fought, the vict'ry won,
  Enter thy Master's joy."
The voice at midnight came:
  He started up to hear;
A mortal arrow pierced his frame:
  He fell, - but felt no fear.

2 His sword was in his hand
  Still warm with recent fight,
Ready that moment, at command,
  Through rock and steel to smite.
Bent on such glorious toils,
  The world to him was loss,

Yet all his trophies, all his spoils,
He hung upon the cross.

3 At midnight came the cry,
"To meet thy God prepare!"
He woke,—and caught his Captain's eye,
Then, strong in faith and prayer,
His spirit, with a bound,
Left its encumb'ring clay;
His tent, at sunrise, on the ground
A darken'd ruin lay.

4 The pains of death are past,
Labor and sorrow cease;
And, life's long warfare closed at last,
His soul is found in peace.
Soldier of Christ, well done!
Praise be thy new employ;
And while eternal ages run,
Rest in thy Saviour's joy. *Montgomery.*

487 *Life, the day of grace.* L. M.

LIFE is the time to serve the Lord,
　The time t' insure the great reward;
And while the lamp holds out to burn,
The vilest sinner may return.

2 Life is the hour that God has given
To escape from hell, and fly to heaven;
The day of grace, and mortals may
Secure the blessings of the day.

3 The living know that they must die,
But all the dead forgotten lie;
Their mem'ry and their sense is gone,
Alike unknowing and unknown.

4 Their hatred and their love is lost,
Their envy buried in the dust;

FUNERALS AND OTHER OCCASIONS.

They have no share in all that's done
Beneath the circuit of the sun.

5 Then what my thoughts design to do,
My hands, with all your might pursue;
Since no device nor work is found,
Nor faith, nor hope, beneath the ground.

6 There are no acts of pardon pass'd
In the cold grave, to which we haste;
But darkness, death, and long despair,
Reign in eternal silence there. *Watts.*

488 *Funeral of a youth.* L. M.
1 Peter i. 24, 25.

THE morning flowers display their sweets,
And gay their silken leaves unfold,
As careless of the noontide heats,
As fearless of the evening cold.

2 Nipp'd by the wind's untimely blast,
Parch'd by the sun's directer ray,
The momentary glories waste,
The short-liv'd beauties die away.

3 So blooms the human face divine,
When youth its pride of beauty shows;
Fairer than spring the colors shine,
And sweeter than the virgin rose.

4 Or worn by slowly-rolling years,
Or broke by sickness in a day,
The fading glory disappears,
The short-lived beauties die away.

5 Yet these, new-rising from the tomb,
With lustre brighter far shall shine,
Revive with ever-during bloom,
Safe from diseases and decline.

6 Let sickness blast, let death devour,
   If heaven must recompense our pains:
Perish the grass, and fade the flower,
   If firm the word of God remains.
                              S. Wesley, Jr.

489   *Disembodied saints.*   L. M

THE saints who die of Christ possess'd
    Enter into immediate rest;
For them no further test remains
Of purging fires and torturing pains.

2 Who trusting in their Lord depart,
Cleans'd from all sin and pure in heart,
The bliss unmix'd, the glorious prize,
They find with Christ in paradise.

3 Close followed by their works they go,
Their Master's purchas'd joy to know;
Their works enhance the bliss prepar'd,
And each hath its distinct reward.

4 Yet glorified by grace alone,
They cast their crowns before the throne:
And fill the echoing courts above
With praises of redeeming love. *C. Wesley.*

490   *Dies iræ.*   L. M.

THE day of wrath, that dreadful day,
    When heaven and earth shall pass away!
What power shall be the sinner's stay?
How shall he meet that dreadful day—

2 When, shriv'lling like a parched scroll,
The flaming heavens together roll;
And louder yet, and yet more dread,
Swells the high trump that wakes the dead?

3 O, on that day, that wrathful day,
   When man to judgment wakes from clay,
   Be thou, O Christ, the sinner's stay,
   Though heaven and earth shall pass away.
   W. Scott.

491 *Death welcome to the Christian.* L. M.

SHRINKING from the cold hand of death,
   I soon shall gather up my feet;
Shall soon resign this fleeting breath,
   And die,—my father's God to meet.

2 Number'd among thy people, I
   Expect with joy thy face to see:
Because thou didst for sinners die,
   Jesus, in death remember me!

3 O that without a lingering groan
   I may the welcome word receive!
My body with my charge lay down,
   And cease at once to work and live!

4 Walk with me through the dreadful shade,
   And, certified that thou art mine,
My spirit calm and undismayed,
   I shall into thy hands resign.

5 No anxious doubt, no guilty gloom,
   Shall damp whom Jesus' presence cheers:
My light my life, my God is come,
   And glory in his face appears!

492 *The peaceful death.* L. M.

WHY should we start and fear to die?
   What tim'rous worms we mortals are!
Death is the gate to endless joy,
   And yet we dread to enter there.

2 The pains, the groans, the dying strife,
   Fright our approaching souls away;

And we shrink back again to life,
Fond of our prison and our clay.

3 O if my Lord would come and meet,
My soul would stretch her wings in haste,
Fly fearless through death's iron gate,
Nor feel the terrors as she passed.

4 Jesus can make a dying-bed
Feel soft as downy pillows are,
While on his breast I lean my head,
And breathe my life out sweetly there.
Watts.

493   *God eternal, and man mortal.*   L. M.
Ps. 90.

THROUGH every age, eternal God,
Thou art our rest, our safe abode:
High was thy throne ere heaven was made,
Or earth, thy humble footstool, laid.

2 Long hadst thou reign'd ere time began
Or dust was fashion'd into man:
And long thy kingdom shall endure,
When earth and time shall be no more.

3 But man, weak man, is born to die,
Made up of guilt and vanity:
Thy dreadful sentence, Lord, is just—
"Return ye sinners, to your dust."

4 Death, like an ever-flowing stream,
Sweeps us away: our life's a dream—
An empty tale—a morning flower
Cut down and wither'd in an hour.

5 Teach us, O Lord, how frail is man,
And kindly lengthen out our span,
Till, cleans'd by grace, we all may be
Prepar'd to die, and dwell with thee.   *Watts.*

494   "*I would not live alway.*"   11s.

I WOULD not live alway: I ask not to stay
Where storm after storm rises dark o'er the way;
The few lurid mornings that dawn on us here,
Are enough for life's woes, full enough for its cheer.

2 I would not live alway: no—welcome the tomb;
Since Jesus hath lain there, I dread not its gloom;
There, sweet be my rest, till he bid me arise,
To hail him in triumph descending the skies.

3 Who, who would live alway, away from his God,—
Away from yon heaven, that blissful abode,
Where rivers of pleasure flow o'er the bright plains,
And the noontide of glory eternally reigns:

4 Where the saints of all ages in harmony meet,
Their Saviour and brethren transported to greet;
While the anthems of rapture unceasingly roll,
And the smile of the Lord is the feast of the soul!   *Muhlenberg.*

495   *Funeral of a Christian Brother.*   10, 5, 11.

HOSANNA to God, in his highest abode:
All heaven be join'd
T' extol the Redeemer and Friend of mankind!
He claims all our praise, who in infinite grace
Again hath stoop'd down
And caught up a worm to inherit a crown.

2 Our friend is restor'd to the joy of his Lord,
   With triumph departs,
   But speaks by his death to our echoing hearts:
   Follow after, he cries, as he mounts to the skies,
   Follow after your friend
   To the blissful enjoyments that never shall end.

3 Through Jesus's name our comrade o'ercame,
   And Jesus is ours,
   And arms us with all his invincible powers:
   He looks from the skies, he shows us the prize,
   And gives us a sign
   That we shall o'ercome by the mercy Divine.

4 For us is prepar'd the angelical guard;
   The convoy attends—
   A minist'ring host of invisible friends—
   Ready-wing'd for their flight to the regions of light,
   The horses are come,
   The chariots of Israel, to carry us home.
                                           C. Wesley.

196 *Funeral of a Christian.* Rev. xiv. 13. 7s.

HARK! a voice divides the sky,
   Happy are the faithful dead!
In the Lord who sweetly die,
   They from all their toils are freed.

2 Them the Spirit hath declar'd
   Blest, unutterably blest;
Jesus is their great reward,
   Jesus is their endless rest.

3 Follow'd by their works, they go
   Where their Head has gone before;

FUNERALS AND OTHER OCCASIONS.

 Reconcil'd by grace below,
  Grace hath open'd Mercy's door.
4 Justified through faith alone,
  Here they knew their sins forgiven;
 Here they laid their burden down,
  Hallow'd, and made meet for heaven.
C. Wesley.

497 *Death of a Relative.* 8, 8, 6.

IF death my friend and me divide,
 Thou dost not, Lord, my sorrow chide,
  Or frown, my tears to see;
Restrain'd from passionate excess.
Thou bidd'st me mourn in calm distress
  For them that rest in thee.

2 I feel a strong, immortal hope,
Which bears my mournful spirit up,
  Beneath its mountain-load;
Redeem'd from death, and grief, and pain,
I soon shall find my friend again
  Within the arms of God.

3 Pass a few fleeting moments more,
And death the blessing shall restore
  Which death has snatch'd away;
For me thou wilt the summons send,
And give me back my parted friend
  In that eternal day. *C. Wesley.*

498 *Longing to be glorified.* Rev. xxii. 17. 8s.

THE Church in her militant state
 Is weary, and cannot forbear!
The saints in an agony wait,
 To see him again in the air!
The Spirit invites in the bride
 Her heavenly Lord to descend.

And place her enthron'd at his side,
In glory that never shall end.

2 The news of his coming I hear,
And join in the catholic cry:
O Jesus, in triumph appear;
Appear in the clouds of the sky!
Whom only I languish to love,
In fulness of majesty come;
And give me a mansion above;
And take to my heavenly home!
C. Wesley.

499   *The Shining Shore.*   8, 7

MY days are gliding swiftly by,
    And I, a pilgrim stranger,
Would not detain them as they fly,
    Those hours of toil and danger.
CHORUS.—For O, we stand on Jordan's strand,
    Our friends are passing over,
And just before, the shining shore
    We may almost discover.

2 We'll gird our loins, my brethren dear,
    Our heavenly home discerning;
Our absent Lord has left us word,
    Let every lamp be burning.

3 Should coming days be cold and dark,
    We need not cease our singing;
That perfect rest naught can molest
    Where golden harps are ringing.

4 Let sorrow's rudest tempest blow,
    Each chord on earth to sever;
Our King says come, and there's our home,
    Forever, O forever.

FUNERALS AND OTHER OCCASIONS.

500 *The heavenly Jerusalem.* C. M.

JERUSALEM, my happy home!
   Name ever dear to me!
When will my sorrows have an end?
   Thy joys, when shall I see?

2 Thy walls are all of precious stone,
   Most glorious to behold;
Thy gates are richly set with pearl,
   Thy streets are pav'd with gold.

3 Thy garden and thy pleasant walks,
   My study long have been;
Such dazzling views by human sight
   Have never yet been seen.

4 If heaven be thus so glorious, Lord,
   Why should I stay from thence?
What folly's this that I should dread
   To die and go from hence?

5 Reach down, O Lord, thine arm of grace,
   And cause me to ascend,
Where congregations ne'er break up,
   And Sabbaths never end.

6 Jesus, my Lord, to glory's gone,
   Him will I go and see;
And all my brethren here below,
   Will soon come after me.

7 My friends, I bid you all adieu,
   I leave you in God's care,
And if I never more see you,
   Go on, I'll meet you there. *Dickson.*

501 *Death the gate to Heaven.* C. M.

WHY do we mourn departing friends,
   Or shake at death's alarms?

'Tis but the voice that Jesus sends
To call them to his arms.

2 Are we not tending upward too,
As fast as time can move?
Nor should we wish the hours more slow
To keep us from our Love.

3 Why should we tremble to convey
Their bodies to the tomb?
There once the flesh of Jesus lay,
And left a long perfume.

4 The graves of all his saints he bless'd,
And soften'd every bed:
Where should the dying members rest,
But with their dying Head? *Watts.*

502 *Faith contemplating Heaven.* C. M.

THERE is a house not made with hands,
Eternal and on high;
And here my spirit waiting, stands,
Till God shall bid it fly.

2 Shortly this prison of my clay
Must be dissolved and fall;
Then, O my soul, with joy obey
Thy heavenly Father's call.

3 'Tis he, by his almighty grace,
That forms thee fit for heav'n;
And, as an earnest of the place,
Has his own Spirit giv'n.

4 We walk by faith of joys to come;
Faith lives upon his word;
But while the body is our home,
We're absent from the Lord.

5 'Tis pleasant to believe thy grace,
  But we had rather see;
  We would be absent from the flesh,
  And present, Lord, with thee. *Watts.*

503 *Looking from earth to Heaven.* C. M.

DEATH may dissolve my body now,
  And bear my spirit home:
Why do my days so sluggish move,
  Nor my salvation come?

2 God has laid up in heaven for me
  A crown which cannot fade;
The righteous Judge, at that great day,
  Shall place it on my head.

3 Jesus, the Lord, will guard me safe
  From every ill design,
And to his heavenly kingdom take
  This feeble soul of mine.

4 God is my everlasting aid,
  My portion and my friend,
To him be highest glory paid,
  Through ages without end. *Watts.*

504 *What are these?* Rev. vii. 13–17. 7s.

WHAT are these arrayed in white,
  Brighter than the noonday sun?
Foremost of the sons of light,
  Nearest the eternal throne?
These are they that bore the cross,
  Nobly for their Master stood,
Suff"rers in his righteous cause,
  Foll'wers of the dying God.

2 Out of great distress they came,
 Wash'd their robes by faith below,
In the blood of yonder Lamb,
 Blood that washes white as snow;
Therefore are they next the throne,
 Serve their Maker day and night,
God resides among his own.
 God doth in his saints delight.

3 More than conquerors at last,
 Here they find their trials o'er;
They have all their suff'rings past,
 Hunger now and thirst no more:
No excessive heat they feel
 From the sun's directer ray;
In a milder clime they dwell,
 Region of eternal day. *C. Wesley.*

505 *A city that hath foundations.* 8s.

AWAY with our sorrow and fear!
 We soon shall recover our home;
The city of saints shall appear;
 The day of eternity come.
From earth we shall quickly remove,
 And mount to our native abode;
The house of our Father above,
 The palace of angels and God.

2 Our mourning is all at an end,
 When rais'd by the life-giving word,
We see the new city descend,
 Adorn'd as a bride for her Lord:
The city so holy and clean,
 No sorrow can breathe in the air:
No gloom of affliction or sin,
 No shadow of evil is there!

506   *The redeemed in heaven.*   L. M.

LO! round the throne, a glorious band,
   The saints in countless myriads stand;
Of every tongue redeemed to God,
Arrayed in garments washed in blood.

2 Through tribulation great they came;
They bore the cross, despised the shame;
But now from all their labors rest,
In God's eternal glory blest.

3 They see the Saviour face to face;
They sing the triumph of his grace;
And day and night, with ceaseless praise,
To him their loud hosannas raise.

4 O may we tread the sacred road
That holy saints and martyrs trod;
Wage to the end the glorious strife,
And win, like them, a crown of life!
                              Mary L. Duncan.

507   L. M.
" They shall behold the land that is very far off."
                Isa. xxxiii. 17.

THERE is a land mine eye hath seen
   In visions of enraptured thought,
So bright, that all which spreads between
   Is with its radiant glories fraught.

2 A land upon whose blissful shore
   There rests no shadow, falls no stain;
There those who meet shall part no more,
   And those long parted meet again.

3 Its skies are not like earthly skies,
   With varying hues of shade and light;
It hath no need of suns to rise
   To dissipate the gloom of night.

4 There sweeps no desolating wind
  Across that calm, serene abode;
  The wanderer there a home may find
  Within the paradise of God.
                    Gurdon Robins.

508   *The last great day.*   L. M.

METHINKS the last great day is come,
  Methinks I hear the trumpet sound,
That shakes the earth, rends every tomb,
  And wakes the prisoners under ground.

2 The mighty deep gives up her trust,
  Aw'd by the Judge's high command;
Both small and great now quit their dust
  And round the dread tribunal stand.

3 Behold the awful books displayed,
  Big with th' important fates of men;
Each deed a word more public made,
  As wrote by heaven's unerring pen.

4 To every soul the books assign
  The joyous or the dread reward;
Sinners in vain lament and pine—
  No plea the Judge will here regard.

5 Lord, when these awful leaves unfold,
  May life's fair book my soul approve!
There may I read my name enroll'd,
  And triumph in redeeming love!

509   *The Heavenly Zion.*   L. M.

ARM of the Lord, awake, awake!
  Thine own immortal strength put on!
With terror clothed, hell's kingdom shake,
  And cast thy foes with fury down.

2 By death and hell pursued in vain,
  To thee the ransomed seed shall come;
  Shouting, their heavenly Zion gain,
  And pass through death triumphant home

3 The pain of life shall then be o'er,
  The anguish and distracting care;
  There sighing grief shall weep no more,
  And sin shall never enter there.

4 Where pure, essential joy is found,
  The Lord's redeemed their heads shall raise,
  With everlasting gladness crowned,
  And filled with love, and lost in praise.
                              Charles Wesley.

510   *The land of peace.*   S. M.

COME to the land of peace;
  From shadows come away;
Where all the sounds of weeping cease,
  And storms no more have sway.

2 Fear hath no dwelling here;
    But pure repose and love
  Breathe through the bright, celestial air
    The spirit of the dove.

3 Come to the bright and blest,
    Gathered from every land;
  For here thy soul shall find its rest
    Amid the shining band.

4 In this divine abode
    Change leaves no saddening trace;
  Come, trusting spirit, to thy God,
    Thy holy resting-place.

5 "Come to our peaceful home,"
    The saints and angels say,

DEATH—THE JUDGMENT—HEAVEN.

"Forsake the world, no longer roam ;
O wanderer, come away!"   *Unknown.*

511   *At home in Heaven.*   S. M.

"FOREVER with the Lord!"
  Amen, so let it be!
Life from the dead is in that word,
  'Tis immortality.

2 Here in the body pent,
  Absent from him I roam,
Yet nightly pitch my moving tent
  A day's march nearer home.

3 "Forever with the Lord!"
  Father, if 'tis thy will,
The promise of that faithful word,
  E'en here to me fulfill.

4 So when my latest breath
  Shall rend the vail in twain,
By death I shall escape from death,
  And life eternal gain.

5 Knowing as I am known,
  How shall I love that word,
And oft repeat before the throne,
  "Forever with the Lord!"
        James Montgomery.

512   *The goodly land.*   S. M.

FAR from these scenes of night,
  Unbounded glories rise,
And realms of joy and pure delight,
  Unknown to mortal eyes.
2 Fair land! could mortal eyes
  But half its charms explore,

How would our spirits long to rise,
 And dwell on earth no more!

3 No cloud those regions know,
 Realms ever bright and fair;
 For sin, the source of mortal woe,
 Can never enter there.

4 O, may the prospect fire
 Our hearts with ardent love,
 Till wings of faith and strong desire,
 Bear every thought above.

5 Prepared, by grace divine,
 For thy bright courts on high,
 Lord, bid our spirits rise and join
 The chorus of the sky. *Anne Steele.*

513   *No night in Heaven.*   S. M.

THERE is no night in heaven;
 In that blest world above
Work never can bring weariness,
 For work itself is love.

2 There is no grief in heaven;
 For life is one glad day,
And tears are of those former things
 Which all have passed away.

3 There is no sin in heaven;
 Behold that blessed throng,
All holy in their spotless robes,
 All holy in their song.

4 There is no death in heaven;
 For they who gain that shore
Have won their immortality,
 And they can die no more.
      Frederick D. Huntington.

SECTION XVII.
Devotional Miscellany.

514   *Surrendering all for Christ.*   C. M.

HOW vain are all things here below!
　How false, and yet how fair!
Each pleasure hath its poison, too,
　And every sweet a snare.

2 The brightest things below the sky
　Give but a flatt'ring light:
We should suspect some danger nigh
　Where we possess delight.

3 Our dearest joys and nearest friends,
　The partners of our blood,
How they divide our wav'ring minds,
　And leave but half for God!

4 The fondness of a creature's love,
　How strong it strikes the sense!
Thither the warm affections move,
　Nor can we call them thence.

5 Dear Saviour, let thy beauties be
　My soul's eternal food;
And grace command my soul away
　From all created good.   *Watts.*

515   *The Pilgrim's Song.*   8s & 6s.

YE weary, heavy laden souls,
　Who are oppressed sore,
Ye trav'lers through the wilderness,
　To Canaan's peaceful shore:

Through chilling winds and beating rain,
　The waters deep and cold,
And enemies surrounding you,
　Take courage and be bold.

2 Though storms and hurricanes arise,
　The desert all around,
And fiery serpents oft appear
　Through the enchanted ground.
Dark nights, and clouds, and gloomy fear,
　And dragons often roar;
But while the gospel trump we hear,
　We'll press for Canaan's shore.

3 Methinks I now begin to see
　The borders of that land;
The trees of life, with heav'nly fruit,
　In beauteous order stand;
The wintry time is past and gone,
　Sweet flowers now appear.
The fiftieth year hath now rolled round,
　The great Sabbatic year.　　*Unknown.*

516　　　*Remember me.*　　　C. M.

JESUS! thou art the sinner's friend,
　As such I look to thee;
Now in the bowels of thy love,
　O Lord! remember me.

2 Remember thy pure word of grace,
　Remember Calvary;
Remember all thy dying groans,
　And then remember me.

3 Thou wondrous Advocate with God!
　I yield myself to thee;
While thou art sitting on thy throne,
　O Lord! remember me.

4 I own I'm guilty, own I'm vile,
  Yet thy salvation's free;
  Then, in thy all-abounding grace,
  O Lord! remember me.

5 Howe'er forsaken, or distress'd,
  Howe'er oppress'd I be,
  Howe'er afflicted here on earth,
  Do thou remember me. *Unknown.*

617   *Admission into the Church.*   C. M.

INQUIRE, ye pilgrims, for the way
  That leads to Sion's hill,
And thither set your steady face,
  With a determin'd will.

2 Invite the strangers all around
  Your pious march to join,
And spread the sentiments you feel
  Of faith and love divine.

3 O come, and to his temple haste,
  And seek his favor there:
Before his footstool humbly bow,
  And pour your fervent prayer.

4 O come, and join your souls to God
  In everlasting bands:
Accept the blessings he bestows,
  With thankful hearts and hands.
    Doddridge.

518   *Scenes of the Resurrection.*   C. M.

HOW long shall Death, the tyrant, reign,
  And triumph o'er the just?
How long the blood of martyrs slain
  Lie mingled with the dust?

2 Lo! I behold the scatter'd shades:
　The dawn of heaven appears:
　The bright, immortal morning spreads
　　Its blushes round the spheres.
3 I see the Lord of glory come,
　And flaming guards around:
　The skies divide to make him room:
　　The trumpet shakes the ground.
4 I hear the voice, "Ye dead, arise!"
　And, lo! the graves obey;
　And waking saints, with joyful eyes,
　　Salute th' expected day.
5 O may our humble spirits stand
　Among them, cloth'd in white:
　The meanest place at his right hand
　　Is infinite delight. *Watts.*

519 "*Thy kingdom come.*" Matt. vi. 10. C. M.

FATHER of me. and all mankind
　And all the hosts above,
　Let every understanding mind
　　Unite to praise thy love:
2 To know thy nature and thy name,
　One God in persons three;
　And glorify the great I AM
　　Through all eternity.
3 Thy kingdom come, with power and grace,
　To every heart of man:
　Thy peace, and joy, and righteousness,
　　In all our bosoms reign. *C. Wesley.*

520 "*Lighten mine eyes.*" Psl. xiii. 3. C. M.

O SUN of righteousness, arise
　With healing in thy wing!

To my diseas'd, my fainting soul,
Life and salvation bring

2 These clouds of pride and sin dispel,
By thine all-piercing beam:
Lighten mine eyes with faith, my heart
With holy hope inflame.

3 My mind, by thy all-quickening power,
From low desires set free:
Unite my scatter'd thoughts, and fix
My love entire on thee.

4 Father, thy long-lost son receive;
Saviour, thy purchase own;
Blest Comforter, with peace and joy
Thy new-made creature crown.

5 Eternal, undivided Lord,
Coëqual One and Three,
On thee all faith, all hope be placed,
All love be paid to thee. *C. Wesley.*

521 *Evening.* C. M.

THE work of one more day is done—
Is done, as best we could,
And yet, O Lord, we must confess
'Tis not done as we would.

2 We would have lived throughout the hours
As though we saw thee near,
That thou shouldst know each thought and word,
Should bring to us no fear.

3 But as we retrospect the day,
Our heart is made to grieve.
In pity, Lord, we pray look down,
Our burden'd souls relieve.

4 O make us not to close our eyes,
   Till we shall feel thy love,
Hear thou our song, hear thou our pray'r,
   "Come quickly from above."
5 With this assurance sweetly given,
   We each to each may say,
Good-night, Good-night, God keep us safe
   Until the break of day.   *B. T. Tanner.*

522 *"See how these Christians love."* C. M.

GIVER of concord, Prince of peace,
   Meek, lamb-like Son of God,
Bid our unruly passions cease,
   By thy atoning blood.
2 Rebuke our rage, our passions chide,
   Our stubborn wills control,
Beat down our wrath, root out our pride,
   And calm our troubl'd soul.
3 Subdue in us the carnal mind,
   Its enmity destroy,
With cords of love our spirits bind,
   And melt us into joy.
4 Us into closest union draw,
   And in our inward parts
Let kindness sweetly write her law,
   And love command our hearts. *C. Wesley.*

523   *The Farewell*   C. M.

YE golden lamps of heaven, farewell,
   With all your feeble light:
Farewell, thou ever-changing moon,
   Pale empress of the night.
2 And thou, refulgent orb of day,
   In brighter flames array'd,

My soul, that springs beyond thy sphere
No more demands thy aid.

3 Ye stars are but the shining dust
Of my divine abode,
The pavement of those heavenly courts,
Where I shall see my God.

4 No more the drops of piercing grief
Shall swell into mine eyes;
Nor the meridian sun decline
Amidst those brighter skies.

5 There all the millions of his saints
Shall in one song unite;
And each the bliss of all shall view,
With infinite delight. *Doddridge.*

524 C. M.
A minister or brethren parting on earth.
Acts xx. 36-38.

DEAR friends, farewell, I do you tell,
Since you and I must part;
I go away but here you stay;
But still we're joined in heart.

2 Your love to me has been so free,
Your conversation sweet;
How can I bear to journey, where
With you I cannot meet!

3 Yet I do find my heart inclined
To lo my work below;
When Christ doth call, I trust I shall
Be ready then to go.

4 I leave you all, both great and small,
To Christ's encircling arms,
Which can you save from hell's dark grave,
And shield you from all harms.

5 I long to go where pleasures flow,
   My soul shall be at rest,
  No more complain or sigh again,
   But be forever blest.

6 There we shall meet in bliss complete,
   And long together dwell,
  To love the Lord with one accord;
   So, brethren, all farewell. *Unknown.*

525   *Patriot's Song.*   C. M.

LORD, while for all mankind we pray,
   Of every clime and coast,
  O hear us for our native land,—
   The land we love the most.

2 O guard our shores from every foe,
   With peace our borders bless,
  With prosp'rous times our cities crown,
   Our fields with plenteousness.

3 Here may religion shed her light
   On days of rest and toil;
  And piety and virtue reign,
   And bless our native soil.

4 Lord of the nations, thus to thee
   Our country we commend;
  Be thou her refuge and her trust,
   Her everlasting friend. *Wreford.*

526   *Nearer to Thee.*   6s & 4s.

Then shall the Lord be my God; and this stone shall be God's house.—Gen. xxviii. 21, 22.

NEARER, my God, to thee,
   Nearer to thee!
  E'en though it be a cross
   That raiseth me;

Still all my song shall be—
Nearer, my God to thee,
Nearer to thee!

2 Though, like the wanderer,
The sun go down,
Darkness be over me,
My rest a stone;
Yet in my dreams I'd be—
Nearer, my God, to thee!
Nearer to thee!

3 There let the way appear
Steps unto heaven;
All that thou sendest me
In mercy given;
Angels to beckon me—
Nearer, my God, to thee!
Nearer to thee!

4 Then with my waking thoughts,
Bright with thy praise,
Out of my stony griefs,
Bethel I'll raise;
So by my woes to be—
Nearer, my God, to thee!
Nearer to thee!

5 Or if on joyful wing,
Cleaving the sky,
Sun, moon, and stars forgot
Upward I fly;
Still all my song shall be—
Nearer, my God, to thee!
Nearer to thee! *Mrs. S. F. Adams.*

527 *The dying Christian to his Soul.* 7s, 8s.

VITAL spark of heavenly flame,
Quit, O quit this mortal frame;

Trembling, hoping, lingering, flying,
O, the pain, the bliss of dying!
Cease, fond nature, cease thy strife,
And let me languish into life.

2 Hark!—they whisper; angels say,
"Sister spirit, come away;"
What is this absorbs me quite?—
Steals my senses, shuts my sight,
Drowns my spirits, draws my breath?—
Tell me, my soul, can this be death?

3 The world recedes; it disappears;
Heaven opens on my eyes; my ears
With sounds seraphic ring:
Lend, lend your wings! I mount! I fly!
"O Grave, where is thy victory?
O Death, where is thy sting?" *Pope.*

528 *Birthday of a Consort.* 11, 9.

COME away to the skies, my beloved arise,
And rejoice in the day thou wast born:
On this festival day, come exulting away,
And with singing to Sion return.

2 We have laid up our love and our treasure above.
Though our bodies continue below:
The redeem'd of our Lord, we remember his word,
And with singing to paradise go.

3 With singing we praise the original grace
By our heavenly Father bestow'd;
Our being receive from his bounty, and live
To the honor and glory of God.

4 For thy glory we are created to share
Both the nature and kingdom divine:

Created again, that our souls may remain
In time and eternity thine.

5 With thanks we approve the design of thy love,
Which hath joined us in Jesus's name;
So united in heart that we never can part,
Till we meet at the feast of the Lamb.
C. Wesley.

529 "*He beheld the city, and wept over it.*" S. M.

DID Christ o'er sinners weep,
And shall our cheeks be dry?
Let floods of penitential grief
Burst forth from every eye.

2 The Son of God in tears
The woud'ring angels see:
Be thou astonished, O my soul;
He shed those tears for thee.

3 He wept that we might weep:
Each sin demands a tear:
In heaven alone no sin is found,
And there's no weeping there.
Beddome.

530 *Household consecrated to God.* S. M.

THE power to bless my house
Belongs to God alone;
Yet rend'ring him my constant vows,
He sends his blessings down.

2 Shall I not then engage
My house to serve the Lord,
To search the soul-converting page,
And feed upon his word,—

3 To ask with faith and hope
The grace which he supplies,

In prayer and praise to offer up
Their daily sacrifice?

4 Let each his sin eschew,
Through thy restraining grace,
Our father Abrah'm's steps pursue,
And walk in all thy ways.

5 Saviour of men, incline
The hearts which thou hast made,
Which thou hast bought with blood Divine,
To ask thy promis'd aid.

6 Me and my house receive,
Thy family t' increase,
And let us in thy favor live,
And let us die in peace. *C. Wesley.*

631   *General Thanksgiving.*   S. M.

THROUGH all the lofty sky,
Through all the inferior ground,
Th' Almighty Maker shines confess'd,
And pours his blessings round.

2 Each year the teeming earth
With flowers and fruits is crown'd;
And grass, and herbs, and harvests, grow
And send their joys around.

3 The world of waters yields
A rich supply of food,
And distant lands their treasures send
Upon the rolling flood.

4 To serve and bless our land
The elements conspire;
And mercies mix themselves with earth,—
With ocean, air and fire.

5 O that the sons of men
   To God their songs would raise,
And celebrate his power and love
   In never-ceasing praise!   *Gibbons.*

532   *"Glorious in holiness."*   S. M.

GOD is in Judah known,
   Israel extols his name,
In Salem he has placed his throne,
   In Zion lives his fame.

2 There did he break the shield,
   The battle and the bow;
There to his glorious might shall yield
   The desolating foe.

3 There is the spoiler spoil'd,
   The proud have slept their sleep;
There are the men of battle foil'd,
   In one promiscuous heap.

4 When thy rebuke is heard,
   Both horse and car expire;
Thou God of Jacob shalt be fear'd;
   O who shall meet thine ire?

5 Heaven utter'd thy decree,
   Earth, trembling, paused to hear:
Soon shall the world thy judgments see,
   Thy saints no more shall fear.   *Marsh.*

533   *On changing place of abode.*   L. M.

SOLE Sov'reign of the earth and skies,
   Supremely good, supremely wise,
Fix thou the place of our abode,
But let it still be near our God.

2 On earth we weary pilgrims roam,
Nor find, nor hope, a lasting home;

DEVOTIONAL MISCELLANY.

We seek a house not made with hands,
A heavenly house which ever stands.
8 Yet while we sojourn here below,
Let streams of mercy round us flow;
And when our destin'd race is run,
Assign us mansions near thy throne.
Unknown.

534 *The Prosperous Saint.* L. M.
Rev. vii. 13–17.

COME, ye that love the Lord indeed,
Who are from sin and bondage freed,
Submit to all the ways of God,
And walk that narrow happy road.
2 Great tribulation you shall meet,
But soon shall walk the golden street;
Though hell may rage and vent her spite,
Yet Christ will save his heart's delight.
8 That happy day will soon appear,
When Gabriel's trumpet you shall hear
Sound through the earth, yea, down to hell,
To call the nations great and small.
4 Behold the earth in burning flames,
The trumpet louder still proclaims;
The earth must hear and know her doom,
The separation day is come.
5 Behold the righteous marching home,
And all the angels bid them come;
When Christ himself these words proclaims,
Here come my saints, I know their names.
Unknown

535 *Self-dedication.* L. M
LORD, I am thine, entirely thine,
Purchased and saved by blood Divine;

With full consent thine would I be,
And own thy sovereign right in me.

2 Grant one poor sinner more a place
Among the children of thy grace;
A wretched sinner, lost to God,
But ransom'd by Immanuel's blood.

3 Thine would I live, thine would I die,
Be thine through all eternity;
The vow is past beyond repeal,
Now will I set the solemn seal.

4 Here at that cross where flows the blood
That bought my guilty soul for God,
Thee, my new Master, now I call,
And consecrate to thee my all.

5 Do thou assist a feeble worm
The great engagement to perform:
Thy grace can full assistance lend,
And on that grace I dare depend. *Davies.*

536   *National Praise.*   L. M.

WE bless thy name, Almighty God,
    For all the kindness thou hast shown,
To this fair land our fathers trod,
    This land we fondly call our own.

2 Here freedom spreads her banner wide,
    And casts her soft and hallow'd ray;
For thou our country's arms didst guide,
    And lead them on their conqu'ring way.

3 We praise thee, that the gospel light
    Through all our land its radiance sheds;
Scatters the shades of error's night,
    And heavenly blessings round us spreads.

4 When foes without and foes within,
  With threatening ills our land have press'd,
  Thou hast our nation's bulwark been,
  And, smiling, sent us peaceful rest.

5 O God, preserve us in thy fear,
  In troublous times our helper be;
  Diffuse thy truth's bright precepts here,
  And may we worship only thee.
                              Presb. Hymns.

537   *The Triumphs of Prayer.*
          FIRST PART.

COME, brothers and sisters, who love one another,
  And have done for years that are gone,
  How often we've met him in sweet heavenly union,
  Which opens the way to God's throne.

2 With joy and thanksgiving we'll praise him who loved us.
  While we run the bright shining way,
  Though we part here in body we are bound for one glory,
  And bound for each other to pray.

3 There were Joshua and Joseph, Elias and Moses,
  That prayed and God heard from his throne;
  There were Abraham and Isaac, and Jacob and David,
  And Solomon, and Stephen, and John.

4 There were Simeon and Anna, and I don't know how many,
  That prayed as they journeyed along:

Some cast among lions, some bound with rough irons,
Yet glory and praises they sung.

538 - SECOND PART.

SOME tell us that praying and also that praising
Is labor that's all spent in vain,
But we have such a witness that God hears with swiftness,
From praying we will not refrain.

2 There was old father Noah, and ten thousand more,
Who witnessed that God heard them pray;
There were Samuel and Hannah, Paul, Silas and Peter,
And Daniel and Jonah, we'll say.

3 That God by his Spirit, or an angel, does visit
Their souls and their bodies while praying:
Shall we all go fainting, while they all go praising,
And glorify God in the flame?

4 God grant us to inherit the same praying spirit
While we are a-journeying below,
Then when we cease praying we shall not cease praising,
But round God's bright throne we shall bow. *Unknown.*

539 10, 11, 10, 11.
"Come thou with us." Numb. x. 29.

O TELL me no more of this world's vain store,
The time for such trifles with me now is o'er;

A country I've found where true joys abound,
To dwell I'm determined on that happy ground.

2 The souls that believe, in paradise live,
And me in that number will Jesus receive:
My soul, don't delay—he calls thee away,
Rise, follow thy Saviour, and bless the glad day.

3 No mortal doth know what he can bestow,
What light, strength, and comfort—go after him, go;
Lo, onward I move to a city above,
None guesses how wondrous my journey will prove.

4 Great spoils I shall win from death, hell, and sin,
Midst outward afflictions shall feel Christ within;
And when I'm to die, receive me, I'll cry,
For Jesus hath lov'd me, I cannot tell why.

5 But this I do find, we two are so join'd,
He'll not live in glory and leave me behind:
So this is the race I'm running through grace,
Henceforth—till admitted to see my Lord's face.

6 And now I'm in care, my neighbors may share
These blessings: to seek them will none of you dare?
In bondage, O why, and death will you lie,
When one here assures you free grace is so nigh? *Gambold.*

540   FIRST PART.   11s and 6s.

BY faith I view my Saviour dying
On the tree; on the tree

DEVOTIONAL MISCELLANY.

To every nation he is crying,
  Look to me! look to me!
He bids the guilty now draw near,
Repent, believe, dismiss their fear;—
Hark! hark! what precious words I hear!
  Mercy's free! mercy's free!

2 Did Christ, when I w s sin pursuing,
  Pity me? pity me?
And did he snatch my soul from ruin?
Can it be? can it be?
O yes! he did salvation bring:
He is my Prophet, Priest, and King;
And now my happy soul can sing,—
  Mercy's free! mercy's free!

3 Jesus my weary soul refreshes;—
  Mercy's free! mercy's free!
And every moment, Christ is precious
  Unto me! unto me!
None can describe the bliss I prove,
While through this wilderness I rove:
All may enjoy the Saviour's love,
  Mercy's free! mercy's free!

541   SECOND PART.   11s & 6s.

JESUS, the mighty God, hath spoken
  Peace to me, peace to me:
Now all my chains of sin are broken—
  I am free, I am free:
Soon as I in his name believed,
The Holy Spirit I received,
And Christ from death my soul retrieved:
  Mercy's free! mercy's free!

2 This precious truth, ye sinners, hear it—
  Mercy's free! mercy's free!

Ye ministers of God, declare it—
Mercy's free! mercy's free!
Visit the heathen's dark abode,
Proclaim to all the love of God,
And spread the glorious news abroad—
Mercy's free! mercy's free!

2 Long as I live I'll still be crying,
Mercy's free! mercy's free!
And this shall be my theme when dying,
Mercy's free! mercy's free!
And when the vale of death I've pass'd,
When lodg'd above the stormy blast,
I'll sing, while endless ages last,
Mercy's free! mercy's free! *Unknown.*

612 *Will you go?* 8, 6.

WE'RE traveling home to heaven above,
   Will you go? will you go?
To sing the Saviour's dying love,
   Will you go? will you go?
Millions have reach'd that blest abode,
Anointed kings and priests to God;
And millions more are on the road,
   Will you go? will you go?

2 We're going to walk the plains of light,
Where perfect day excludes the night:
Our sun will there no more go down,
In that blest world of great renown,
Our days of mourning past and gone.

3 The way to heaven is free for all,
For Jew and Gentile, great and small.
Make up your mind, give God your heart,
With every sin and idol part,
And now for glory make a start.

4 The way to heaven is straight and plain:
Repent, believe, be born again:
The Saviour cries aloud to thee:
Take up thy cross and follow me,
And thou shalt my salvation see. *Unknown.*

543 *Opening Worship.* 8s, 7s.

BRETHREN, we have met to worship
And adore our God the Lord:
Will you pray with all your power,
While we try to preach the word?
All is vain unless the Spirit
Of the Holy One come down:
Brethren, pray, and holy manna
Will be shower'd all around.

2 Brethren, see poor sinners round you
Slumbering on the brink of woe:
Death is coming, hell is moving,
Can you bear to let them go?
See our fathers, and our mothers,
And our children sinking down:
Brethren, pray, and holy manna
Will be shower'd all around.

3 Sisters, will you join and help us?
Moses' sister join'd with him:
While you see the trembling sinners,
Have you no concern for them?
Tell them all about the Saviour,
Tell them that he will be found:
Pray on, sisters, and the manna
Will be shower'd all around.

4 Let us love our God supremely,
Let us love each other, too:
Let us love and pray for sinners,
Till our God makes all things new

Then he'll call us home to heaven,
At his table we'll sit down:
Christ will gird himself, and serve us
With sweet manna all around.
Unknown.

544 *" The unity of the Spirit."* Eph. iv. 3. 7s.

CHRIST, from whom all blessings flow,
Perfecting the saints below,
Hear us who thy nature share.
Who thy mystic body are.
Join us in one spirit join,
Let us still receive of thine:
Still for more on thee we call,
Thou who fillest all in all.

2 Move, and actuate, and guide:
Divers gifts to each divide:
Placed according to thy will,
Let us all our work fulfil:
Never from our office move,
Needful to each other prove:
Use the grace on each bestow'd,
Temp'red by the art of God!

3 Sweetly may we all agree,
Touch'd with softest sympathy;
Kindly for each other care;
Every member feel its share.
Many are we now and one,
We who Jesus have put on:
Names, and sects, and parties, fall:
Thou, O Christ, art all in all. *C. Wesley*

545   *Cleaving to God.*   7s.

GOD of love, that hear'st the pray'r,
Kindly for thy people care,

DEVOTIONAL MISCELLANY.

Who on thee alone depend:
Love us, save us to the end.
2 Save us in the prosp'rous hour,
From the flatt'ring tempter's power;
From his unsuspected wiles,
From the world's pernicious smiles.
3 Men of worldly, low design,
Let not these thy people join,
Poison our simplicity,
Drag us from our trust in thee.
4 Save us from the great and wise,
Till they sink in their own eyes,
Tamely to thy yoke submit,
Lay their honors at thy feet.
5 Never let the world break in,
Fix a mighty gulf between:
Keep us little and unknown,
Priz'd and lov'd by God alone. *C. Wesley*

546 *Prayer for the Salvation of Children.* 7s.

GOD of mercy, hear our pray'r
    For the children thou hast giv'n;
Let them all thy blessings share—
    Grace on earth and bliss in heaven.
2 In the morning of their days
    May their hearts be drawn to thee;
Let them learn to lisp thy praise
    In their earliest infancy.
3 When we see their passions rise,
    Sinful habits unsubdued,
Then to thee we lift our eyes,
    That their hearts may be renew'd.
4 Cleanse their souls from every stain,
    Through the Saviour's precious blood;

Let them all be born again,
 And be reconciled to God.

' For this mercy, Lord, we cry;
 Bend thine ever-gracious ear:
 While on thee our souls rely,
 Hear our prayer—in mercy hear.
Campbell's Col.

647   *Revivals.*

PASS me not, O gentle Saviour,
 Hear my humble cry;
While on others thou art smiling,
 Do not pass me by.

CHO.—Saviour, Saviour, hear my humble cry,
 While on others thou art calling,
 Do not pass me by.

2 Let me at a throne of mercy
 Find a sweet relief,
Kneeling there in deep contrition,
 Help my unbelief.

3 Trusting only in thy merit,
 Would I seek thy face:
Heal my wounded, broken spirit,
 Save me by thy grace.

4 Thou the Spring of all my comfort,
 More than life to me,
Whom have I on earth beside thee?
 Whom in heaven but thee?   *Sankey's Col.*

548   *Scenes of Glory.*   8, 7.

DARK and thorny is the desert
 Through which pilgrims make their way;
Yet beyond this vale of sorrow
 Lie the fields of endless day:

DEVOTIONAL MISCELLANY.

Fiends, loud howling through the desert,
   Make them tremble as they go;
And the fiery darts of Satan
   Often bring their courage low.

2 O young pilgrims, are you weary
   Of the roughness of the way?
Does your strength begin to fail you,
   And your vigor to decay?
Jesus, Jesus, will go with you:
   He will lead you to his throne:—
He who dyed his garments for you,
   And the wine-press trod alone.

3 There, on flowery hills of pleasure,
   Lie the fields of endless rest:
There shall love and joy forever
   Reign and triumph in your breast:
Hail, ye happy, happy spirits!
   Death no more shall make you fear.
Grief or sorrow, pain or anguish,
   Never shall distress you there. *Unknown*

549   *The open gate.*

THERE is a gate that stands ajar,
   And through its portals gleaming,
A radiance from the cross afar,
   The Saviour's love revealing.

REF.—Oh, depth of mercy! can it be
   That gate was left ajar for me?
For me, for me?
Was left ajar for me?

2 That gate ajar stands free for all
   Who seek through it salvation;
The rich and poor, the great and small,
   Of every tribe and nation.

3 Press onward, then, though foes may frown,
While mercy's gate is open;
Accept the cross, and win the crown,
Love's everlasting token.

4 Beyond the river's brink we'll lay
The cross that here is given,
And bear the crown of life away,
And love him more in heaven.

From Gospel Hymns

550   *Hesitation.*

"ALMOST persuaded" now to believe;
"Almost persuaded" Christ to receive;
Seems now some soul to say,
"Go, Spirit go thy way;
Some more convenient day
On thee I'll call."

2 "Almost persuaded," come, come to-day;
"Almost persuaded," turn not away;
Jesus invites you here,
Angels are lingering near,
Prayers rise from hearts so dear;
"O wanderer, come."

3 "Almost persuaded," harvest is past!
"Almost persuaded," doom comes at last!
"Almost" cannot avail;
"Almost" is but to fail!
Sad, sad, that bitter wail—
"Almost—*but lost!*"   *P. P. Bliss.*

551   *My Beloved.*   11s & 8s.

O THOU, in whose presence my soul takes delight,
On whom in affliction I call,

My comfort by day, and my song in the night,
My hope, my salvation, my all!

2 Where dost thou, dear Shepherd, resort with
thy sheep,
To feed them in pastures of love?
Say, why in the valley of death should I weep,
Or alone in this wilderness rove?

3 O why should I wander an alien from thee,
Or cry in the desert for bread?
Thy foes will rejoice when my sorrows they see,
And smile at the tears I have shed.

4 Ye daughters of Zion, declare have you seen
The star that on Israel shone?
Say, if in your tents my Beloved has been,
And where with his flocks he is gone.

5 He looks! and ten thousands of angels rejoice,
And myriads wait for his word;
He speaks! and eternity, filled with his voice,
Re-echoes the praise of the Lord.

6 Dear Shepherd, I hear, and will follow thy call;
I know the sweet sound of thy voice:
Restore and defend me, for thou art my all,
And in thee I will ever rejoice. *Unknown.*

552 *The Rock that is higher than I.* P. M.

OH, sometimes the shadows are deep,
   And rough seems the path to the goal,
And sorrows, how often they sweep
   Like tempests down over the soul.
CHO.—‖:Oh, then to the Rock let me fly,
    To the Rock that is higher than I.:‖

2 Oh, sometimes how long seems the day,
   And sometimes how weary my feet;
   But toiling in life's dusty way,
   The Rock's blessed shadow, how sweet

3 Oh, near to the Rock let me keep,
   Or blessings, or sorrows prevail;
   Or climbing the mountain-way steep
   Or walking the shadowy vale. *E. Johnson*

553 *Is my name written there?* 7s. & 6s

LORD, I care not for riches,
   Neither silver nor gold;
I would make sure of heaven,
   I would enter the fold.
In the book of thy kingdom,
   With its pages so fair,
Tell me, Jesus, my Saviour,
   Is my name written there?

Cho.—Is my name written there,
   On the page white and fair?
In the book of thy kingdom,
   Is my name written there?

2 Lord, my sins they are many,
   Like the sands of the sea,
But thy blood, O my Saviour,
   Is sufficient for me;
For thy promise is written,
   In bright letters that glow,
"Though your sins be as scarlet,
   I will make them like snow."

3 Oh! that beautiful city,
   With its mansions of light,
With its glorified beings,
   In pure garments of white;

DEVOTIONAL MISCELLANY.

Where no evil thing cometh,
To despoil what is fair;
Where the angels are watching,—
Is my name written there?
M. A. Kidder.

554   *I love thee, thou art mine forever.*   11s.

MY Jesus, I love thee, I know thou art mine,
For thee all the follies of sin I resign;
My gracious Redeemer, my Saviour art thou,
If ever I loved thee, my Jesus, 'tis now.

2 I love thee because thou hast first lovéd me,
And purchased my pardon on Calvary's tree;
I love thee for wearing the thorns on thy brow,
If ever I loved thee, my Jesus, 'tis now.

3 I'll love thee in life, I will love thee in death,
And praise thee as long as thou lendest me breath:
And say when the death-dew lies cold on my brow,
If ever I loved thee, my Jesus, 'tis now,

4 In mansions of glory and endless delight,
I'll ever adore thee in heaven so bright:
I'll sing with the glittering crown on my brow,
If ever I loved thee, my Jesus, 'tis now.
English Baptist Col.

555   *The thought of Thee.*   C. M.

JESUS, the very thought of thee
With sweetness fills the breast;
But sweeter far thy face to see,
And in thy presence rest.

2 No voice can sing, no heart can frame,
    Nor can the memory find
A sweeter sound than Jesus' name,
    The Saviour of mankind.

3 O Hope of every contrite heart,
    O Joy of all the meek,
To those who ask, how kind thou art!
    How good, to those who seek!

4 But what to those who find? Ah, this
    Nor tongue nor pen can show:
The love of Jesus, what it is,
    None but his loved ones know.

5 Jesus, our only joy be thou,
    As thou our prize wilt be;
In thee be all our glory now,
    And through eternity. *Bernard.*

556   "*All things are of God.*"   C. M.
    1 Sam. iii. 18.

IT is the Lord—enthroned in light,
    Whose claims are all divine,
Who has an undisputed right
    To govern me and mine.

2 It is the Lord—who gives me all—
    My wealth, my friends, my ease;
And of his bounties may recall
    Whatever part he please.

3 It is the Lord—my covenant God,
    Thrice bléssed be his name;
Whose gracious promise, sealed with blood,
    Must ever be the same.

4 Can I, with hopes so firmly built,
    Be sullen, or repine?
No! gracious God, take what thou wilt,
    To thee I all resign. *Green.*

557 *Lord, grant my Prayer.* C. M.

GRANT me within thy courts a place,
  Among thy saints a seat,
For ever to behold thy face,
  And worship at thy feet;
2 In thy pavilion to abide
  When storms of trouble blow,
And in thy tabernacle hide,
  Secure from every foe.
3 Then leave me not when griefs assail
  And earthly comforts flee;
When father, mother, kindred fail,
  My God! remember me. *Montgomery.*

558 *The Saviour welcomed.* C. M.
Prov. xxiii. 26.

WELCOME, O Saviour! to my heart;
  Possess thine humble throne;
Bid every rival hence depart,
  And claim me for thine own.
2 The world and Satan I forsake—
  To thee I all resign;
My longing heart, O Jesus! take,
  And fill with love divine.
3 Oh! may I never turn aside,
  Nor from thy bosom flee;
Let nothing here my heart divide—
  I give it all to thee. *Bourne.*

559 *Desiring salvation.* Ps. li. C. M.

O GOD of mercy! hear my call,
  My load of guilt remove;
Break down this separating wall,
  That bars me from thy love.

2 Give me the presence of thy grace;
   Then my rejoicing tongue
Shall speak aloud thy righteousness,
   And make thy praise my song.
3 No blood of goats, nor heifer slain,
   For sin could e'er atone:
The death of Christ shall still remain
   Sufficient and alone.
4 A soul, oppressed with sin's desert,
   My God will ne'er despise;
An humble groan, a broken heart,
   Is our best sacrifice.   *Watts.*

560   *Zeal. John xii. 43.*   L. M.

GO, labor on; spend and be spent,—
   Thy joy to do the Father's will;
It is the way the Master went;
   Should not the servant tread it still?
2 Go, labor on; 'tis not for naught;
   Thine earthly loss is heavenly gain;
Men heed thee, love thee, praise thee not;
   The Master praises,—what are men?
3 Go, labor on; enough, while here,
   If he shall praise thee, if he deign
Thy willing heart to mark and cheer:
   No toil for him shall be in vain.
4 Toil on, and in thy toil rejoice;
   For toil comes rest, for exile home;
Soon shalt thou hear the Bridegroom's voice,
   The midnight peal: "Behold, I come!"
                                          Bonar.

561   *Zeal. John ix. 4.*   L. M.

GO, labor on, while it is day;
   The world's dark night is hastening on:

DEVOTIONAL MISCELLANY.

Speed, speed thy work,—cast sloth away!
   It is not thus that souls are won.

2 Men die in darkness at your side,
   Without a hope to cheer the tomb;
Take up the torch and wave it wide—
   The torch that lights time's thickest gloom.

3 Toil on,—faint not; keep watch and pray!
   Be wise the erring soul to win;
Go forth into the world's highway;
   Compel the wanderer to come in.

4 Go, labor on; your hands are weak;
   Your knees are faint, your soul cast down;
Yet falter not; the prize you seek
   Is near,—a kingdom and a crown! *Bonar.*

562   "*Though thou slay me, yet will I*   L. M.
     trust in thee." Heb. vii. 11.

I BLESS thee, Lord, for sorrows sent
   To break the dream of human power,
For now my shallow cistern's spent,
   I find thy fount and thirst no more.

2 I take thy hand, and fears grow still;
   Behold thy face, and doubts remove;
Who would not yield his wavering will
   To perfect truth and boundless love!

3 That truth gives promise of a dawn,
   Beneath whose light I am to see,
When all these blinding veils are drawn,
   This was the wisest path for me.

4 That love this restless soul doth teach
   The strength of thy eternal calm;
And tunes its sad and broken speech,
   To sing ev'n now the angels' psalm. *Anon.*

DEVOTIONAL MISCELLANY.

563　　*God is love.* Heb. xii. 6.　　L. M.

I CANNOT always trace the way
　Where thou, Almighty One, dost move;
But I can always, always say,
　That God is love, that God is love.

2 When fear her chilling mantle flings
　O'er earth, my soul to heaven above,
As to her native home, upsprings,
　For God is love, for God is love.

3 When mystery clouds my darkened path,
　I'll check my dread, my doubts reprove:
In this my soul sweet comfort hath,
　That God is love, that God is love.

4 Yes, God is love;—a thought like this
　Can every gloomy thought remove,
And turn all tears, all woes, to bliss,
　For God is love, for God is love.　　*Anon.*

564　　*O draw near us.* John viii. 36.　　8s & 7s.

SAVIOUR, hear us, through thy merit;
　Lowly bending at thy feet;
Oh, draw near us by thy Spirit;
　Prostrate at thy mercy-seat.

2 For the joys of thy salvation,
　Still we raise our cries to thee;
Hear the voice of supplication,
　Set our souls at liberty.　　*Anon.*

565　　*The Sower.* Ps. cxxvi. 6.　　8s & 7s.

HE that goeth forth with weeping,
　Bearing precious seed in love,
Never tiring, never sleeping,
　Findeth mercy from above.

2 Soft descend the dews of heaven,
    Bright the rays celestial shine;
  Precious fruits will thus be given,
    Through an influence all divine.
3 Sow thy seed, be never weary,
    Let no fears thy soul annoy;
  Be the prospect ne'er so dreary,
    Thou shalt reap the fruits of joy.
4 Lo, the scene of verdure brightening!
    See the rising grain appear;
  Look again! the fields are whitening.
    For the harvest time is near. *Hastings.*

566   *Glorying in the cross.*   8s, 7s.

IN the cross of Christ I glory,
    Towering o'er the wrecks of time;
  All the light of sacred story
    Gathers round its head sublime.
2 When the woes of life o'ertake me,
    Hopes deceive, and fears annoy,
  Never shall the cross forsake me;
    Lo! it glows with peace and joy.
3 When the sun of bliss is beaming
    Light and love upon my way,
  From the cross the radiance streaming
    Adds more lustre to the day.
4 Bane and blessing, pain and pleasure,
    By the cross are sanctified;
  Peace is there, that knows no measure,
    Joys that through all time abide.
              Sir John Bowring.

567   *Only Jesus.* Matt. xvii. 8.   8s, 7s.

JESUS only, when the morning
    Beams upon the path I tread;

Jesus only, when the darkness
  Gathers round my weary head.
' Jesus only, when the billows
  Cold and sullen o'er me roll;
Jesus only, when the trumpet
  Rends the tomb and wakes the souL

3 Jesus only, when in judgment
  Boding fears my heart appall;
Jesus only, when the wretched
  On the rocks and mountains call.

4 Jesus only, when, adoring,
  Saints their crowns before him bring;
Jesus only, I will, joyous,
  Through eternal ages sing. *Nason.*

568 *Lover of Sinners.* Prov. xviii. 24. 8s, 7s.

ONE there is, above all others,
  Well deserves the name of Friend;
His is love beyond a brother's,
  Costly, free, and knows no end.

2 Which of all our friends, to save us,
    Could or would have shed his blood?
  But our Jesus died to have us
    Reconciled in him to God.

3 When he lived on earth abaséd,
    Friend of sinners was his name;
  Now above all glory raiséd,
    He rejoices in the same.

4 Oh! for grace our hearts to soften,
    Teach us, Lord, at length, to love;
  We, alas! forget too often
    What a friend we have above. *Newton.*

569   *The Heavenly Home.*   L. M.

MY heavenly home is bright and fair;
   Nor pain nor death can enter there;
Its glittering towers the sun outshine;
That heavenly mansion shall be mine.

   I'm going home, I'm going home,
   I'm going home to die no more;
   To die no more, to die no more,
   I'm going home to die no more.

2 My Father's house is built on high,
Far, far above the starry sky.
When from this earthly prison free,
That heavenly mansion mine shall be.

3 While here, a stranger far from home,
Affliction's waves may round me foam;
Although, like Lazarus, sick and poor,
My heavenly mansion is secure.

4 Let others seek a home below,
Which flames devour, or waves o'erflow,
Be mine the happier lot to own
A heavenly mansion near the throne.

5 Then fail the earth, let stars decline,
And sun and moon refuse to shine,
All nature sink and cease to be,
That heavenly mansion stands for me.
                          William Hunter.

570   *Rapturous Anticipation.*   12, 9.

COME, let us ascend,
   My companion and friend,
To a taste of the banquet above:

If thy heart be as mine,
If for Jesus it pine,
Come up into the chariot of love.

2 Who in Jesus confide,
We are bold to outride
The storms of affliction beneath;
With the prophet we soar
To the heavenly shore,
And outfly all the arrows of death.

3 By faith we are come
To our permanent home;
By hope we the rapture improve:
By love we still rise,
And look down on the skies,
For the heaven of heavens is love.

4 Who on earth can conceive
How happy we live
In the palace of God the great King?
What a concert of praise,
When our Jesus's grace
The whole heavenly company sing!

5 What a rapturous song,
When the glorified throng
In the spirit of harmony join;
Join all the glad choirs,
Hearts, voices and lyres,
And the burden is, "Mercy divine!"

6 "Hallelujah," they cry,
To the King of the sky,
To the great everlasting I AM;
To the Lamb that was slain,
And that liveth again,—
"Hallelujah to God and the Lamb!"

Charles Wesley.

THE SABBATH.

SECTION XVIII.
The Sabbath.

571 *Christ's Resurrection.* Psalm cxviii. 24. C.M.

THIS is the day the Lord hath made,
   He calls the hours his own;
Let heaven rejoice, let earth be glad,
   And praise surround the throne.

2 To-day he rose and left the dead,
   And Satan's empire fell;
To-day the saints his triumphs spread,
   And all his wonders tell.

3 Hosanna to the anointed King,
   To David's holy Son!
Help us, O Lord! descend and bring
   Salvation from thy throne.

4 Blest be the Lord who comes to men
   With messages of grace;
Who comes in God his Father's name,
   To save our sinful race.

5 Hosanna in the highest strains
   The church on earth can raise;
The highest heavens, in which he reigns,
   Shall give him nobler praise.   *Watts.*

572 *O come, let us worship and bow down.* C. M.

COME, let us join with one accord
   In hymns around the throne!
This is the day our rising Lord
   Hath made and called his own.

THE SABBATH.

2 This is the day which God hath blessed,
  The brightest of the seven,
Type of that everlasting rest
  The saints enjoy in heaven.

3 Then let us in his name sing on,
  And hasten to that day
When our Redeemer shall come down,
  And shadows pass away.

4 Not one, but all our days below,
  Let us in hymns employ;
And in our Lord rejoicing, go
  To his eternal joy.   *C. Wesley.*

573   *In the Spirit.* Rev. i. 10.   C. M.

MAY I throughout this day of thine
  Be in thy Spirit, Lord:
Spirit of humble fear divine,
  That trembles at thy word;—

2 Spirit of faith, my heart to raise,
  And fix on things above;
Spirit of sacrifice and praise,
  Of holiness and love.   *C. Wesley.*

574   *In the Sanctuary.*   L. M.

FAR from my thoughts, vain world, begone!
  Let my religious hours alone:
Fain would my eyes my Saviour see;
I wait a visit, Lord, from thee.

2 My heart grows warm with holy fire,
And kindles with a pure desire:
Come, my dear Jesus, from above,
And feed my soul with heavenly love.

THE SABBATH.

3 Blest Jesus, what delicious fare!
How sweet thine entertainments are!
Never did angels taste above
Redeeming grace and dying love. *Watts.*

575 *The day of rest.* L. M.

ANOTHER six days' work is done;
Another Sabbath is begun:
Return, my soul, enjoy thy rest;
Improve the day thy God hath blessed.

2 O that our thoughts and thanks may rise,
As grateful incense, to the skies;
And draw from Christ that sweet repose
Which none but he that feels it knows!

3 This heavenly calm within the breast
Is the dear pledge of glorious rest,
Which for the Church of God remains,
The end of cares, the end of pains.

4 In holy duties let the day,
In holy comforts, pass away:
How sweet, a Sabbath thus to spend,
In hope of one that ne'er shall end!
J. Stennett.

576 *Sweet is the work.* Psalm xcii. L. M.

SWEET is the work, my God, my King,
To praise thy name give thanks, and sing,
To show thy love by morning light,
And talk of all thy truth by night.

2 Sweet is the day of sacred rest:
No mortal cares shall seize my breast:
O may my heart in tune be found,
Like David's harp of solemn sound!

THE SABBATH.

3 My heart shall triumph in my Lord,
And bless his works, and bless his word:
Thy works of grace, how bright they shine!
How deep thy counsels! how divine!

4 Then I shall share a glorious part
When grace hath well refined my heart,
And fresh supplies of joy are shed,
Like holy oil, to cheer my head.

5 Then shall I see, and hear, and know,
All I desired or wished below;
And every hour find sweet employ
In that eternal world of joy. *Watts.*

577 *The Eternal Sabbath.* L. M.

THINE earthly Sabbaths, Lord, we love;
But there's a nobler rest above;
To that our lab'ring souls aspire,
With ardent pangs of strong desire.

2 No more fatigue, no more distress:
Nor sin nor hell shall reach the place;
No sighs shall mingle with the songs
Which warble from immortal tongues.

3 No rude alarms of raging foes;
No cares to break the long repose;
No midnight shade, no clouded sun,
But sacred, high, eternal noon.

4 O long expected day, begin;
Dawn on these realms of woe and sin:
Fain would we leave this weary road,
And sleep in death, to rest with God.
Doddridge.

THE SABBATH.

578 *Welcome Sabbath.* S. M.

WELCOME, sweet day of rest,
  That saw the Lord arise:
Welcome to this reviving breast,
  And these rejoicing eyes!

2 The King himself comes near,
  And feasts his saints to-day;
Here we may sit, and see him here,
  And love, and praise, and pray.

3 One day within the place
  Which thou dost, Lord, frequent,
Is sweeter than ten thousand days
  In sinful pleasures spent.

4 My willing soul would stay
  In such a frame as this,
And sit and sing herself away
  To everlasting bliss *Watts.*

579 *The Eternal Sabbath.* S. M.

HAIL to the Sabbath day!
  The day divinely given,
When men to God their homage pay,
  And earth draws near to heaven.

2 Lord, in this sacred hour,
  Within thy courts we bend,
And bless thy love, and own thy power,
  Our Father and our Friend.

3 But thou art not alone
  In courts by mortals trod;
Nor only is the day thine own
  When man draws near to God:

THE SABBATH.

4 Thy temple is the arch
  Of yon unmeasured sky;
  Thy Sabbath, the stupendous march
  Of vast eternity.

5 Lord, may that holier day
  Dawn on thy servants' sight;
  And purer worship may we pay
  In heaven's unclouded light.
  Stephen G. Bulfinch.

580 C. M.
But now is Christ risen from the dead. 1 Cor. xv. 20.

THIS is the day, the sacred day
  When Jesus left the grave:
  Of him we sing, and well we may,
  His arm is strong to save.

2 'Tis sweet to know that by his death
  We live—this grace is sweet:
  The Saviour, with his dying breath,
  Proclaim'd his work complete.

3 He lives, he reigns the God of love,
  He reigns for evermore:
  His throne, all other thrones above;
  His name, all names before.

4 To him who died and rose again,
  The Lord of earth and heav'n:
  To him, by angels and by men,
  Be endless glory giv'n:

5 The glory due to him alone,
  Who reigns in heav'n above;
  Who fills the everlasting throne;
  The God of grace and love.
  Kelley's Hymns.

THE SABBATH.

581   C. M.
Hitherto hath the Lord helped us. 1 Sam. vii. 12.

ANOTHER week is past and gone,
   Rejoice, we're nearer home,
Our gracious Lord has led us on;
   And thus far have we come.

2 Our Ebenezer here we'll raise:
   The Lord our help has been:
We'll publish, to our Saviour's praise,
   The things our eyes have seen..

3 We've seen our foes before us flee,
   They turned and fled apace:
To God alone the glory be;
   We'll sing his pow'r and grace.

4 We've seen the timid lose their fears,
   And valiant wax in fight;
We've seen the mourners dry their tears,
   And put their griefs to flight.

5 We've seen the pris'ners burst their chains,
   And walk at liberty;
We've seen the guilty lose his stains,
   And without blemish be.

6 His word, on which we rest, is true,
   Himself a faithful friend:
And he, who kept us hitherto,
   Will keep us to the end.
              Kelley's Hymns.

582   8s, 7s.
Seeing him who is invisible. Heb. xi. 27.

NEITHER "voice" we have nor "vision,"
   Yet we walk as if we had;

Objects of the world's derision;
  Sorrowful, yet always "glad."
On the word of truth relying,
  Word of him who cannot lie,
We go on, the foe defying,
  Knowing that the Lord is nigh.

2 One "unseen" we own as master,
  And with him we look to be;
Fly, ye seasons, fly still faster,
  Till our "Lord from heav'n" we see.
Never can we rest, no never,
  Till the day when he appears,
Then we cease from sin forever,
  And he wipes away our tears.

3 Then we shall be what we should be,
  Which, till then, can never be;
Then we shall be where we would be,
  Dwelling, Lord, in heav'n with thee.
What a hope! To be forever
  In thy presence, Lord, above;
To behold thee there, and never
  Cease to sing thy grace and love
            Kelley's Hymns.

Selections from the Psalms.

[NOTE.—These Psalms are selected from the revised arrangement by the United Presb. Ch.]

583   *Psalm* lxxxii.   C. M.

AMONG assembled men of might,
    The mighty God doth stand:
He stands to order judgment right
    To judges of the land.

2 How long will ye, with wrongful aid,
   The oppressor's cause protect?
   How long, by gift and favor swayed,
   The wicked man respect?
3 Protect the fatherless and weak,
   Defend the poor distressed;
   And give deliv'rance to the meek
   By lawless power oppressed.
4 They will not know nor understand,
   In darkness on they go:
   Quake all the pillars of the land;
   They totter to and fro.
5 "True, ye are gods, ye kings," I said;
   "And sons of God Most High;
   Yet as the sons of men ye fade,
   And as the princes die."
6 Arise, O God, assert thy right,
   Pronounce thy just decree;
   The heritage of earth by right
   Belongs, O Lord, to thee.

584 *Psalm* xci. **C. M.**

THE man that doth in secret place
   Of God Most High reside,
Beneath the shade of him that is
   Th' Almighty shall abide.
2 I of the Lord my God will say,
   He is my refuge still,
   He is my fortress, and my God;
   And trust in him I will.
3 Assuredly he shall thee save,
   And give deliverance
   From cunning fowler's snare, and **from**
   The deadly pestilence.

SELECTIONS FROM THE PSALMS.

4 His feathers shall thee hide; thy trust
　Beneath his wings shall be:
His faithfulness shall be a shield
　And buckler unto thee.

5 Thou shalt not need to be afraid
　For terrors of the night;
Nor for the arrow that doth fly
　By day, while it is light;

6 Nor for the pestilence, that walks
　In darkness secretly;
Nor for destruction, that doth waste
　At noon-day openly.

7 A thousand at thy side shall fall,
　On thy right hand shall lie
Ten thousand dead; yet unto thee
　It shall not once come nigh.

585　　　　*Psalm* lxxxiv.　　　　**C. M.**
　　　　　FIRST PART.

O LORD of hosts, how lovely is
　The place where thou dost dwell!
The tabernacles of thy grace
　In pleasantness excel.

2 My soul doth long, yea even faint,
　Jehovah's courts to see;
My heart and flesh are crying out,
　O living God, for thee.

3 Behold, the sparrow findeth out
　A house wherein to rest;
The swallow also for herself
　Hath found a peaceful nest.

4 And there securely sheltered she
　Her young ones forth may bring·

SELECTIONS FROM THE PSALMS.

So thine own altars, Lord of Hosts,
I seek, my God and King.

5 Blest all who dwell within thy house,
They ever give thee praise,
And blest the man whose strength thou art,
In whose heart are the ways:

6 Who passing on through Baca's vale,
Do make of it a well;
And copious rains descending there,
The pools with water fill.

586   SECOND PART.   C. M.

SO they from strength unwearied go
Still forward unto strength;
And they in Zion shall appear
Before the Lord at length.

8 Lord God of hosts, my prayer now hear;
O Jacob's God, give ear.
See, God, our shield, look on the face
Of thy anointed dear.

9 For in thy courts one day excels
A thousand; rather in
My God's house will I keep a door,
Than dwell in tents of sin.

10 For God the Lord's a sun and shield,
He'll grace and glory give;
And no good thing will he withhold
From them that justly live.

11 O thou that art the Lord of hosts,
That man is truly blest,
Who with unshaken confidence
On thee alone doth rest.

SELECTIONS FROM THE PSALMS.

587   *Psalm cxi.*   C. M.

PRAISE ye the Lord: with all my heart
 I will God's praise declare,
Ev'n where assemblies of the just
 And congregations are.

2 Jehovah's works are very great,
 The wonders of his might;
Sought out they are of every one
 Who in them takes delight.

3 His work most honorable is,
 Most glorious and pure,
And his untainted righteousness
 Forever doth endure.

4 His works of wonder he hath made
 To be remembered well:
In grace and in compassion great
 Jehovah doth excel.

5 The Lord provideth food for all
 Who truly do him fear;
And evermore his covenant
 He in his mind will bear.

6 He did the power of his works
 To his own people show,
That he the heathen's heritage
 Upon them might bestow.

588   *Psalm ciii.*   8s & 7s.

O my soul, bless thou Jehovah,
 All within me bless his name,
Bless Jehovah, and forget not
 All his mercies to proclaim.

2 Who forgives all thy transgressions,
 Thy diseases all who heals;

Who redeems thee from destruction,
Who with thee so kindly deals.

3 Who with tender mercies crowns thee,
Who with good things fills thy mouth,
So that even like the eagle
Thou hast been restored to youth.

4 In his righteousness, Jehovah
Will deliver those distressed;
He will execute just judgment
In the cause of all oppressed.

5 He made known his ways to Moses,
And his acts to Isr'el's race;
God is plentiful in mercy,
Slow to anger, rich in grace.

6 He will not forever chide us,
Nor keep anger in his mind,
Hath not dealt as we offended,
Nor rewarded as we sinned.

589 *Psalm vi.* 8s & 7s.

LORD, in anger do not chasten;
Thy fierce wrath from me restrain;
I am weak; in mercy hasten,
O relieve my flesh from pain.

2 Sorrows deep my soul are grieving;
Lord, how long!—O pity take;
Lord, return, my soul relieving;
Save me for thy mercy's sake.

3 Thee the grave no more remembers:
Who gives thanks among the dead?
Weary groans distract my slumbers,
Tears have overflowed my bed.

4 Sorely vexed by my oppressors,
   Grief like age has dimmed my eye,
  Hence, and leave me, all transgressors,
   For the Lord hath heard my cry.
5 God hath heard my supplication;
   My petition will not spurn.
  Let my foes, with sore vexation,
   Back in sudden shame return.

590 *Psalm lxx.* 11s & 8s.

MAKE haste, O my God, to deliver I pray,
   O Lord, to my succor make haste:
  Let them be confounded who seek me to slay,
   And in their own folly disgraced.

2 Let them be turned back in confusion, O Lord,
   Who wish my destruction to see;
  Let shame and defeat be their only reward,
   Who laugh in derision at me.

3 Let all them that seek thee be glad and rejoice,
   And who thy salvation would see;
  In anthems of praise let them lift up the voice,
   And constantly magnify thee.

4 But I, poor and needy, still trust in thy word;
   Make haste to the rescue, I pray;
  My helper thou art, and my Saviour, O Lord,
   No longer thy coming delay.

591 *Psalm ii.* L. M.
FIRST PART.

WHY do the heathen storm with ire?
   The people vanity devise?

SELECTIONS FROM THE PSALMS.

The rulers craftily conspire,
The kings of earth rebellious rise.
2 Against the Lord they lift their hands,
Against him and his Christ they say,
"Asunder let us break their bands,
And from us cast their cords away."
3 He that in heaven sits shall laugh,
Jehovah shall deride them all;
Then as he speaks in burning wrath,
Dismay and dread shall on them fall.
4 "Yet notwithstanding I ordain,"
Thus shall he speak his sov'reign will,
"He my anointed King shall reign,
On Zion, my own holy hill."

592   SECOND PART.   L. M.

THUS spake to me the Holy One,
I utter now the Lord's decree,
"Thou art proclaimed my only Son,
This day have I begotten thee.
6 "Ask for inheritance of me,
And I will make the heathen thine,
And for possession, give to thee
The earth to its remotest line.
7 "An iron sceptre thou shalt sway,
And with it break and crush them all;
E'en like the potter's brittle clay,
Thou shalt them dash in pieces small."
8 And now, ye kings, be wise and hear;
Be warned, ye judges of the earth;
See that ye serve the Lord with fear,
And mingle trembling with your mirth.

593   *Psalm* xcvii.   L. M.

JEHOVAH reigns, let earth be glad,
  And all her islands clap their hands;
With clouds and darkness he is clad,
  His throne in right and judgment stands.

2 A fiery stream before him goes,
  And burns around him all his foes;
His lightning shafts, in vengeance hurled,
  Blaze lurid o'er the trembling world.

3 Like wax the mountains melt away,
  Before his majesty divine;
The heavens his righteousness display,
  All nations see his glory shine.

4 Be shamed who idols serve and boast,
  Fear him, ye gods, with all your host;
When Zion glad, thy judgments heard,
  Then Judah's daughters praised the Lord.

5 Exalted is thy throne, O Lord,
  Above all gods, above all lands;
Hate evil, ye who love his word,
  His saints he frees from wicked hands.

6 For all the righteous sown is light,
  And joy for men in heart upright,
Ye saints rejoice in God; him bless,
  When musing on his holiness.

594   *Psalm* xcviii.   L. M.

COME, let us sing unto the Lord,
  New songs of praise with sweet accord;
For wonders great by him are done;
His hand and arm have vict'ry won.

2 The great salvation of our God
  Is seen through all the earth abroad;
  Before the heathen's wondering sight,
  He hath revealed his truth and right.

3 He called to mind his truth and grace
  In promise made to Isr'el's race;
  And unto earth's remotest bound,
  Glad tidings of salvation sound.

4 All lands to God lift up your voice;
  Sing praise to him, with shouts rejoice;
  With voice of joy and loud acclaim,
  Let all unite and praise his name.

5 Praise God with harp, with harp sing praise,
  With voice of psalms his glory raise;
  With trumpets, cornets, gladly sing,
  And shout before the Lord, the King.

6 Let earth be glad, let billows roar,
  And all that dwell from shore to shore;
  Let floods clap hands with one accord,
  Let hills rejoice before the Lord.

595   *Psalm* c.   L. M.

ALL people that on earth do dwell,
  Sing to the Lord with cheerful voice.
Him serve with mirth, his praise forth tell,
  Come ye before him and rejoice.

2 Know that the Lord is God indeed;
    Without our aid he did us make:
  We are his flock, he doth us feed,
    And for his sheep he doth us take.

3 O enter then his gates with joy,
    Within his courts his praise proclaim;

SELECTIONS FROM THE PSALMS.

Let thankful songs your tongues employ,
O bless and magnify his name.

4 Because the Lord our God is good,
His mercy is forever sure;
His truth at all times firmly stood,
And shall from age to age endure.

596 *Psalm* xix. H. M.
FIRST PART.

THE glory of the Lord
The heavens declare abroad;
The firmament displays
The handiwork of God;
Day unto day declareth speech,
And night to night doth knowledge teach.

2 Aloud they do not speak,
They utter forth no word,
Nor into language break;
Their voice is never heard.
Their line through all the earth extends,
Their words to earth's remotest ends.

3 In them he for the sun
Hath set a dwelling-place;
Rejoicing as a man
Of strength to run a race;
He, bridegroom-like in his array,
Comes from his chamber, bringing day.

4 His daily going forth
Is from the end of heaven;
The firmament to him
Is for his circuit given—
His circuit reaches to its ends,
And everywhere his heat extends.

SELECTIONS FROM THE PSALMS.

597   *Psalm* xix.   H. M.
SECOND PART.

GOD'S perfect law converts
    The soul in sin that lies;
His testimony sure
    Doth make the simple wise;
His statutes just delight the heart;
His holy precepts light impart.

6   The fear of God is clean,
    And ever doth endure;
His judgments all are truth,
    And righteousness most pure.
To be desired are they far more
Than finest gold in richest store.

7   God's judgments to the taste
    More sweet than honey are,
Than honey from the comb
    That droppeth, sweeter far.
With counsel they thy servant guard;
In keeping them is great reward.

8   Who can his errors know?
    From secret faults me cleanse;
Thy servant keep thou back
    From all presumptuous sins.
O let them not my way control,
Nor gain dominion o'er my soul.

9   Then in thy righteous way
    My life shall upright be;
I shall be innocent—
    From great transgression free.
Accept my words, and thoughts of heart;
Lord, thou my strength and Saviour art.

SELECTIONS FROM THE PSALMS.

598   Psalm xxiii.   L. M

MY Shepherd is the Lord Most High,
    And all my wants shall be supplied;
In pastures green he makes me lie,
    And leads by streams which gently glide.

2 He in his mercy doth restore
    My soul when sinking in distress;
For his name's sake he evermore
    Leads me in paths of righteousness.

3 Yea, though I walk through death's dark
        vale,
    Ev'n there no evil will I fear,
Because thy presence shall not fail,
    Thy rod and staff my soul shall cheer.

4 For me a table thou hast spread,
    Prepared before the face of foes;
With oil thou dost anoint my head;
    My cup is filled and overflows.

5 Goodness and mercy shall not cease
    Through all my days to follow me;
And in God's house my dwelling place
    With him forevermore shall be.

599   Psalm xxiv.   11s.

THE earth and the fulness with which it is
    stored,
The world and its dwellers belong to the Lord;
For he on the seas its foundation hath laid,
And firm on the waters its pillars hath stayed.

2 What man shall the hill of Jehovah ascend?
And who in the place of his holiness stand?
The man of pure heart, and of hands without
        stain,
Who swears not to falsehood, nor loves what
    is vain.

3 He shall from Jehovah the blessing receive,
  The God of salvation shall righteousness give;
  For this is the people, yea, this is the race,
  The Israel true who are seeking thy face.

4 Ye gates, lift your heads, and an entrance display,
  Ye doors everlasting, wide open the way;
  The King of all glory high honors await,
  The King of all glory shall enter in state.

5 What King of all glory is this that ye sing?
  The Lord, strong and mighty, the conquering King.
  Ye gates, lift your heads, and an entrance display,
  Ye doors everlasting, wide open the way.

6 The King of all glory high honors await,
  The King of all glory shall enter in state.
  What King of all glory is this that ye sing?
  Jehovah of hosts, he of glory is King.

600   *Psalm xxv.*   **C. M.**

TO thee I lift my soul, O Lord
  My God, I trust in thee;
  O let me never be ashamed,
  Nor foes exult o'er me.

2 O Lord, let none be put to shame
  Upon thee who attend;
  But make all those to be ashamed
  Who causelessly offend.

3 Thy ways, Lord, show; teach me thy paths;
  Lead me in truth, teach me;
  For of my safety thou art God;
  All day I wait on thee.

SELECTIONS FROM THE PSALMS.

4 Thy mercies that most tender are,
  To mind, O Lord, recall,
  And loving-kindnesses, for they
  Have been through ages all.

5 Let not the errors of my youth,
  Nor sins remembered be;
  In mercy, for thy goodness' sake,
  O Lord, remember me.

6 Jehovah good and upright is,
  The way he'll sinners show;
  The meek in judgment he will guide
  And make his path to know.

601   C. M.
A Prayer for deliverance from Oppression.

REGARD in tenderness, O Lord,
  The ills thy children bear;
Do thou thy gracious help afford,
  And answer this our prayer.

2 We trust not in the arms of flesh,
  We lean upon thy word;
  For thine own arm omnipotent,
  Is mightier than the sword.

3 What care we for the midnight foe?
  Or arrows winged with light?
  Or pestilence's fatal touch,
  Since thou, Lord, art our might?

4 We need not fear the cruel hate
  Of those we've done no wrong;
  We look to thee, our Advocate,
  For weapons sure and strong.

403

5 In common Fatherhood above,
   Thou reignest o'er the world;
  The poor thou liftest from the dust,
   The proud are downward hurled.
                    Rev. H. T. Johnson.

602 *Cold Gethsemane.* Luke xxii. 44. C. M.

COLD Gethsemane! the sweat and tears,
   Witnessed by thee, from him
  Who came to save and calm our fears,
   And bring us back to heav'n.

2 *The thought of that sad hour*—the day,
   So chill; the night so cold,
  The amazing grief that on him lay,
   Might well amaze my soul.

3 They all forsake him now, weak men!
   Alas! men always do,
  Forsake their God, always—ah then,
   Can sinful man be true?

4 How shall I thee requite, my Lord
   For all thy grief and pain,
  How magnify thy gracious word,
   Or how, extend thy fame?

5 I'll take the cup of blessing now,
   And drink before thy face,
  And sound throughout the world below,
   The wonders of thy grace. *J. C. Embry.*

603 *The mystery of power—wisdom—* 9s & 8s.
   love. Gen. i. 1–5 & 2 Cor. viii. 9.

IN deep eternity, out-lying,
   The ages mark'd by circling bands,
  Our God, in cycles still out-vieing,
   Creation wrought by his own hands.

2 He spake, and said, let light go flying,
   Beneath, from the eternal throne.
  Creation heard his voice with crying,
   Behold, the mighty work is done.
3 His plans in wisdom now arranging,
   For darkness he hath given light,
  His perfect law shall know no changing,
   And brings the morning after night.
4 The morning stars began with singing,
   An anthem to his wondrous name,
  And flaming clusters join in ringing,
   The chorus, through the shining frame.
5 Let men unite their humbler voices,
   With those that hymn his praise above,
  And sing—the universe rejoices—
   The mystery of life is love!
6 O love of God in Jesus bringing.
   Bright image of the Father's face.
  Let earth and heaven continue ringing,
   O love and grace to answer grace.
                     J. C. Embry.

604   *Courage.*

AM I a soldier of the cross,—
   A follower of the Lamb,—
And shall I fear to own His cause,
   Or blush to speak His name?

2 Must I be carried to the skies
   On flowery beds of ease,
  While others fought to win the prize,
   And sailed through bloody seas?

3 Are there no foes for me to face?
   Must I not stem the flood?

Is this wild world a friend to grace,
 To help me on to God?
4 Sure I must fight if I would reign:
 Increase my courage, Lord;
 I'll bear the toil, endure the pain,
 Supported by Thy word.
5 Thy saints, in all this glorious war,
 Shall conquer, though they die:
 They see the triumph from afar,
 By faith they bring it nigh.
6 When that illustrious day shall rise,
 And all thy armies shine,
 In robes of vict'ry, through the skies,
 The glory shall be Thine. *Watts.*

605 *The Pilgrimage.* 8, 7, 8, 7, 4, 7.

GUIDE me, O thou great Jehovah,
 Pilgrim through this barren land:
I am weak, but Thou art mighty;
 Hold me with thy powerful hand:
 Bread of heaven,
 Feed me till I want no more,
2 Open, Lord, the crystal fountain
 Whence the healing waters flow:
Let the fiery, cloudy pillar,
 Lead me all my journey through:
 Strong Deliv'rer!
 Be Thou still my strength and shield.
3 When I tread the verge of Jordan,
 Bid my anxious fears subside:
Death of death, and hell's destruction,
 Land me safe on Canaan's side;
 Songs of praises
 I will ever give to Thee. *Williams.*

606 *"For ye are members one of another."* S. M.

BLEST be the tie that binds
  Our hearts in Jesus' love;
The fellowship of Christian minds
  Is like to that above.

2 Before our Father's throne
  We pour united prayers;
Our fears, our hopes, our aims are one;
  Our comforts and our cares.

3 We share our mutual woes,
  Our mutual burdens bear;
And often for each other flows
  The sympathizing tear.

4 When we at death must part,
  Not like the world's, our pain:
But one in Christ, and one in heart,
  We part to meet again.

5 From sorrow, toil, and pain,
  And sin we shall be free;
And perfect love and friendship reign
  Throughout eternity. *Fawcett.*

607 *Before His cross.* 8, 7.

SWEET the moments, rich in blessing,
  Which before the cross I spend;
Life, and health, and peace possessing,
  From the sinner's dying Friend.

2 Truly blessed is this station,
  Low before His cross to lie,
While I see divine compassion
  Beaming in His gracious eye.

3 Here it is I find my heaven
  While upon the cross I gaze;

Love I much? I've much forgiven;
Ι'm a miracle of grace.

4 Love and grief my heart dividing,
With my tears His feet I'll bathe:
Constant still, in faith abiding,
Life deriving from His death.

5 Here in tender, grateful sorrow
With my Saviour will I stay;
Here new hope and strength will borrow;
Here will love my fears away.
James Allen.

608 *What a Friend we have in Jesus!* 8, 7.

WHAT a Friend we have in Jesus,
All our sins and griefs to bear!
What a privilege to carry
Every thing to God in prayer!
O what peace we often forfeit,
O what needless pain we bear,
All because we do not carry
Every thing to God in prayer!

2 Have we trials and temptations?
Is there trouble anywhere?
We should never be discouraged,
Take it to the Lord in prayer.
Can we find a friend so faithful
Who will all our sorrows share?
Jesus knows our every weakness,
Take it to the Lord in prayer.

3 Are we weak and heavy laden,
Cumbered with a load of care?—
Precious Saviour, still our refuge,—
Take it to the Lord in prayer.

Do thy friends despise forsake thee?
Take it to the Lord in prayer;
In His arms He'll take and shield thee,
Thou wilt find a solace there.
Unknown.

609

IN Thy cleft, O Rock of Ages,
  Hide Thou me:
When the fitful tempest rages,
  Hide Thou me;
Where no mortal arm can sever,
From my heart Thy love forever,
Hide me, O Thou Rock of Ages,
  Safe in Thee.

2 From the snare of sinful pleasure,
  Hide Thou me;
Thou my soul's eternal treasure,
  Hide Thou me;
When the world its power is wielding,
And my heart is almost yielding,
Hide me, O Thou Rock of Ages,
  Safe in Thee.

3 In the lonely night of sorrow,
  Hide Thou me;
Till in glory dawns the morrow,
  Hide Thou me;
In the sight of Jordan's billow,
Let Thy bosom be my billow,
Hide me, O Thou Rock of Ages,
  Safe in Thee. *Fanny J. Crosby.*

610

SHALL we meet beyond the river,
  Where the surges cease to roll?
Where, in all the bright forever,
  Sorrow ne'er shall vex the soul?

Cho.—Shall we meet, shall we meet,
Shall we meet beyond the river?
Shall we meet beyond the river,
Where the surges cease to roll?

2 Shall we meet in that blest harbor,
When our stormy voyage is o'er,
Shall we meet and cast the anchor
By the fair celestial shore?

Cho.—Shall we meet, etc.

3 Shall we meet in yonder city,
Where the towers of crystal shine?
Where the walls are all of jasper,
Built by workmanship Divine?

Cho.—Shall we meet, etc.

4 Shall we meet with Christ our Saviour,
When He comes to claim His own?
Shall we know His blessed favor
And sit down upon His throne?

Cho —Shall we meet, etc.

H. L. Hastings. 1858.

611
L. M.
Rest.

1 Asleep in Jesus! Blessed sleep,
From which none ever wakes to weep—
A calm and undisturbed repose,
Unbroken by the last of foes.

2 Asleep in Jesus! Oh how sweet
To be for such a slumber meet,
With holy confidence to sing
That death has lost his venomed sting!

3 Asleep in Jesus! Peaceful rest,
Whose waking is supremely blest:
No fear, no woe, shall dim that hour
That manifests the Saviour's power.

4 Asleep in Jesus! Far from thee
Thy kindred and their graves may be,
But thine is still a blessed sleep,
From which none ever wakes to weep

612
C. M.

The Heavenly Canaan.

1 On Jordan's stormy banks I stand,
    And cast a wishful eye
To Canaan's fair and happy land,
    Where my possessions lie.

2 O the transporting, rapt'rous scene
    That rises to my sight
Sweet fields array'd in living green,
    And rivers of delight!

3 There gen'rous fruits that never fail
    On trees immortal grow:
There rocks, and hills, and brooks, and vales,
    With milk and honey flow.

4 All o'er those wide-extended plains
    Shines one eternal day;
There God the Son for ever reigns,
    And scatters night away.

5 No chilling winds nor pois'nous breath
Can reach that healthful shore;
Sickness and sorrow, pain and death,
Are felt and fear'd no more.

6 When shall I reach that happy place,
And be for ever blest?
When shall I see my Father's face,
And in his bosom rest?

7 Filled with delight, my raptur'd soul
Would here no longer stay!
Though Jordan's waves around me roll
Fearless I'd launch away.

S. Stennett.

613

L. M.

Before receiving appointments.

1 Jesus, the truth and power Divine,
Send forth these messengers of thine,
Their hands confirm, their hearts inspire,
And touch their lips with hallowed fire.

2 Be thou their mouth and wisdom, Lord;
Thou, by the hammer of thy word,
The rocky hearts in pieces break,
And bid the sons of thunder speak.

3 To those who would their Lord embrace,
Give them to preach the word of grace,—
Sweetly their yielding bosoms move,
And melt them with the fire of love.

4 Let all with thankful hearts confess
  Thy welcome messengers of peace,
  Thy power in their report be found,
  And let thy feet behind them sound.

614
C. M.
A Warning from the Grave.

1 Beneath our feet and o'er our head
    Is equal warning given;
  Beneath us lie the countless dead,
    And far above is heaven.

2 Death rides on every passing breeze,
    And lurks in every flower;
  Each season has its own disease,
    Its peril every hour.

3 Turn, sinner, turn: thy danger know:
    Where,er thy foot can tread,
  The earth rings hollow from below,
    And warns thee of her dead.

4 Turn, Christian, turn: thy soul apply
    To truths which hourly tell
  That they who underneath thee lie
    Shall live in heaven—or hell.

615
S. M.
Prepare us for that day.

1 Behold! with awful pomp
    The Judge prepares to come;

The' archangel sound the dreadful trump
And wakes the gen'ral doom.

2 Nature, in wild amaze,
　　Her dissolution mourns;
　Blushes of blood the moon deface,
　　The sun to darkness turns.

3 The living look with dread;
　　The frighted dead arise,
　Start from the monumental bed,
　　And lift their ghastly eyes.

4 Horrors all hearts appal;
　　They quake, they shriek, they cry;
　Bid rocks and mountain on them fall;
　　But rocks and mountains fly.

5 Great God, in whom we live,
　　Prepare us for that day:
　Help us in Jesus to believe,—
　　To watch, and wait, and pray.

616
L. M.

The living and the dead.

1 Where are the dead? In heaven or hell
Their disembodied spirits dwell!
Their perish'd forms in bonds of clay,
Reserv'd until the judgment day.

2 Who are the dead? The sons of time
In every age and state and clime—
Renown'd, dishonour'd, or forgot—
The place that knew them knows them **not.**

3 Where are the living? On the ground
Where prayer is heard and mercy found,
Where, in the compass of a span,
The mortal makes th' immortal man.

4 Who are the living? They whose breath
Draws every moment nigh to death:
Of endless bliss or wo the heirs,
O what a solemn state is theirs!

5 Then, timely warn'd, let us begin
To follow Christ, and flee from sin,
Daily grow up in him our Head;
Lord of the living and the dead·
Montgomery.

617
L. M·

A Burial Hymn.

1 Unveil thy bosom, faithful tomb!
   Take this new treasure to thy trust,
And give these sacred relics room
   To slumber in the silent dust.

·2 Nor pain, nor grief, nor anxious fear
   Invade thy bounds; no mortal woes
Can reach the peaceful sleeper here,
   While angels watch the soft repose.

3 So Jesus slept;—God's dying Son
   Passed through the grave, and blessed the bed!
Rest here, blest saint, till from his throne,
   The morning break, and pierce the shade.

618

6s & 4s·
Self-consecration.

1 My faith looks up to thee,
Thou Lamb of Calvary,
  Saviour divine;
Now hear me while I pray;
Take all my guilt away
Oh let me from this day
  Be wholly thine.

2 May thy rich grace impart
Strength to my fainting heart,
  My zeal inspire
As thou hast died for me,
O may my love to thee
Pure, warm, and changeless be—
  A living fire.

3 While life's dark maze I tread,
And griefs around me spread,
  Be thou my guide;
Bid darkness turn to day,
Wipe sorrow's tear away,
Nor let me ever stray
  From thee aside.

4 When ends life's transient dream,
When death's cold, sullen stream
  Shall o'er me roll;
Bless'd Saviour, then, in love,
Fear and distress remove;
O bear me safe above—
  A ransomed soul

619

6,3.

1 What wondrous love is this, O my soul! O my soul!
What wondrous love is this, O my soul!
What wondrous love is this, that caus'd the Lord of bliss,
To send this precious peace to my soul, to my soul,
To send this precious peace to my soul.

2 When I was sinking down, O my soul, O my soul,
When I was sinking down, O my soul.
When I was sinking down, beneath God's righteous frown,
Christ laid aside his crown, for my soul, for my soul,
Christ laid aside his crown, for my soul!

3 Ye friends of Zion's King, join his praise, join his praise,
Ye friends of Zion's King join his praise,
Ye friends of Zion's King, with hearts and voices sing,
And strike each tuneful string in his praise,
And strike each tuneful string in his praise.

4 To God and to the Lamb, I will sing, I will sing,
To God and to the Lamb, I will sing,
To God and to the Lamb who is the great I AM!
While millions join the theme, I will sing, I will sing,
While millions join the theme, I will sing.

5 And when from death I'm free, I'll sing on,
I'll sing on;
And when from death I'm free, I'll sing on,
And when from death I'm free, I'll sing
and joyful be;
And through eternity I'll sing on, I'll sing
on,
And through eternity I'll sing on.

620 L. M
Camp-meeting.

1 A twelve month more has roll'd around,
Since we were on this tented ground:
Ten thousand scenes have mar'd the year,
Since we last met to worship here

2 Relentless death has hurl'd his darts,
And lodged them deep in noblest hearts:
O'er old and young, in every sphere,
He's triumph'd since we worshipp'd here.

3 Yet we are spared, to Heaven be praise,
Our God has lengthen'd out our days:
We've left our homes with hearts sincere,
And met, once more, to worship here.

4 My Father's children — heirs of heaven,
Let all your hearts to prayer be given,
That God may lend a listening ear
And answer, while we worship here.

5 Come sinners, come, your pardoning God
Now waits t' impart his cleansing blood:
O! loathe your sins, to Christ draw near,
And seek him while we worship here.

6 Ye mourners, raise your languid eyes:
Your homes's beyond the starry skies!
Your Saviour smiles, renounce your fear,
And praise him while we worship here.
A. Means.

621
C. M.
Heaven.

1 Arise and shine, oh Zion fair,
   Behold thy light is come!
Thy glorious conq'ring King is near
   To take his exiles home:
The trumpet sounding through the sky,
   To set poor captives free;
The day of wonder now is nigh;
   The year of Jubilee.

2 Ye heralds, blow your trumpets loud
   The earth must know her doom;
Go spread the news from pole to pole,
   Behold the Judge is come:
Blow out the sun! burn up the earth!
   Consume the rolling flood!
While every star shall disappear,
   Go turn the moon to blood!

3 Arise ye nations under ground,
   Before the Judge appear:
All tongues and languages shall come,
   Their final doom to hear!
King Jesus on his dazzling throne.
   Ten thousand angels round;
And Gabriel with a silver trump,
   Echoes the awful sound!

4 The glorious news of gospel grace
   To sinners now is o'er;
   The trump in Zion now is still,
   And to be heard no more!
   The watchmen all have left their walls,
   And with their flocks above,
   On Canaan's peaceful shore they sing,
   And shout redeeming love!

5 Come on my brethren in the Lord,
   Whose hearts are join'd in one;
   Hold up your heads with courage bold,
   Your race is almost run:
   Above the clouds behold him stand,
   And smiling, bid you come,
   And angels whispering you away
   To your eternal home. *Anon.*

622

Will You Meet Us. 8,8,8,6·

1 Say, brothers, will you meet us,
  Say, brothers, will you meet us,
  Say, brothers, will you meet us,
   On Canaan's happy shore?

2 By the grace of God we'll meet you,
  By the grace of God we'll meet you,
  By the grace of God we'll meet you,
   Where parting is no more.

3 Jesus lives and reigns for ever,
  Jesus lives and reigns for ever,
  Jesus lives and reigns for ever,
   On Canaan's happy shore.

4 Glory, glory, hallelujah,
  Glory, glory, hallelujah,
  Glory, glory, hallelujah,
   For ever, evermore.

Doxologies.

1   L. M.

PRAISE God, from whom all blessings flow;
   Praise him, all creatures here below;
Praise him above, ye heavenly host;
Praise Father, Son, and Holy Ghost. *T. Ken.*

2   C. M.

TO Father, Son, and Holy Ghost,
   The God whom we adore,
Be glory, as it was is now,
   And shall be evermore. *Tate and Brady.*

3   C. M.

THE God of mercy be adored,
   Who calls our souls from death,
Who saves by his redeeming word,
   And new-creating breath;
To praise the Father, and the Son,
   And Spirit all-divine,—
The One in Three, and Three in One,—
   Let saints and angels join. *Isaac Watts.*

4   S. M.

TO God, the Father, Son,
   And Spirit, One in Three,
Be glory, as it was, is now,
   And shall forever be. *John Wesley.*

5   L. M. 6*l.*

IMMORTAL honor, endless fame,
   Attend the almighty Father's name
The Saviour Son be glorified,
Who for lost man's redemption died,
And equal adoration be,
Eternal Comforter, to thee! *John Dryden.*

6   L. P. M.

NOW to the great and sacred Three,
   The Father, Son, and Spirit, be
Eternal praise and glory given,
Through all the worlds where God is known,
By all the angels near the throne,
And all the saints in earth and heaven. *Watts.*

7   TO God the Father's throne   P. M.
     Your highest honors raise;
  Glory to God the Son;
    To God the Spirit, praise:
With all our powers, eternal King,
Thy everlasting praise we sing.
                     Isaac Watts, alt.

8   C. P. M.

TO Father, Son, and Holy Ghost,
   The God whom heaven's triumphant host
And saints on earth adore;
Be glory as in ages past,
And now it is, and so shall last,
When time shall be no more.
                     Tate & Brady.

9   7s.

SING we to our God above,
   Praise eternal as his love;
Praise him, all ye heavenly host,
Father, Son, and Holy Ghost!
                     C. Wesley.

10   7s, 6l.

PRAISE the name of God most high;
   Praise him, all below the sky;
Praise him, all ye heavenly host,
Father, Son, and Holy Ghost!
As through countless ages past,
Evermore his praise shall last.   *Unknown.*

11 8s, 7s, 4s.

GREAT Jehovah! we adore thee,
  God the Father, God the Son,
God, the Spirit, joined in glory
  On the same eternal throne:
    Endless praises
  To Jehovah, Three in One!
             William Goode.

12 8s, 7s.

PRAISE the God of our salvation;
  Praise the Father's boundless love;
Praise the Lamb, our expiation;
  Praise the Spirit from above,
    Author of the new creation,
  Him by whom our spirits live;
Undivided adoration
  To the one Jehovah give! *Josiah Conder.*

THE LITURGY.

Order of Baptism.

ORDER FOR THE ADMINISTRATION OF BAPTISM TO INFANTS.

The Minister, coming to the Font, which is to be filled with pure Water, shall use the following:

DEARLY BELOVED: Forasmuch as all men are conceived and born in sin, and that our Saviour Christ saith, Except a man be born of water and of the Spirit he cannot enter into the kingdom of God; I beseech you to call upon God the Father, through our Lord Jesus Christ, that having, of his bounteous mercy, redeemed *this child* by the blood of his Son, he will grant that *he*, being baptized with water, may also be baptized with the Holy Ghost, be received into Christ's holy Church, and become *a lively member* of the same.

Then shall the Minister say:

Let us pray.

Almighty and everlasting God, who of thy great mercy hast condescended to enter into covenant relations with man, wherein thou hast included children as partakers of its gracious benefits, declaring that of such is thy kingdom: and in thy ancient Church didst appoint divers baptisms, figuring thereby the renewing of the Holy Ghost; and by thy well-beloved Son Jesus Christ gavest commandment to thy holy apostles to go into all the world and disciple all nations, baptizing them in the name of the Father, and of the Son, and of the Holy Ghost: We beseech thee, that of thine infinite mercy thou wilt look upon *this child:* wash *him* and sanctify *him;* that *he,* being saved by thy grace, may be received into Christ's holy Church, and being steadfast in faith, joyful through hope, and rooted in love, may so overcome the evils of this present world, that finally *he* may attain to everlasting life, and reign with thee, world without end, through Jesus Christ our Lord. *Amen.*

O merciful God, grant that all carnal affections may die in *him,* and that all things belonging to the Spirit may live and grow in *him. Amen.*

Grant that *he* may have power and strength to have victory, and to triumph against the devil, the world, and the flesh. *Amen.*

Grant that whosoever is dedicated to thee by

THE LITURGY.

our office and ministry may also be endued with heavenly virtues, and everlastingly rewarded through thy mercy, O blessed Lord God, who dost live, and govern all things, world without end. *Amen.*

Almighty, ever-living God, whose most dearly beloved Son Jesus Christ, for the forgiveness of our sins, did shed out of his most precious side both water and blood, regard, we beseech thee, our supplications. Sanctify this water for this holy sacrament; and grant that *this child,* now to be baptized, may receive the fullness of thy grace, and ever remain in the number of thy faithful and elect children, through Jesus Christ our Lord. *Amen.*

Then shall the Minister address the Parents [or Guardians] as follows:

DEARLY BELOVED: Forasmuch as *this child is* now presented by you for Christian baptism, you must remember that it is your part and duty to see that *he* be taught, as soon as *he* shall be able to learn, the nature and end of this holy sacrament. And that *he* may know these things the better, you shall call upon *him* to give reverent attendance upon the appointed means of grace, such as the ministry of the word and the public and private worship of God; and further, ye shall provide that *he* shall read the Holy Scriptures, and learn the Lord's Prayer, the Ten Commandments, the Apostles' Creed, the Catechism, and all other things which a Christian ought to know and believe to his soul's health, in order that *he* may be brought up to lead a virtuous and holy life, remembering always that baptism doth represent unto us that inward purity which disposeth us to follow the example of our Saviour Christ; that as he died and rose again for us, so should we, who are baptized, die unto sin and rise again unto righteousness, continually mortifying all corrupt affections and daily proceeding in all virtue and godliness.

Do you therefore solemnly engage to fulfill these duties, so far as in you lies, the Lord being your helper?

Answ. We do.

Then shall the people stand up, and the Minister shall say:

Hear the words of the Gospel, written by St. Mark. [Chap. x. 13–16.]

They brought young children to Christ, that he should touch them. And his disciples rebuked those that brought them. But when Jesus saw it, he was much displeased, and said untc them, Suffer the little children to come unto me, and forbid them not, for of such is the kingdom of God. Verily I say unto you, Whosoever sh'l

THE LITURGY.

not receive the kingdom of God as a little child, he shall not enter therein. And he took them up in his arms, put his hands upon them, and blessed them.

Then the Minister shall take the Child into his hands, and say to the friends of the Child,

Name this child.

And then, naming it after them, he shall sprinkle or pour Water upon it, or, if desired, immerse it in Water, saying,

N., I baptize thee in the name of the Father, and of the Son, and of the Holy Ghost. *Amen.*

Then may the Minister offer extemporary prayer.

Then shall be said, all kneeling :

Our Father who art in heaven, hallowed be thy name. Thy kingdom come. Thy will be done in earth, as it is in heaven. Give us this day our daily bread: and forgive us our trespasses, as we forgive them that trespass against us: and lead us not into temptation, but deliver us from evil: for thine is the kingdom, and the power, and the glory, forever. *Amen.*

ORDER FOR THE ADMINISTRATION OF BAPTISM TO SUCH AS ARE OF RIPER YEARS.

DEARLY BELOVED: Forasmuch as all men are conceived and born in sin; and that which is

BAPTISM OF INFANTS.

born of the flesh is flesh, and they that are in the flesh cannot please God, but live in sin, committing many actual transgressions; and our Saviour Christ saith, Except a man be born of water and of the Spirit he cannot enter into the kingdom of God: I beseech you to call upon God the Father, through our Lord Jesus Christ, that of his bounteous goodness he will grant to *these persons* that which by nature *they* cannot have; that *they*, being baptized with water, may also be baptized with the Holy Ghost, and being received into Christ's holy Church, may continue lively *members* of the same.

Then shall the Minister say:

Let us pray.

Almighty and immortal God, the aid of all that need, the helper of all that flee to thee for succor, the life of them that believe, and the resurrection of the dead: we call upon thee for *these persons,* that *they*, coming to thy holy baptism, may also be filled with thy Holy Spirit. Receive *them*, O Lord, as thou hast promised by thy well-beloved Son, saying, Ask, and ye shall receive; seek, and ye shall find; knock, and it shall be opened unto you: so give now unto us that ask: let us that seek, find: open the gate unto us that knock; that *these persons* may enjoy the everlasting benediction of thy heavenly

THE LITURGY.

washing, and may come to the eternal kingdom which thou hast promised by Christ our Lord. *Amen.*

Then shall the people stand up, and the Minister shall say:

Hear the words of the Gospel, written by St. John. [Chap. iii. 1-8.]

There was a man of the Pharisees, named Nicodemus a ruler of the Jews: the same came to Jesus by night, and said unto him, Rabbi, we know that thou art a teacher come from God; for no man can do these miracles that thou doest except God be with him. Jesus answered and said unto him, Verily, verily, I say unto thee, Except a man be born again, he cannot see the kingdom of God. Nicodemus saith unto him, How can a man be born when he is old? Can he enter the second time into his mother's womb, and be born? Jesus answered, Verily, verily, I say unto thee, Except a man be born of water and of the Spirit, he cannot enter into the kingdom of God. That which is born of the flesh is flesh, and that which is born of the Spirit is spirit. Marvel not that I said unto thee, Ye must be born again. The wind bloweth where it listeth, and thou hearest the sound thereof, but canst not tell whence it cometh, and whither it goeth: so is every one that is born of the Spirit.

Then the Minister shall speak to the persons to be baptized on this wise:

Well Beloved, who *have* come hither desiring to receive holy baptism, you have heard how the congregation hath prayed that our Lord Jesus Christ would vouchsafe to receive you, to bless you, and to give you the kingdom of heaven and everlasting life. And our Lord Jesus Christ hath promised in his holy word to grant all those things that we have prayed for: which promise he for his part will most surely keep and perform.

Wherefore, after this promise made by Christ, you must also faithfully, for your part, promise in the presence of this whole congregation, that you will renounce the devil and all his works, and constantly believe God's holy word, and obediently keep his commandments.

Then shall the Minister demand of each of the persons to be baptized:

Quest. Dost thou renounce the devil and all his works, the vain pomp and glory of the world, with all covetous desires of the same, and the carnal desires of the flesh, so that thou wilt not follow nor be led by them?

Answ. I renounce them all.

THE LITURGY.

Quest. Dost thou believe in God the Father Almighty, Maker of heaven and earth;

And in Jesus Christ his only-begotten Son our Lord; and that he was conceived by the Holy Ghost, born of the Virgin Mary; that he suffered under Pontius Pilate, was crucified, dead and buried; that he rose again the third day; that he ascended into heaven, and sitteth at the right hand of God the Father Almighty; and from thence shall come again at the end of the world, to judge the quick and the dead?

And dost thou believe in the Holy Ghost; the holy catholic* Church, the communion of saints; the forgiveness of sins; the resurrection of the body, and everlasting life after death?

Answ. All this I steadfastly believe.

Quest. Wilt thou be baptized in this faith?

Answ. Such is my desire.

Quest. Wilt thou then obediently keep God's holy will and commandments, and walk in the same all the days of thy life?

Answ. I will endeavor so to do, God being my helper.

Then shall the Minister say:

O merciful God, grant that all carnal affections may die in *these persons*, and that all things

---

* The one universal Church of Christ.

BAPTISM OF ADULTS.

belonging to the Spirit may live and grow in them. *Amen.*

Grant that *they* may have power and strength to have victory, and triumph against the devil, the world, and the flesh. *Amen.*

Grant that *they*, being here dedicated to thee by our office and ministry, may also be endued with heavenly virtues, and everlastingly rewarded, through thy mercy, O blessed Lord God, who dost live, and govern all things, world without end. *Amen.*

Almighty, ever-living God, whose most dearly beloved Son Jesus Christ, for the forgiveness of our sins, did shed out of his most precious side both water and blood; and gave commandment to his disciples that they should go teach all nations, and baptize them in the name of the Father, and of the Son, and of the Holy Ghost; regard, we beseech thee, our supplications; and grant that the *persons* now to be baptized may receive the fullness of thy grace, and ever remain in the number of thy faithful and elect children, through Jesus Christ our Lord. *Amen.*

Then shall the Minister ask the name of each person to be baptized: and shall sprinkle or pour water upon him, (or, if he shall desire it, shall immerse him in water,) saying:

THE LITURGY.

N., I baptize thee in the name of the Father, and of the Son, and of the Holy Ghost. *Amen.*

Then shall be said the Lord's Prayer, all kneeling:

Our Father who art in heaven, hallowed be thy name. Thy kingdom come. Thy will be done in earth as it is in heaven. Give us this day our daily bread: and forgive us our trespasses, as we forgive them that trespass against us: and lead us not into temptation, but deliver us from evil: for thine is the kingdom, and the power, and the glory, forever. *Amen.*

Then may the Minister conclude with extemporary prayer.

Reception of Members.

FORM FOR RECEIVING PERSONS INTO THE CHURCH AFTER PROBATION.

On the day appointed, all that are to be received into the Church shall be called forward, and the Minister, addressing the congregation, shall say:

DEARLY BELOVED BRETHREN: The Scriptures teach us that the Church is the household of God, the body of which Christ is the Head; and that it is the design of the Gospel to bring together in one all who are in Christ. The fellowship of the Church is the communion that its members enjoy one with another. The ends of this fellowship are, the maintenance of sound doctrine and of the ordinances of Christian worship, and the exercise of that power of godly admonition and discipline which Christ has committed to his Church for the promotion of holiness. It is the duty of all men to unite in this fellowship, for it is only those that "be planted in the house of the Lord" that "shall flourish in the courts of our God." Its more particular duties are, to promote peace and unity; to bear one another's burdens; to prevent each other's stumbling; to seek the intimacy of friendly society among themselves; to continue steadfast in the faith and worship of the Gospel; and to pray and sympathize with each other. Among its privileges are, peculiar incitements to holiness from the hearing of God's word and sharing in Christ's ordinances; the being placed under the watchful care of pastors, and the enjoyment of the blessings which are promised only to those who are of the household of faith. Into this holy fellowship the *persons* before you, who *have* already received the Sacrament of Baptism, and *have* been under the care of *proper leaders* for six months on *trial, come* seeking admission. We now propose, in the fear of God, to question *them* as to *their* faith and purposes, that you may know that *they* are *proper persons* to be admitted into the Church.

Then addressing the applicants for admission, the Minister shall say:

Dearly Beloved: You are come hither seeking the great privilege of union with the Church our Saviour has purchased with his own blood. We rejoice in the grace of God vouchsafed unto you in that he has called you to be his *followers*, and that thus far you have run well. You have heard how blessed are the privileges, and how solemn are the duties, of membership in Christ's Church; and before you are fully admitted thereto, it is proper that you do here publicly renew your vows, confess your faith, and declare your purpose, by answering the following questions:

Q. 1. Do you here, in the presence of God and of this congregation, renew the solemn promise contained in the baptismal covenant, ratifying and confirming the same, and acknowledging *yourself* bound faithfully to observe and keep that covenant?

Answ. I do.

Q. 2. Have you saving faith in the Lord Jesus Christ?

Answ. I trust I have.

Q. 3. Do you entertain friendly feelings toward all the members of this Church?

RECEPTION OF MEMBERS.

Answ. I do.

Q. 4. Do you believe in the doctrines of the Holy Scriptures, as set forth in the Articles of Religion of the African Methodist Episcopal Church?

Answ. I do.

Q. 5. Will you cheerfully be governed by the rules of the African Methodist Episcopal Church; hold sacred the ordinances of God; and endeavor, as much as in you lies, to promote the welfare of your brethren and the advancement of the Redeemer's kingdom?

Answ. I will.

Q. 6. Will you contribute of your earthly substance according to your ability, to the support of the Gospel and the various benevolent enterprises of the Church?

Answ. I will.

Then the Minister, addressing the Church, shall say:

Brethren, *these persons* having given satisfactory responses to our inquiries, have any of you reason to allege why *they* should not be received into full membership in the Church?

No objection being alleged, the Minister shall say to the candidates:

We welcome you to the communion of the

THE LITURGY.

Church of God; and, in testimony of our Christian affection and the cordiality with which we receive you, I hereby extend to you the right hand of fellowship: and may God grant that you may be a faithful and useful member of the Church militant till you are called to the fellowship of the Church triumphant, which is "without fault before the throne of God."

Then shall the Minister offer extemporary prayer

The Lord's Supper.

[Whenever practicable, let none but the pure, unfermented juice of the grape be used in administering the Lord's Supper.]

ORDER FOR THE ADMINISTRATION OF THE LORD'S SUPPER.

The Elder shall say one or more of these sentences, during the reading of which the persons appointed for that purpose shall receive the alms for the poor:

LET your light so shine before men, that they may see your good works, and glorify your Father which is in heaven. [Matt. v. 16.]

Lay not up for yourselves treasures upon earth, where moth and rust doth corrupt, and where thieves break through and steal: but lay up for yourselves treasures in heaven, where neither moth nor rust doth corrupt, and where thieves do not break through nor steal. [Matt. vi. 19, 20.]

Whatsoever ye would that men should do to you, do ye even so to them: for this is the law and the prophets. [Matt. vii. 12.]

Not every one that saith unto me, Lord, Lord, shall enter into the kingdom of heaven; but he that doeth the will of my Father which is in heaven. [Matt. vii. 21.]

Zaccheus stood, and said unto the Lord: Behold, Lord, the half of my goods I give to the poor; and if I have taken any thing from any man by false accusation, I restore him fourfold. [Luke xix. 8.]

He which soweth sparingly shall reap also sparingly; and he which soweth bountifully shall reap also bountifully. Every man according as he purposeth in his heart, so let him give; not grudgingly, or of necessity, for God loveth a cheerful giver. [2 Cor. ix. 6, 7.]

As we have therefore opportunity, let us do good unto all men, especially unto them who are of the household of faith. [Gal. vi. 10.]

Godliness with contentment is great gain; for we brought nothing into this world, and it is certain we can carry nothing out. [1 Tim. vi. 6, 7.]

THE LITURGY.

Charge them that are rich in this world, that they be not high-minded, nor trust in uncertain riches, but in the living God, who giveth us richly all things to enjoy; that they do good, that they be rich in good works, ready to distribute, willing to communicate; laying up in store for themselves a good foundation against the time to come, that they may lay hold on eternal life. [1 Tim. vi. 17–19.]

God is not unrighteous to forget your work and labor of love, which ye have showed toward his name, in that ye have ministered to the saints, and do minister. [Heb. vi. 10.]

To do good and to communicate forget not; for with such sacrifices God is well pleased. [Heb. xiii. 16.]

Whoso hath this world's good, and seeth his brother have need, and shutteth up his bowels of compassion from him, how dwelleth the love of God in him? [1 John iii. 17.]

He that hath pity upon the poor, lendeth unto the Lord; and that which he hath given will he pay him again. [Prov. xix. 17.]

Blessed is he that considereth the poor: the Lord will deliver him in time of trouble. [Psa. xli. 1.]

After which the Elder shall give the following INVITATION, *the people standing:*

If any man sin, we have an advocate with

THE LORD'S SUPPER.

the Father, Jesus Christ the righteous: and he is the propitiation for our sins: and not for ours only, but also for the sins of the whole world.

Wherefore ye that do truly and earnestly repent of your sins, and are in love and charity with your neighbors, and intend to lead a new life, following the commandments of God, and walking from henceforth in his holy ways; draw near with faith, and take this holy sacrament to your comfort: and, devoutly kneeling, make your humble confession to Almighty God.

Then shall this general CONFESSION *be made by the Minister in the name of all those who are minded to receive the holy communion, both he and all the people devoutly kneeling, and saying:*

Almighty God, Father of our Lord Jesus Christ, Maker of all things, Judge of all men: we acknowledge and bewail our manifold sins and wickedness, which we from time to time most grievously have committed, by thought, word, and deed, against thy Divine Majesty, provoking most justly thy wrath and indignation against us. We do earnestly repent, and are heartily sorry for these our misdoings; the remembrance of them is grievous unto us,

THE LITURGY.

Have mercy upon us, have mercy upon us, most merciful Father; for thy Son, our Lord Jesus Christ's sake, forgive us all that is past, and grant that we may ever hereafter serve and please thee in newness of life, to the honor and glory of thy name, through Jesus Christ our Lord. *Amen,*

Then shall the Elder say:

Almighty God, our heavenly Father, who of thy great mercy hast promised forgiveness of sins to all them that with hearty repentance and true faith turn unto thee, have mercy upon us; pardon and deliver us from all our sins; confirm and strengthen us in all goodness, and bring us to everlasting life through Jesus Christ our Lord. *Amen.*

The Collect.

Almighty God, unto whom all hearts are open, all desires known, and from whom no secrets are hid; cleanse the thoughts of our hearts by the inspiration of thy Holy Spirit, that we may perfectly love thee, and worthily magnify thy holy name through Jesus Christ our Lord. *Amen.*

Then shall the Elder say:

We do not presume to come to this thy table, O merciful Lord, trusting in our own righteous-

THE LORD'S SUPPER.

ness, but in thy manifold and great mercies. We are not worthy so much as to gather up the crumbs under thy table. But thou art the same Lord, whose property is always to have mercy: Grant us, therefore, gracious Lord, so to eat the flesh of thy dear Son, Jesus Christ, and to drink his blood, that we may live and grow thereby, and that, being washed through his most precious blood, we may evermore dwell in him, and he in us. *Amen.*

Then the Elder shall offer the prayer of CONSE-CRATION *as followeth:*

Almighty God, our heavenly Father, who of thy tender mercy didst give thine only Son Jesus Christ to suffer death upon the cross for our redemption; who made there, by his oblation of himself once offered, a full, perfect and sufficient sacrifice, oblation and satisfaction for the sins of the whole world; and did institute, and in his holy Gospel command us to continue, a perpetual memory of his precious death until his coming again: hear us, O merciful Father, we most humbly beseech thee, and grant that we, receiving these thy creatures of bread and wine, according to thy Son our Saviour Jesus Christ's holy institution, in remembrance of his death and passion, may be partakers of his most blessed body and blood:

THE LITURGY.

Who, In the same night that he was betrayed, took bread; [*here the Elder may take the plate of bread in his hand*] and when he had given thanks, he brake it, and gave it to his disciples, saying, Take. eat; this is my body which is given for you: do this in remembrance of me.

Likewise after supper he took [*here he may take the cup in his hand*] the cup; and when he had given thanks, he gave it to them, saying, Drink ye all of this; for this is my blood of the New Testament, which is shed for you, and for many, for the remission of sins; do this, as oft as ye shall drink it, in remembrance of me. *Amen.*

Then shall the Minister receive the communion in both kinds, and proceed to deliver the same to the other Ministers, if any be present; after which he shall say:

It is very meet, right, and our bounden duty, that we should at all times, and in all places, give thanks unto thee, O Lord, holy Father, almighty, everlasting God.

Therefore, with angels and archangels, and with all the company of heaven. we laud and magnify thy glorious name, evermore praising thee, and saying, Holy, holy, holy Lord God of hosts, heaven and earth are full of thy glory. Glory be to thee, O Lord most high. *Amen.*

THE LORD'S SUPPER.

The Minister shall then proceed to administer the communion to the people in order, kneeling, into their uncovered hands. And when he delivereth the bread, he shall say:

The body of our Lord Jesus Christ, which was given for *thee,* preserve *thy soul* and *body* unto everlasting life. Take and eat this in remembrance that Christ died for *thee,* and feed on him in *thy heart* by faith, with thanksgiving.

And the Minister that delivereth the cup shall say:

The blood of our Lord Jesus Christ, which was shed for *thee,* preserve *thy soul* and *body* unto everlasting life. Drink this in remembrance that Christ's blood was shed for *thee,* and be thankful.

[If the consecrated bread or wine be all spent before all have communed, the Elder may consecrate more by renewing the Prayer of Consecration.]

[When all have communed, the Minister shall return to the Lord's table and place upon it what remaineth of the consecrated elements, covering the same with a fair linen cloth.]

Then shall the Elder say the Lord's Prayer; the people kneeling and repeating after him every petition:

Our Father, who art in heaven, hallowed be thy name. Thy kingdom come. Thy will be done in earth, as it is in heaven. Give us this

THE LITURGY.

day our daily bread: and forgive us our trespasses, as we forgive them that trespass against us: and lead us not into temptation, but deliver us from evil: for thine is the kingdom, and the power, and the glory, forever. *Amen.*

After which shall be said as followeth:

O Lord our heavenly Father, we thy humble servants desire thy Fatherly goodness mercifully to accept this our sacrifice of praise and thanksgiving; most humbly beseeching thee to grant, that, by the merits and death of thy Son Jesus Christ, and through faith in his blood, we and thy whole Church may obtain forgiveness of our sins, and all other benefits of his passion. And here offer and present unto thee, O Lord, ourselves, our souls and bodies, to be a reasonable, holy, and lively sacrifice unto thee; humbly beseeching thee that all we who are partakers of this holy communion may be filled with thy grace and heavenly benediction. And although we be unworthy, through our manifold sins, to offer unto thee any sacrifice, yet we beseech thee to accept this our bounden duty and service; not weighing our merits, but pardoning our offenses, through Jesus Christ our Lord; by whom, and with whom, in the unity of the Holy Ghost, all honor and glory be unto thee, O Father Almighty, world without end. *Amen.*

THE LORD'S SUPPER.

Then shall be said or sung•

Glory be to God on high, and on earth peace, good-will toward men! We praise thee, we bless thee, we worship thee, we glorify thee, we give thanks to thee for thy great glory, O Lord God, heavenly King, God the Father Almighty!

O Lord, the only-begotten Son Jesus Christ; O Lord God, Lamb of God, Son of the Father, that takest away the sins of the world, have mercy upon us. Thou that takest away the sins of the world, have mercy upon us. Thou that takest away the sins of the world, receive our prayer. Thou that sittest at the right hand of God the Father, have mercy upon us. For thou only art holy; thou only art the Lord; thou only, O Christ, with the Holy Ghost, art most high in the glory of God the Father. *Amen.*

Then the Elder if he see it expedient, may put up an extemporary prayer; and afterward he shall let the people depart with this blessing•

May the peace of God, which passeth all understanding, keep your hearts and minds in the knowledge and love of God, and of his Son Jesus Christ our Lord, and the blessing of God Almighty, the Father, the Son, and the Holy Ghost, be among you, and remain with you always. *Amen.*

THE LITURGY.

N. B —If the Elder be straitened for time in the usual administration of the Holy Communion, he may omit any part of the service except the Invitation, the Confession and the Prayer of Consecration : and in its administration to the Sick, he may omit any part of the service except the Confession, the Prayer of Consecration, and the usual sentences in de ivering the Bread and Wine, closing with the Lord's Prayer. extempore supplication, and the Benediction

INDEX OF FIRST LINES TO HYMNS.

A.

A broken heart, my God, my King 183
According to thy gracious word 315
A charge to keep I have 12
Ah! whither should I go 186
Alas! and did my Saviour bleed 189
Alas! what hourly dangers rise 22
Almighty God of love 443
Almost persuaded 550
Always with us, always with us 387
All hail the power of Jesus' name 110
All people that on earth do dwell 595
All praise to him who dwells in bliss 403
All things are ready, come 100
Amazing grace! how sweet the sound 223
Am I a soldier of the cross 604
Among assembled men of might 583
And am I born to die 475
And are we yet alive 295
And can I yet delay? 187
And let our bodies part 296
And let this feeble body fail 482
And must I be to judgment brought 468
And must this body die 474
And now, my soul, another year 415
And will the great eternal God 418
And will the Judge descend? 144
And will the mighty God 145
Another six days' work is done 575
Another week is past and gone 581
Arise, and bless the Lord 21

INDEX OF FIRST LINES TO HYMNS.

Arise, my soul, arise 23
Arise, my soul, on wings sublime 241
Arise, my tenderest thoughts, arise 158
Arise, O King of grace, arise 427
Arm of the Lord, awake, awake ! 509
At the Lamb's high feast we sing 322
Author of faith, we seek thy face 407
Awake, and sing the song 13
Awake, glad soul, awake, awake 116
Awake, Jerusalem, awake 175
Awake, my soul, and with the sun 373
Awake, my soul, in joyful lays 6
Awake, my soul, stretch every nerve 330
Awake, my soul, to meet the day 379
Awake, my tongue, thy tribute bring 75
Awake, ye saints, and raise your eyes 416
Away, my unbelieving fear 335
Away with our sorrow and fear 505

B.

Before Jehovah's awful throne 8
Before thy mercy seat, O Lord 4
Begin, my soul, th' exalted lay 78
Behold a stranger at the door 179
Behold the expected time draws near 450
Behold the heathen waits to know 441
Behold the mountain of the Lord 440
Behold the Saviour of mankind 109
Behold the servant of the Lord 264
Behold the throne of grace 287
Behold thy temple, God of grace 420
Behold what condescending love 305
Behold what wondrous grace 208
Being of beings, God of love 249
Be thou exalted, O my God 7
Blessed be our everlasting Lord 54

INDEX OF FIRST LINES TO HYMNS.

Blest be the dear uniting love 410
Blest be the tie that binds 606
Blest hour when mortal man retires 41
Blow ye the trumpet, blow 150
Brethren, we have met to worship 543
Brightest and best of the sons of 102
Bright was the guiding star that led 83
By faith I view my Saviour dying 540

C.

Children of the heavenly king 339
Christ, from whom all blessings flow 544
Christ, the Lord, is risen again 118
Christ, the Lord, is risen to-day 119
Christ, whose glory fills the skies 124
Cold Gethsemane, the sweat and tears 602
Come and let us sweetly join 456
Come away to the skies, my beloved, arise 528
Come, brothers and sisters, who love one another . . 537
Come, Father, Son, and Holy Ghost 302
Come, gracious Spirit, heavenly Dove 136
Come, happy souls, approach your God 199
Come, Holy Ghost, our hearts inspire 130
Come, Holy Ghost, our hearts inspire and lighten . . 139
Come, Holy Ghost, set to thy seal 320
Come, Holy Spirit, come; Let thy bright beams . . . 126
Come, Holy Spirit, come, with energy divine 127
Come, Holy Spirit, heavenly Dove 133
Come, humble sinner, in whose breast 147
Come, let our voices join to raise 35
Come, let us anew, our journey pursue 385
Come, let us ascend 570
Come, let us join our friends above 471
Come, let us join our cheerful songs 122
Come, let us join with one accord 572
Come, let us lift our joyful eyes 37
Come, let us sing unto the Lord 594

INDEX OF FIRST LINES TO HYMNS.

Come, let us use the grace divine 25
Come, let us who in Christ believe 19
Come, Lord, and tarry not 453
Come, O my soul, in sacred lays 9
Come, O thou all victorious Lord 205
Come, O thou greater than my heart 235
Come on, my partners in distress 354
Come, Saviour Jesus, from above 234
Come, sinners, to the gospel feast 140
Come, sound his praise abroad 68
Come, thou Almighty King 15
Come, thou desire of all thy saints 20
Come, thou fount of every blessing 351
Come, thou high and lofty Lord 457
Come, thou long expected Jesus 165
Come to Calvary's holy mountain 163
Come to the land of peace 510
Come, ye disconsolate 162
Come ye sinners, poor and needy 170
Come, ye that love the Lord 32
Come, ye that love the Lord indeed 534
Comfort, ye ministers of grace 272
Commit thou all thy griefs 401

D.

Dark and thorny is the desert 548
Day of judgment, day of wonders 177
Dear friends, farewell, I do you tell 524
Death may dissolve my body now 503
Did Christ o'er sinners weep 520
Depth of mercy, can there be 193
Draw near, O Son of God, draw near 273
Dread Sovereign, let my evening song 405

E.

Early, my God, without delay 2
Equip me for the war 369

INDEX OF FIRST LINES TO HYMNS.

Eternal beam of light divine 334
Eternal depth of love divine 57
Eternal power, whose high abode 62
Eternal source of every joy 395
Eternal Spirit, God of truth 132

F.

Far as thy name is known 274
Far from my thoughts, vain world, begone 57%
Far from these scenes of night 512
Father above the concave sky 55
Father, behold with gracious eyes 358
Father, I dare believe 232
Father, I stretch my hands to thee 188
Father of all, in whom alone 46
Father of all, whose powerful voice 76
Father of Jesus Christ my Lord 227
Father of life, descend 430
Father of me, and all mankind 379
Father of mercies, in thy word 48
Father of Spirits, nature's God 74
Father, our hearts we lift 87
Forever here, my rest shall be 229
Forever with the Lord 511
Fountain of life, to all below 218
Frequent the day of God returns 51
From all that dwell below the skies 10
From every stormy wind that blows 409
From Greenland's icy mountains 431
Full of trembling expectation 356

G.

Gently, Lord, O gently lead us 351
Give me the wings of faith to rise 481
Giver and guardian of my sleep 386
Giver of concord, Prince of peace 521

INDEX OF FIRST LINES TO HYMNS.

Glorious things of thee are spoken 280
Glory to God on high. 318
God is gone up on high 66
God is in Judah known. 532
God is love, his mercy brightens 77
God is the refuge of his saints. 270
God moves in a mysterious way. 28
God of all power, and truth, and grace 211
God of almighty love. 388
God of love, that hear'st the prayer 545
God of mercy, hear my prayer 546
God of my life, through all my days. 34
God of my life, to thee I call 362
God of thine Israel true 423
God of thunder, and the lightning. 422
God's perfect law converts 597
Go forth ye heralds, in my name 288
Go, labor on; spend and be spent 560
Go. labor on, while it is day. 561
Go, messengers of peace and love 449
Go, preach my gospel, saith the Lord 290
Grace is a plant where'er it grows 156
Grace! 'tis a charming sound 152
Gracious Redeemer, shake 368
Gracious Spirit, love divine. 130
Grant me within thy courts 557
Great God, attend while Zion sings 5
Great God, indulge my humble claim 405
Great God, the nations of the earth. 299
Great God, we sing thy mighty hand 396
Great is the Lord our God 431
Great King of glory, come 424
Guide me, O thou great Jehovah 605

H.

Hail, holy, holy, holy Lord 52
Hail the day that sees him rise 117

INDEX OF FIRST LINES TO HYMNS.

Hail to the brightness of Zion's glad morning 438
Hail to the Sabbath day 579
Happy the heart where graces reign 464
Happy the man who finds the grace 154
Happy the souls to Jesus joined 39
Hark, a voice divides the sky 496
Hark, from the tombs a doleful sound 467
Hark, how the watchmen cry 292
Hark, my soul, it is the Lord 255
Hark, ten thousand harps and voices 17
Hark, the glad sound, the Saviour comes 106
Hark, the herald angels sing 91
Hark, the song of jubilee 434
Hark, the voice of Jesus crying 437
Hark, the voice of love and mercy 101
Hark, what mean those holy voices 104
Hasten Lord the glorious time 435
Hasten, sinners, to be wise 180
Haste traveler, haste, the night comes on 169
Hearts of stone, relent . . . . 173°
Hear what God the Lord hath spoken 281
He dies, the friend of sinners dies 96
He leadeth me, O blessed thought 333
He that goeth forth with weeping 565
He wills that I should holy be 240
Help, Lord, to whom for help we fly 246
Here in thy name, eternal God 421
High in the heavens eternal God 58
High on his everlasting throne 289
Hither, ye faithful, haste with songs 103
Holy and true, and righteous Lord 236
Holy Ghost, with light divine 137
Ho! every one that thirsts, draw nigh 178
Hosanna to God in the highest 495
How beauteous are their feet 293
How can a sinner know 206

INDEX OF FIRST LINES TO HYMNS.

How did my heart rejoice to hear 279
How do thy mercies close me round 375
How great the wisdom, power and grace 300
How happy ev'ry child of grace 38
How happy, gracious Lord, are we 476
How large the promise, how divine 306
How long shall death, the tyrant, reign 518
How pleasant, how divinely fair 268
How sad our state by nature is 196
How sweet and heavenly is the sight 460
How sweet the name of Jesus sounds 123
How sweetly flowed the gospel sound 155
How tedious and tasteless the hour 353
How vain are all things here below 514

I.

I ask the gift of righteousness 202
I bless thee, Lord, for sorrows sent 562
I cannot always trace the way 563
I heard the voice of Jesus say 204
I know that my Redeemer lives 231
I lift my soul to God 207
I long to behold him arrayed 478
I love thy kingdom, Lord 284
I love to steal awhile away 404
I thank thee, uncreated Sun 265
I the good fight have fought 310
I thirst, thou wounded Lamb of God 209
I want a heart to pray 258
I would be thine, thou knowest I would 230
I would not live alway 494
If death my friend and me divide 497
If human kindness meets return 319
If, Lord, I have acceptance found 239
I'm not ashamed to own my Lord 278
In deep eternity 603
In the cross of Christ I glory 566

INDEX OF FIRST LINES TO HYMNS.

Inquire, ye pilgrims, for the way 517
In thy cleft, O Rock of Ages 609
It is the Lord, enthroned in light 556

J.

Jehovah reigns, let earth be glad 593
Jerusalem, my happy home 500
Jesus, all-redeeming Lord 321
Jesus, and shall it ever be 393
Jesus, at whose supreme command 316
Jesus, from whom all blessings flow 267
Jesus hath died that I might live 248
Jesus, great shepherd of the sheep 465
Jesus, immortal King, arise 298
Jesus, I my cross have taken 215
Jesus invites his saints 309
Jesus, in whom the Godhead's rays 238
Jesus is our common Lord 214
Jesus, Lord, we look to thee 459
Jesus, lover of my soul 201
Jesus, my advocate above 203
Jesus, my all, to heaven is gone 111
Jesus, my great High Priest 106
Jesus, my Lord, attend 195
Jesus, my Saviour, brother, friend 345
Jesus, my strength, my hope 251
Jesus, my truth, my way 233
Jesus, one word from thee 346
Jesus only, when the morning 561
Jesus, Redeemer of mankind 151
Jesus the Conqueror reigns 82
Jesus, the life, the truth, the way 252
Jesus, the mighty God hath spoken 541
Jesus, the name high over all 277
Jesus, the very thought of thee 555
Jesus, thou all-redeeming Lord 197
Jesus, thou art the sinner's friend 516
Jesus, thou joy of loving hearts 365

INDEX OF FIRST LINES TO HYMNS.

Jesus, thy blood and righteousness 210
Jesus, thy boundless love to me 266
Jesus, we look to thee 14
Jesus, we on the word depend 135
Jesus, we thus obey 324
Join all the glorious names 99
Joy to the world, the Lord is come 80
Just as I am, without one plea 217

L.

Laden with guilt and full of fears 49
Let all who truly bear 323
Let earth and heaven agree 151
Let every mortal ear attend 146
Let every tongue thy goodness speak 72
Let him to whom we now belong 262
Let us join, 'tis God's command 458
Let Zion's watchmen all awake 297
Life is the time to serve the Lord 487
Lift your eyes of faith and see 479
Light of life, seraphic fire 384
Look unto him, ye nations, own 213
Lord, all I am is known to thee 56
Lord, how secure and blest are they 361
Lord, I am thine, entirely thine 535
Lord, I believe a rest remains 359
Lord, I believe thy every word 328
Lord, I care not for riches, neither, etc 553
Lord, I hear of showers of blessings 166
Lord, if at thy command 444
Lord, in anger do not chasten 589
Lord, in the morning thou shalt hear 381
Lord, it belongs not to thy care 329
Lord of hosts, to thee we raise 425
Lord of the harvest, hear 275
Lord, teach thy servants how to pray 418

INDEX OF FIRST LINES TO HYMNS.

Lord, thou on earth didst love thine own 461
Lord, thou wilt hear me when I pray 402
Lord, when thou didst ascend on high 363
Lord, while for all mankind we pray 525
Lo! round the throne a glorious band 506
Love divine, all loves excelling 352

M.

Make haste, O man to live 371
Make haste, O my God, to deliver I pray 590
May I, throughout this day of thine 573
Methinks the last great day is come 508
Mighty God, while angels bless thee 350
Mortals, awake, with angels join 82
Must Jesus bear the cross alone 331
My days are gliding swiftly by 499
My dear Redeemer and my Lord 90
My head is low, my heart is sad 176
My heavenly home is bright and fair 569
My hope is built on nothing less 219
My God, accept my early vows 374
My God accept my heart this day 261
My God, my God, to thee I cry 225
My God, my life, my love 67
My God, my portion and my love 360
My shepherd is the Lord most high 598
My God, the spring of all my joys 212
My thoughts surmount these lower skies 483
My God, what gentle cords are thine 463
My Jesus, I love thee, I know thou art mine 554
My Lord, how full of sweet content 367
My Saviour, my almighty friend 332
My Saviour's pierced side 308
My son, know thou the Lord 161
My soul, be on thy guard 370
My soul, repeat his praise 30

INDEX OF FIRST LINES TO HYMNS.

My spirit, on thy care 341
My times are in thy hand 340

N.

Nearer my God, to thee 526
Neither voice we have, nor vision 582
Not all the blood of beasts 86
Not all the outward forms on earth 131
Not to condemn the sons of men 94
Now let my soul, eternal King 44
Now the shades of night are gone 382
Now to the Lord, a noble song 114
Now to the Lord, who makes us know 408

O.

O bless the Lord, my soul 70
O could I speak the matchless worth 480
O for a closer walk with God 192
O for a faith that will not shrink 327
O for a glance of heavenly day 182
O for a heart to praise my God 226
O for a thousand seraph tongues 29
O for a thousand tongues to sing 1
O God, most merciful and true 242
O God of mercy, hear my call 559
O God, our help in ages past 377
O God thou art my God alone 366
O God thou bottomless abyss 61
O God, what offering shall I bring 263
O glorious hope of perfect love 243
O happy day that fixed my choice 222
O happy, happy place 276
O how happy are they, who their Saviour 216
O how the thought of God attracts 250
O Jesus, at thy feet we wait 227

INDEX OF FIRST LINES TO HYMNS.

O Jesus, full of grace	194
O Jesus, full of truth and grace	237
O joyful sound of gospel grace	247
O Lord of hosts how lovely is	585
O Lord our God, arise	286
O Lord, thy work revive	454
O Lord, while we confess the worth	304
O love divine, how sweet thou art	244
O Love divine, O matchless grace	314
O Love divine, that stooped to share	337
O my soul, bless thou Jehovah	588
O Spirit of the living God	291
O Sun of righteousness, arise	520
O tell me no more of this world's vain store	539
O that I could look to thee	92
O that I knew the secret place	191
O that my load of sin were gone	185
O thou in whose presence	551
O thou our Saviour, Brother, Friend	36
O thou that wouldst not have	191
O thou to whom all creatures bow	73
O thou whom all thy saints adore	60
O thou whom we adore	152
O thou to whose all-searching sight	221
O when shall I see Jesus	344
O when shall we sweetly remove	477
O what amazing words of grace	301
O where shall rest be found	167
Of Him who did salvation bring	120
Oh! for the happy hour	455
Oh! sometimes the shadows are deep	552
Omnipresent God, whose aid	383
Once more, my soul, the rising day	378
Once more we come before our God	26
One there is above all others	568
On thee each morning, O my God	417

INDEX OF FIRST LINES TO HYMNS.

On the mountain tops appearing 282
O'er the gloomy hills of darkness 445
Our heavenly Father, hear 398
Over the ocean wave 436
O what delight is this 317

P.

Pass me not, O gentle Saviour 547
Pilgrim, burdened with sin 171
Plunged in a gulf of dark despair 107
Praise to thee, thou great Creator 16
Praise waits in Zion, Lord, for thee 40
Praise ye the Lord, y' immortal choirs 21
Praise ye the Lord, my heart shall join 113
Praise ye the Lord, 'tis good to raise 59
Praise ye the Lord; with all my heart 587
Prayer is appointed to convey 372
Precious volume what thou doest 50

R.

Regard in tenderness, O Lord 601
Rejoice, the Lord is King 99
Rest for the toiling hand 485
Rock of ages, cleft for me 125

S.

Salvation, O the joyful sound 200
Saviour hear us through thy merit 564
Saviour, on me the grace bestow 245
Saviour, sprinkle many nations 448
Say sinner, hath a voice within 168
See from on high, a light divine 81
See how great a flame aspires 433
See Israel's gentle Shepherd stand 307
Serene, I laid me down 409
Servant of God, well done 484

INDEX OF FIRST LINES TO HYMNS.

Shall we meet beyond the river 610
Shepherd of souls, with pitying eye 159
Show pity Lord, O Lord forgive 184
Shrinking from the cold hand of death 491
Sing O ye ransomed of the Lord 325
Sing to the great Jehovah's praise 413
Sinners, obey the gospel word 141
Sinners turn, why will you die 172
Sinners, will you scorn the message? 164
Sole sovereign of the earth and skies 533
Some tell us that praying, and also 538
Sometimes a light surprises 345
So they from strength unwearied go 586
Spirit divine, attend our prayer 129
Spirit of faith, come down 128
Spirit of peace, celestial Dove 252
Still for thy loving-kindness, Lord 190
Sweet hour of prayer, sweet hour of prayer 364
Sweet is the work, my God, my King 576
Sweet the moments, rich in blessing 607

T.

Take the name of Jesus with you 357
Take up the cross, the Saviour said 11
Talk with us Lord, thyself reveal 326
Teach me the measure of my days 376
That awful day will surely come 470
That doleful night, before his death 313
The church in her militant state 498
The counsels of redeeming grace 47
The countless multitude on high 33
The day of Christ, the day of God 112
The day is past and gone 399
The day of wrath, that dreadful day 490
The earth and the fullness with which it is stored . . 599
The glory of the Lord 596
The heavens declare thy glory Lord 43
The King of heaven his table spreads 311

INDEX OF FIRST LINES TO HYMNS.

The Lord declares his will 142
The Lord Jehovah reigns. 65
The Lord my pasture shall prepare 64
The Lord, my shepherd is 69
The Lord of earth and sky 386
The man that doth in secret place. 584
The mighty conqueror leaves the dead 42
The morning flowers display their sweets 488
The nations call from sea to sea. 439
The praise of Zion waits for thee 269
The power to bless my house 530
The saints who die of Christ possessed 489
The Saviour calls, let every ear. 148
The Saviour, when to heaven he rose 271
The Spirit breathes upon the word 134
The Spirit in our hearts 143
The Sun of righteousness appears 115
The truth of God shall still endure 3
The work of one more day is done 521
Thee we adore eternal name 466
There is a fountain filled with blood. 108
There is a gate that stands ajar 549
There is a house not made with hands 502
There is a land mine eye hath seen 507
There is a land of pure delight 481
There is no night in heaven 513
Thine earthly sabbaths, Lord, we love 577
This is the day the Lord hath made. 571
This is the day, the sacred day 580
This is the word of truth and love 174
Thou art, O God, the life and light 63
Thou hidden source of calm repose 348
Thou Judge of quick and dead 472
Thou Lamb of God, thou Prince of peace 338
Thou seest my feebleness 389
Through all the lofty sky 521

INDEX OF FIRST LINES TO HYMNS.

Through every age, eternal God 49a
Thus far, the Lord hath led me on 394
Thus spake to me the Holy One 592
Thy presence Lord, the place shall fill 411
Thy will be done, I will not fear 536
'Tis finished, the Messiah dies 97
To God the only wise 84
To God your every want 390
To our Redeemer's glorious name 27
To thee I lift my soul, O Lord 600
To thee, this temple we devote 429
To us, a child of hope is born 79
To us, a child of royal birth 88
Try us, O God, and search the ground . . . . . , 462
'Twas the commission of our Lord 303

U.
Uphold me, Saviour, or I fall 374

V.
Vain man, thy fond pursuit forbear 469
Vital spark of heavenly flame 527

W.
Walk in the light, so shalt thou know 251
Watchman, tell us of the night 451
We bless thy name, Almighty God 536
We have no outward righteousness 220
We know by faith we know 473
We lift our hearts to thee 392
Welcome, O Saviour, to my heart 558
Welcome, sweet day of rest 578
We're traveling home to heaven above 542
What a friend we have in Jesus 608
What are these arrayed in white? 504
What equal honors shall we bring 121
What glory gilds the sacred page 45
What grace, O Lord, and beauty shone 198

INDEX OF FIRST LINES OF HYMNS.

What is our calling's glorious hope 254
What majesty and grace 153
What shall I render to my God ? 260
What various hinderances we meet 397
When all thy mercies, O my God 18
When Christ doth in my heart appear 28
When I survey the wondrous cross 89
When marshalled on the nightly plain 93
When, my Saviour, shall I be 456
When on Sinai's top I see 426
Where shall I go to seek and find 419
While shepherds watched their flocks by night 105
While thee I seek, protecting power 19
Who, but thou, Almighty Spirit 447
Who in the Lord confide 285
Why do the heathen storm with ire 591
Why do we mourn departing friends 501
Why, O sinner, me profaning 181
Why should we start and fear to die 492
Will God in very deed descend 428
With joy we meditate the grace 312
With my substance I will honor 446
With songs and honors sounding loud 414
Witness ye men and angels, now 259
Would Jesus have the sinner die ? 349

Y.

Ye Christian heralds go, proclaim 442
Ye golden lamps of heaven, farewell 523
Ye messengers of Christ 294
Ye that pass by, behold the man 95
Ye tribes of Adam, join 24
Ye weary, heavy-laden souls 515
Your harps, ye trembling saints 343

Z.

Zion stands with hills surrounded 283

www.ingramcontent.com/pod-product-compliance
Lightning Source LLC
Chambersburg PA
CBHW051849300426
44117CB00006B/325